ADVANCE PRAISE FOR *NO CERTAINTY ATTACHED*

Lurie attempts to come to some kinda understanding of my paradox
that is, I can be so nice
or I can be so not nice
and hardly anything in the middle
and it's funny that Lurie puts the boot in a bit at the end
and he reckons that the fambley manne thing is an act
and my Everyman pose is faux
and really I'm the same old prick
and Rob, you've hit the nail on the head, actually . . .

—Steve Kilbey

It's already yesterday and I still remember the first time I heard "For
a Moment We're Strangers." back in '81. Sometimes stark and edgy,
sometimes sumptuous and fragrant, yet always unique and enticing,
the music of the Church helped to enrich my life in many ways.
It certainly changed the life of Robert Lurie, who has written the
definitive account of the Church and the life of its main protagonist,
the ever creative and artistically complex Steve Kilbey. This is more
than just a band biography; it's also the personal journey of one
Church fanatic, a journey to which we can all relate.

—Ian McFarlane, author of *The Encyclopedia
of Australian Rock and Pop*

(Anthony Collins)

No Certainty Attached

STEVE KILBEY AND THE CHURCH

by Robert Dean Lurie

VERSE CHORUS PRESS   PORTLAND ❧ LONDON ❧ MELBOURNE

Published by Verse Chorus Press
PO Box 14806, Portland OR 97293
info@versechorus.com

Front cover photograph: Wendy McDougall
Back cover photographs: (L-R) courtesy, Nic Ward; Michael Barone/ Dana Valois; Rachel Armstrong/Caroline Barnes; Anthony Collins.
Book and cover design: Steve Connell/Transgraphic Services

The author and the publishers wish to thank all those who supplied photographs and gave permission to reproduce copyright material in this book. Every effort has been made to contact all copyright holders, and the publishers welcome communication from any copyright owners from whom permission was inadvertently not obtained. In such cases, we will be pleased to obtain appropriate permission and provide suitable acknowledgment in future editions.

Printed in China by C & C Offset Printing Co., Ltd.

Library of Congress Cataloging-in-Publication Data

Lurie, Robert Dean, 1974-
    No certainty attached : Steve Kilbey and the Church / by Robert Dean Lurie. – 1st ed.
    p. cm.
    ISBN 978-1-891241-22-2
    1. Kilbey, Steve. 2. Rock musicians–Australia–Biography. 3. Church (Musical group) 4. Rock groups–Australia. I. Title.
ML420.K457L87 2009
782.42166092–dc22
[B]
                                                                    2009003010

CONTENTS

ACKNOWLEDGMENTS

First and foremost I want to thank Steve Kilbey for his full participation in this project. From our first interview onward, he remained on call, always willing to give more information if asked. Without his cooperation, and the many hours of taped interviews it led to, this would have been a very different book indeed.

I am also indebted to the following members of the Kilbey clan for their contributions: John Kilbey, Russell Kilbey, and Joyce Cooper. They helped bring Steve's childhood to life.

Longtime Kilbey co-conspirator Peter Koppes always impressed me with his graciousness and candor. He is truly a sonic magician and deserves a biography of his own.

I owe a large debt of gratitude to the multi-talented (and roguishly charming) Simon Polinski for giving detailed insights into Steve's composition and recording processes.

Nic (formerly Nick) Ward provided detailed reminiscences, photos, and recordings, and this book is much richer for his perspective.

Linda Neil and Sue Campbell deserve special mention for encouraging me to include parts of my own story in the larger narrative. This is a deeply personal book, and they gave me the confidence to be up-front about that. However, I have endeavored to limit my own appearances to those directly related to Steve's larger story. Readers will no doubt be relieved that sections detailing the travails of my first band—the Chowder Monkeys—were dispatched to the cutting room floor during the revision process.

The Church's fans have been a godsend, particularly Brian Smith, creator and maintainer of the *Shadow Cabinet* web site (and early editor of this book), and Victor Gagnon, owner of the largest Church bootleg archive in America. The following fans also helped in crucial ways: Holly Jordan, Anthony Collins, Pablo Vasquez, Brian Hutton, Duane Handy, Tony Pucci, Jeffrey Shiell, Mario and Heather Cordova, Danny Burton, Trevor Boyd, Daniel Watkins, Patrick Boulay, Greg Hatmaker, and many, many others.

Stuart Coupe provided contextual information on the early '80s Australian music scene, as well as his side of the tumultuous story I have come to call "Coupegate." Pryce Surplice also deserves special mention for allowing me to reprint his private e-mail comments on the early '80s Australian scene.

Thank you, too, to my anonymous sources, especially Deep Throat!

I am indebted to several professors from the Creative Writing department of the University of North Carolina–Wilmington, especially David Gessner, my advisor, coach, mentor, and occasional therapist, who midwifed this unwieldy project through its first two incarnations and pushed me to be creative in my approach to my subject. The illustrious and prolific Phil Furia deserves a shout-out for the crucial last-minute line edits he supplied prior to my thesis defense. Philip Gerard and Rebecca Lee are also to be commended for their early suggestions and encouragement.

Seemingly late in the game, Verse Chorus Press came along and helped me pull it all together. The infinitely knowledgeable and eloquent David Nichols became my "Australia Advisor," setting me straight about many things I'd gotten wrong about his country and its musical history. Clinton Walker helped me with some additional fact-checking and generously combed though his archives for Church-related press clippings. My main editor, Steve Connell, operates under a motto of "No cliché left standing." If any have somehow remained in the manuscript, it will be despite his best efforts. He is rigorous, thorough, and has an unerringly correct vision of what good writing should look like. Finally, a very heartfelt thank-you to Harper Piver for providing a constant sounding board and being a moral cheerleader during the darkest hours when there really was no certainty attached.

AUTHOR'S NOTE

While the events depicted in these pages are entirely factual, I have taken certain liberties which should be stated here. Perhaps the most important of these involve the recounting of my interactions with Steve Kilbey. We met quite a few times, in a number of locations, on three different continents. In the interests of coherence and narrative flow, however, some of our meetings have been combined and compressed; for example, a conversation begun in Sydney and finished in Tempe, Arizona has here been confined to a single locale. Also, in the occasional *narrative* scenes—those written in novelistic style, with dialogue—I have added certain imagined details to lend depth and shape to the story.

In a few instances, the names and descriptions of individuals have been changed to protect their privacy.

Steve Kilbey, Berlin, 2002 *(Stefan Horlitz)*

Exasperating, yes. Sometimes eruptive, unreasonable, ferocious, and convulsive, yes. Eloquent, penetrating, exciting, and always—never failingly even at the sacrifice of accuracy and at times his own vanity— witty. Never, never, *never* dull.

—Joseph Cotten, describing Orson Welles
in *Vanity Will Get You Somewhere*

Preface
IT'S A MIRACLE, LET IT ALTER YOU

The Church's concert on the University of Minnesota campus in June 1990 was quite possibly the first spiritual experience of my life. In the two years since I'd discovered their music in 1988, the band had taken its seat at the right hand of the Beatles in my rock-and-roll trinity (the third spot would—over the years—be occupied by a rotating cast including Bauhaus/Love and Rockets, the Cure, and, later, the Afghan Whigs). I could barely sleep at all the night preceding the gig; a fly-on-the-wall observer would have thought *I* was the one who would be taking the stage at Northrop Auditorium the following evening, not the highly touted rock band from Australia.

Andrew Beccone, a fellow musician, accompanied me to the show, along with my friend Pat Curry and a high school classmate named Brian, perhaps the only true Church conversion to my credit. Prior to our first meeting, Brian had been into metal and classic rock, particularly partial to Cinderella, Def Leppard, and Iron Maiden. But after one listen to *Of Skins and Heart* he had thrown all of his old records away and set about collecting the Church catalogue. By the time the concert rolled around, Brian's mullet had been amputated and the only remnant of his former life was a lingering—and, to my mind, unfortunate—appreciation for the music of Rush.

All three of my friends could be described as fans, but none of them shared my all-consuming obsession with the Church, a borderline-unhealthy fixation that necessitated the keeping of Church notebooks: tomes inside which I transcribed Steve Kilbey's lyrics and pondered their meaning;

scrapbooks that contained Church press clippings, xeroxed photographs, and anything else I could find relating to the band.

At sixteen, my friends and I were definitely among the younger members of the audience. Most of the people in attendance appeared to be college-age or older: well-groomed, thoughtful types who had probably been drawn to the subtlety of the Church's music. This audience was quite different from the others I had mingled among during my short stint as a concertgoer; here, it was as if all the Ph.D. candidates within a sixty-mile radius had taken the night off from their studies.

After a wait that seemed like hours, the lights dimmed and fog billowed out from the wings. Four shadowy figures lumbered onto the stage, took up their instruments, and tore into the opening notes of "Pharaoh," pushing the song harder and faster than on record. The music had a very real physical effect on me—the sound man had apparently cranked the PA as high as it could go, causing Steve Kilbey's bass notes to resonate in my chest.

The first thirty minutes of the set consisted entirely of material from the band's recent *Gold Afternoon Fix* album. It was probably my least favorite in the Church oeuvre, but the more aggressive live arrangements improved the songs considerably. This was due in no small part to Jay Dee Daugherty, the band's new drummer. When Marty Willson-Piper (the band's leather-clad, ragged-coiffed guitarist) played the opening notes of *Starfish*'s "Hotel Womb" with his hand suspended above the fretboard and his fingers dangling down across the strings like spiders' legs, my heart began racing. As all four musicians locked into the groove for the first verse, I shivered, a physical reaction conjured in me only by what seemed to me the most sublime musical moments—John Lennon's voice at the beginning of "Mr. Moonlight," for instance, or the crescendo in U2's "Bad." The fact that eight hundred equally enthralled fans shared in this moment only added to its power.

A discernible shift took place as the band segued into material from the *Starfish* album. What had been a very good rock show turned into an electric rapture. This was the type of spiritual communion that eight years of Catholic school had tried—and failed—to elicit from me. I understood now why the band was called the Church.

The final song of the evening—"You Took"—confirmed these four musicians in my mind as icons who would, in many ways, chart the course of my own creative development. The band took the audience on a roller-

Peter Koppes, Steve Kilbey, Marty Willson Piper, 1987 *(Rachel Armstrong/Caroline Barnes)*

coaster ride, stretching the song to three times the length of the studio version. It amazed me how the two guitarists worked together almost telepathically, surfing waves of dissonance and feedback, then emerging into eddies of gentle harmony. Steve anchored the explorations with his bass drone, and Jay Dee controlled the dynamics, nudging the band into edgier, harder terrain whenever they had dallied too long in the sonic ether. Over the course of twenty minutes, the music pulled me through a succession of moods. I had never used LSD, but this seemed the aural equivalent of an acid trip. By the final ringing note of feedback from Marty's guitar, I felt myself transformed.

And as I left the theater that night, I thought to myself: This is my world and this is my language.

For a very brief period at the end of the 1980s, the Church stood poised to become "the next big thing" in America. The quartet had released the critically lauded album *Starfish*, which spawned a Top-20 hit in "Under the Milky Way." Much of the band's magic stemmed from its charismatic and enigmatic frontman—Steve Kilbey. The British-born, Australian-raised singer, bassist, and lyricist had spent the previous fourteen years honing his unique vision to diamond-sharp accuracy, a vision now ensconced in a hypnotic twin-guitar vessel courtesy of two extraordinary musicians—Peter Koppes and Marty Willson-Piper.

To us Americans, the Church seemed to have appeared out of nowhere. In truth, the band had already experienced exhilarating highs and harrowing lows in Australia, going from success to failure and back again. The Church arrived in the United States seasoned and confident, seemingly ready to take over the world.

But it never happened. The fault lies partly with the behavior of Kilbey himself and partly with the ever-fickle tastes of American music consumers. The emergence of Nirvana in 1991 did the music world many favors—chief among them the consigning of "hair metal" to the dustbin of history—but there was also negative fallout from this paradigm shift: in droves, listeners forsook melodic, thoughtful rock music in favor of angst and bombast. The Church and a good number of their contemporaries became casualties of this realignment of popular taste.

These days, the Church have been relegated in mainstream American consciousness to the dreaded category of "one-hit wonder." And that's being generous; large swaths of my country's population have never even heard that one hit. If it weren't for its appearance on the soundtrack of the film *Donnie Darko*, no one under twenty-five would be the least bit familiar with "Under the Milky Way," the Church's signature song.

And yet there are other ways of measuring success. For a core audience who signed on as far back as 1981, the Church never went away. The band may have fallen off of the mainstream radar, but to those listeners in Australia, North America, and Europe who continue to follow their evolving musical career, the Church—after a brief period of soul-searching in the mid-1990s—have gone from strength to strength. It is true that Steve Kilbey, the man whom a fan once hyperbolically described as looking like Jesus but playing and singing like God, had to let go of his dreams of being a rock star—but in doing so he found his true voice. It's just as well, as he was always most comfortable on the margins—sending out sirens' songs to those of us caught in the humdrum of everyday life but yearning for something more.

Through all the ups and downs, the chosen few continue to listen, feeling as if they are in on a very special secret—a secret that could conceivably alter their lives. For those people—and I count myself as one of them—it has been, and will always be, impossible to turn away from the music of Steve Kilbey and the Church.

Steve Kilbey (Wendy McDougall)

This artwork was made in 1991 as my comment on what was then the relatively new technology of CDs, and later shown in *Real Wild Child*, an exhibition at the Powerhouse Museum in Sydney. I made the piece using CD cases as frames—each photo was in a case and they were all stuck on a board. Steve happily agreed to be the face.

I'd been taking photographs for album covers since 1980, but slowly we photographers and artists were losing our beautiful 12-inch-square canvas (which of course could be doubled with a gatefold sleeve). Our canvas was shrinking to something that seemed impossibly small. The transition was somewhat daunting, though I soon came to see it as a new challenge. This piece represents my initial negative response to CDs, though there are positive elements in it, too. Steve's head is shaking from side to side, as if in a "no" gesture, yet by providing the frame and a major part of the artwork, CDs also revealed their potential to be many things.

Steve Kilbey, being in a great, innovative, and thought-provoking band, was the perfect person for this work. I really liked that he and the Church did and said what they believed in, and did it so well.—*WM*

1
YOU ARE A PARADOX TO ME

July 2003: I spent most of the flight to Sydney staring out the window at ever-shifting clouds. As usual I had a Kilbey song in my head; this time it was "Aviatrix," featuring the line "Cumulonimbus like a gray shroud." Having decided to write Steve's story, I was on my way.

I wasn't sure what to expect. For the majority of his career, Steve had given the impression of being an aloof, mysterious man. He spent most interviews claiming he didn't like talking about himself. He refused to explain the meanings of or the inspirations for his songs. On the handful of occasions I had met him personally, he had proved exceedingly difficult to engage in conversation. In some ways he was the J.D. Salinger of rock music: brilliant, reclusive, and insufferable.

In the first e-mail I wrote him about my biography project, I remarked that the number one question people were asking me was how I was going to deal with the subject of his longtime heroin addiction. His response was brief.

> Lurie, it's your book. Write whatever the fuck you want about drugs. You have my blessing.

His brusqueness intimidated me, but—ever the optimist—I chose to interpret the final line as an invitation. Eventually I wrote a second message: "I am going to be in Australia for the month of July working on my project. Would you be available for an interview?"

Again, the response was brief:

Lurie . . . OK. I'll give you a couple hours. In July. If you get here.

★ ★ ★ ★ ★

For years I had wanted to go to Australia. I'm not sure how much of this desire stemmed from a genuine interest in the country, and how much was due to my Church fixation. Steve Kilbey is actually English by birth, but he had grown up in Australia and even though he claimed the place had exerted no influence on his lyrics, I felt it must have—if only as something for him to react against. As silly as this sounds now, I wanted to breathe the air Steve had breathed and see the things he had seen during his formative years. Maybe I was hoping a little of that inspiration would rub off on me.

Australians are often generalized as friendly and gregarious, and that description certainly applied to the first two people I interviewed over the phone for the book. Linda Neil, a violinist who had played on several Church albums in the nineties, talked to me as if we'd grown up together. The same was true of Stuart Coupe, an influential rock writer who had palled around with Steve in the early days. In fact, after twenty minutes on the phone, Stuart offered me a place to stay during my visit. I accepted without hesitation. Later, I tried to put myself in his shoes; for me to do something like that, to invite a complete stranger to stay with me, was inconceivable. Needless to say, my initial impression of Australians was very positive.

The Steve Kilbey I met up with at Bondi Beach only fit the Australian stereotype to a certain extent. He was indeed disarmingly friendly and quite talkative on his home turf, but there was a darker aspect to his personality that could emerge slowly, like clouds gathering ominously on the horizon, or as quickly as a tsunami—a pervasive, buzz-killing melancholy that spread ever outward from its epicenter. Physically, he was quite different from the elfin Pied Piper figure of my adolescence. His thinning grayish-brown hair was pulled back in a ponytail. The earrings—a hallmark of his '80s look— were still there, along with the pointy beard, but the beard was a bit more scraggly now, and flecked with white. There were other physical changes, too. Steve's untucked shirt only partially hid his protruding belly. He stared at me as I approached, crow's feet spreading from the corners of his eyes.

Steve Kilbey and Robert Lurie, 2003 *(John Kilbey)*

"Robert Lurie?" he asked. His voice, a lilting mixture of British and Australian accents, gave me pause. It was a seductive, dangerous voice.

"Yes, it's me. Good to see you, Steve."

"And is that little thing in your brain going?"

"What thing?"

"The little tape recorder? The writer's recorder? Keeping track of every-thing I say?"

"I left the tape recorder at home," I said.

"But the recorder in your brain is on." He smirked. "I know how it's go-ing to start: *He looked a bit older than I remembered, and a bit heavier too.*"

"Something like that." I smiled.

"How's it coming along?"

"I'm just getting started."

"Hmmm." He grabbed the arm of an attractive middle-aged woman who was walking past. "Lindy, this is Robert Lurie. He's writing a book about me."

"Hello darling," she said, flashing a broad smile. I took in her wide toothy grin and cascading blonde curls, and realized this was Lindy Morrison, the former drummer for the Go-Betweens. I was face to face with a bona-fide Australian cult hero.

"Nice to meet you," I said.

"Don't tell him anything bad," Steve said to Lindy.

"Actually," I said, lowering my voice to a conspiratorial tone, "I want all the dirt."

She laughed and looked at Steve. "Watch out, Steven."

Steve and Lindy were at the Bondi Pavilion that day to participate in a songwriting seminar organized by Steve's brother John. Even though I had crashed the party (which local students were paying to attend), the Kilbey brothers incorporated me into the event. Steve introduced me to everyone as "Robert Lurie, an accomplished professional songwriter." He seemed in good spirits.

I played a song I had written titled, appropriately, "Cathedral." Steve critiqued it, praising the fact that it ended on an E-minor chord—"which," he said, "lends it that essential bit of mystery." Other students workshopped their pieces. Kilbey declaimed, gestured, strutted to and fro. Although he was only one of several facilitators, he dominated the workshop, exposing a side of himself I had never seen before. At forty-nine, he appeared ready at last to talk about his life and his music. I resolved to take advantage of this new openness.

Cornering him after the workshop, I said, "So are you still up for an interview?"

He stared at me for a minute, sizing me up. He looked into my eyes.

"You have no axe to grind?" he asked.

"None that I'm aware of."

"I'm going to say this to you because I've been in your shoes. I've met my heroes. I've felt the disappointment when I realized they were human beings. You know this. I'm going to give you the benefit of the doubt, Robert, even though I think no one will ever read this book. No one will want it. No one is interested in me or the Church. But I'll help you with it. I believe in karma."

"So do I," I said.

We shook hands.

And so it began.

2

WHEN I WAS A KID, I'D LOOK AT THE SKY

I always felt incredibly frustrated at being a kid. I felt like, "People should be taking notice of me. I don't want to be this little . . . creature," and I always felt that I was acting at being a kid, and if any old lady picked me up in her arms and said, "Oh Steve," even at four, I felt like, "You don't really know. You think I'm a little boy, but I'm not, I'm this monster inside, and I'm actually . . . maybe I'm looking down your dress or I'm looking at how old you are. Your yellow teeth are disgusting me." So I was never a natural kid.

—Steve Kilbey, July 2003

Steve met me two nights later outside a bookstore/coffee shop called Gertrude & Alice's. As I approached, I could see him pacing back and forth next to a stoplight. He wore a jean jacket, open-necked dress shirt, and black pants that appeared to be splattered with red paint. In his shades he looked iconic, like Bob Dylan crossed with Neil Young.

"How are you, Robert?" he said, gripping my hand.

"Good. I brought something for you." I reached into my backpack and took out the Frank Sinatra CD I had purchased the day before.

"Wow, thank you," he said excitedly, taking the CD, which was titled *Francis Albert Sinatra and Antonio Carlos Jobim.*

"For ten years I was convinced this was where you had gotten your singing style," I said.

He squinted at the cover. "No, I've never heard this one." He scanned the song titles. "Oh, I *have* heard some of these songs. 'Baubles, Bangles, and Beads,' that's a great song. Thank you very much!"

He looked up from the CD case. "Do you know my favorite Sinatra song?" he asked.

"No. What is it?"

He sang his answer softly: "Each place I go . . ."

I continued, ". . . only the lonely go."

He looked at me, then off at some unspecified point behind me. "Where does that sadness come from?" he asked quietly.

"Well," I said, "I like to think he was singing for Ava Gardner."

Steve laughed, and I had the funny feeling I had passed some sort of test. He opened the door and motioned me in.

We were greeted by a pretty, middle-aged woman with short brown hair and horn-rimmed glasses. "Steven," she said, smiling.

"Hello, hello." He turned to me. "What would you like?"

"Hmm. Cappuccino, I guess."

"Right then," he said, "One cappuccino for Mr. Lurie, a soy latte for me."

We made our way to the back of the store, cleared some books off a table, and sat down. Steve removed his sunglasses. I set my tape recorder on the table, pressed record.

"I guess we'll start with your parents," I said. "What can you tell me about them?"

"Ah!" he said, his eyes lighting up. "My dad was a real cockney. He was sort of . . . do you know what a cockney is?"

"Yeah."

"He was kind of like"—Steve segued into a rough Cockney accent—"*If you look after me, I'll look after you.* He'd hold a cigarette like he wouldn't want anyone to see it." As he said this, Steve leapt from his seat, hunched his shoulders, and mimicked someone furtively sucking on a cigarette.

This was my first sense of what Les Kilbey had been like, an image that would be filled out over time by Steve's recollections and childhood photos: handsome, thin, with slicked-back brown hair and a mischievous grin. Les the raconteur. Les the piano player who only played in the key of F-sharp ("That was the only key on his piano in which all of the notes functioned," Steve said.)

As Steve began his story, his physical form faded from my mind, as did
the coffee shop, as did the town of Bondi Beach. In their place was London
just after the end of the Second World War, a place and a time that has taken
on almost mythological resonance: a crossroads of history, with one talkative, charming, slightly roguish marine standing right in the middle of it.

Les Kilbey was twenty-two when he first met Steve's mother, Joyce—who
was only sixteen at the time. Like many young British men, Les had spent
his adult life thus far fighting Germans. And somehow, in the aftermath,
during the euphoric days of celebration and mischief that followed, Les
Kilbey accidentally shot himself in the finger.

It was while he was on sick leave, with his hand bandaged up, that Les
met Joyce. She recounted her first impression of him in her autobiography
The Tale of the Old Iron Pot (published under the pseudonym J. C. Wallop):

> I must say I was far from impressed by this scruffy Marine. He had brown
> suede shoes on (he called them his "brothel creepers"), his beret was
> precariously placed at an impossible angle on the side of his head, he
> slouched and whilst one hand was in his trouser pocket, the other was in a
> sling with a splint about six inches long attached to his index finger.

Nevertheless, Les was quite taken with Joyce and waged a charm of-
fensive, slowly wearing down her resistance. He also managed to ingratiate
himself with Joyce's mother, a wise, no-nonsense matriarch who was at first
skeptical of her young daughter dating a "worldly chap" like Les.

I have seen a picture of the couple in which Joyce—blonde, slim, and
beautiful, with a charmingly lopsided smile—walks arm in arm with Les
along a seaside promenade. Les grins at the camera, his hair flopping about
his face, his suit and slacks just a bit too large for his wiry body.

Joyce Bennett hailed from a large, working-class London family. She was
born in the Old Kent Road, but grew up with her seven brothers and sisters on the Burnt Oak council estate in northwest London. She wrote in
her memoir: "We never had great luxury in our home but Mum and Dad
were always the first to go without. We grew up in a home void of violence
or drunkenness but with plenty of laughter and love." That solid founda-
tion sustained her and her family through the terrifying years of the Blitz,
when bombs were falling all around them. The Bennetts managed to make

it through intact, though they knew many others who weren't so lucky.

When Les's hand healed, he would sit at the piano and play songs for Joyce, often beginning one song before he had finished the previous one. (His son does the same thing when he talks—he begins new sentences before finishing what he is in the middle of saying.)

Les appreciated Joyce's smile, her quick intelligence, the way her curly blonde hair fell about her shoulders, and, most importantly, her sense of humor. The two began courting, and were married in 1948. After living with Joyce's family for a few months, they moved a little further west to Harrow, where Les had lived before the war, and in 1950 to Welwyn Garden City, a "new town" some twenty miles north of London, where Steven, their first child, was born in 1954.

The first thing most people noticed about baby Steven was his silence. He was so taciturn some family guests would pinch him to try and get him to cry. Paradoxically, Steve also displayed an early desire to perform for people—he would alternate between stillness and action, shifting into extrovert mode at moments of his choosing. Another characteristic that manifested itself early—and quite accidentally—was his taste for profanity. One morning, when he was only six months old, he caused a commotion in his neighborhood. Joyce had set Steve outside in his baby carriage, with their neighbor Carole looking after him. After about ten minutes of relative peace and quiet, Joyce heard several loud voices outside. She looked out the front door to discover a group of schoolkids gathered around the carriage and laughing hysterically.

"What's going on?" Joyce asked.

"Listen to this, Mrs. Kilbey."

Carole turned to Steve. "Say 'Ah, baba,' Steve."

Steve slammed his tiny fist against his blanket and yelled, "Ah, bugger!"

In 1957, when Steve was two and a half years old, his family decided to set out for a new life in Australia. Les's only sister had already emigrated there, and after his mother died, Joyce explains, "his sister wrote and said we should move out to Wollongong because it would be a good life for us and our young son."

"The Australian government was very racist in those days," Steve says,

They wanted to fill the country up with English people. So the deal was, you could come over here for ten pounds, and you didn't have to give the money back as long as you stayed for two years. But if you decided, "Oh we don't like it, we're going back," you had to pay back the fare in full, which was a lot of money in those days.

Steve's summary of Australia's immigration policy in the 1950s is over-simplified, but not entirely inaccurate. What was widely known as the "White Australia Policy"—legislation that heavily restricted the ability of non-European immigrants to become Australian citizens—was largely a thing of the past by 1957; however, its legacy lived on in the Australian government's favoritism toward British nationals and its willingness to subsidize their passage. In fact, this selective policy of offering "relocation assistance" to immigrants from Britain was not officially phased out until 1982. It's also interesting to note that the families of Bon Scott and Angus and Malcolm Young (of the iconic Australian band AC/DC) also immigrated from the UK with the help of this program.

Joyce Kilbey and Steven, on the boat to Australia.
(Kilbey family collection)

One of Steve's earliest memories is of an incident that occurred on the boat trip from England. On the evening in question, the sunset cast a glow over both the bobbing cruise ship and the seemingly endless expanse of ocean that surrounded it. The Kilbeys sat on the upper deck, Les on a folding chair, smoking, his brown hair blowing in the breeze. Joyce sat with Steve, explaining to him how to tell time. She pointed to the setting sun, then to her gold watch.

Steve perked up. "Can I hold it?" he asked.

Joyce thought for a minute and then said, "Sure." She unclasped the watch and reached over to place it in Steve's tiny hand. Steve immediately grabbed the watch and hurled it over the ship's railing. Joyce jumped to her feet and gripped the rail just in time to see her expensive anniversary present plunge into the sea.

"Steven Kilbey!" she cried.

Steve laughs now, remembering it. "That was the first real controversial thing I ever did. It actually made the ship's newspaper. It said, *Now the sharks can tell the time.* But I remember thinking, I'm going to throw it into the sea. I also remember thinking, I can't tell her that. And then I threw it in, just for the hell of it."

Australia in the 1950s was a very different place from Australia today. There was still very much a frontier mentality, a sense of building a nation from the ground up. Many immigrants arrived in the country fueled by the romantic notion that a man could get off the boat with ten pounds in his pocket, and by the end of the year own his own home. In the case of the Kilbeys, that scenario proved not far off the mark; within two years of arrival, Les had attained a higher level of prosperity than he had ever enjoyed in England, and the family did in fact have a home (and a mortgage) of their own in the growing city of Wollongong, fifty miles south of Sydney.

In terms of Australia's culture and landscape, the mix of the familiar with the exotic must have been surprising for the new arrivals. It was an odd sensation to have traveled thousands of miles across the ocean to a continent on the far side of the world, and yet find this continent filled with familiar-looking, fair-skinned people who spoke English. It was an Anglo outpost in the middle of the Orient. Yet, in lower-income inner-city neighborhoods and across the outback the original inhabitants of Australia—the Aborigines—were a living reminder that Australia had a people and a culture before the whites arrived.

Mirroring this cultural disorientation, the plant and animal life of Australia is a bewildering mix of species, many of which had been introduced with the best of intentions by the early settlers. In some cases, though, these foreign imports had obliterated, or at least crowded out the indigenous species.

Although this new land became the only home the young Steve would know, traces of England remained in his consciousness. From his early years, he had a sense of being from somewhere else. The melancholy that accompanied this alienation—and the longing for a past that never truly was—would become hallmarks of his writing.

Steve's recollections of his first years in Australia are spotty, but one incident in particular stands out—primarily because it illuminates his early desire to entertain: On a slightly chilly morning during his first-grade year, he found himself at the front of his classroom, soaking up feelings of both exhilaration and terror as his peers gazed at him expectantly. His teacher stood to his left, arms crossed, bifocals poised on the bridge of her nose.

"What joke would you like to tell us today, Steven?" she asked.

"Um . . . " He looked down at his feet, then raised his eyes to look out over the class.

"What did the brassiere say to the top hat?"

Silence greeted him. None of his classmates even knew what a brassiere was.

Steve was looking at his fellow-students and away from his teacher, so he could not see the flush slowly spread across her cheeks. Finally, one of the boys in the front row called out, "What did the brassiere say, Steve?"

Steve smiled and offered up the punchline: "You go on a head, while I give these two a lift."

Silence fell upon the room like a cold, wet blanket. Steve was crestfallen. After all, the joke had gone over so well when his dad had told it to his friends. The sharp grip of his teacher's fingers on his arm shook him from his reverie. "You come with me, Mr. Kilbey," she said curtly. "We're going to the office."

An hour or so later, Steve's chuckling father came and picked him up from school. Steve was gratified that he had his father's approval, even if his classmates had greeted his effort to amuse them with indifference and his teacher had responded with quiet outrage.

★ ★ ★ ★ ★

By his own account, the young Steve was, in many ways, simply a smaller version of the person he is now: mischievous, imaginative, appearing to be detached yet actually quite observant. Early on, he absorbed his father's penchant for puns, and his love of the double entendre continues to this day—evident in such songs as "Pretty Ugly/Pretty Sad" and "Constant in Opal."

The Kilbeys moved a number of times as Les moved up the career ladder. They lived for nine years in Wollongong, then in Shepparton, Victoria for a year, before arriving in Canberra at the end of 1964.

Although Les primarily considered himself a photographer and musician, he had other skills, having worked in the repair shop at the Frigidaire factory in northwest London (where Joyce and several members of her family had also worked during the war, making munitions), and he gravitated towards the appliance repair business on arriving in Australia. In Wollongong, he took over as service manager for H.G. Palmer, a large manufacturer and retailer of electrical appliances. Les never actually fixed their washing machines, televisions, or refrigerators himself, but he oversaw the repairmen who were

Young Steve and young kangaroo, circa 1962 *(Kilbey family collection)*

dispatched to people's homes to do so. He made a decent living, one that allowed him spare time to tinkle away on the piano and log quality hours in his darkroom.

During their years in Wollongong, the family lived in a little fibro cottage built on a new estate just outside of town. "One luxury we were to have," Joyce wrote,

> at extra expense, of course, was a "water closet," which was similar to a septic tank except the toilet system had no bend, and waste just dropped down to a large pit. The flush was two pots of water. A vast improvement on the "dunny," if not exactly sewerage. This little outhouse was placed about six feet from our back door. We had a long back garden but the garden in the front was only small—not too much gardening needed to be done.

Down the street from the cottage, on the corner, stood a small general store owned by an older couple. Steve would trot down there every few days or so and buy himself a candy bar with some money his mother gave him. One day, Joyce stopped at the store and was surprised when the couple offered their sympathy for her crippled boy.

After a long and hilariously confused discussion with the shopkeepers, Joyce finally pieced together the truth: Steve, in order to acquire more chocolate for himself, had been spinning a tale about an ailing younger brother and soliciting extra candy for this unfortunate sibling. Joyce and Les discussed the incident with a doctor, and the conclusion they all reached was that Steve needed a *real* younger brother. The Kilbeys decided to add to their family, though it would be a few years before baby Russell came along.

Steve readily admits that he could be a royal pain in the ass as a young boy. "I reckon I was quite an unlovable kid, actually," he says.

> I was also quite obnoxious. I wasn't a very good friend to my friends because at whatever school I went to, I was oscillating between the nerdy brainy kids who never did anything naughty, and the wild, out-there kids. I wasn't really wild enough to *be* a wild, out-there kid, but I wasn't really brainy enough or focused enough to be with those others, so I was always at a bit of a loose end.

Steve channeled his frustration into attempts to win the approval of adults, but his intelligence, mixed with an already considerable sense of self-worth, got him into hot water. He was often branded as being "cheeky." He didn't recognize the authority of adults. Just because an adult said something didn't necessarily mean it was true, and Steve was quick to point out any discrepancies in their logic. His parents generally respected and understood him, but the same could not be said for members of his extended family, who, according to Steve, didn't quite know what to make of him.

As a result of his frustration with both adults and fellow children, Steve turned inward. From an early age, his active imagination was fueled by a voracious reading habit. One formative influence on Steve's artistic sensibility was C.S. Lewis's fanciful *Chronicles of Narnia* series. The first of the books, *The Lion, the Witch, and the Wardrobe,* featured a mysterious wardrobe that functioned as a portal into another realm: a world of talking animals, witches, and other fantastic creatures. The series followed the adventures of a group of schoolchildren as they traveled through this mystical realm, battling the forces of evil.

They may have been "the antithesis of rock and roll," Steve says,

> . . . but yeah, that whole thing of other worlds, other places, other lives really got to me. I desperately wanted to get out of this world, and I also had this feeling of being in the wrong country. I was reading all these books about the snow, woods and stuff. There were no woods in Australia . . . you go into the bush. There's no snow, there's no lamplight. Australians don't seem to understand what's going on. That added to this whole feeling that I didn't want to be here; I didn't want to be in this mundane, normal world; I wanted something else. So those books took me there. And then music, obviously, and then (later), drugs.

The premise of *The Lion, the Witch and the Wardrobe*—the idea that one could step into a box and journey into another dimension—was expanded on in the popular science-fiction television series *Doctor Who*, a show that Steve watched religiously in the 1960s. The show centered on "the Doctor"—a mysterious alien (in human form) of indeterminate age—and his human companions as they traveled through time and space in a spaceship disguised as a British police telephone box. During their adventures they encountered aliens and robots on other planets, historical figures from past eras on Earth, and fellow time-travelers. Steve would later comment that more than a few of the ideas in his songs could likely be traced back to this program, which has also been cited by such contemporaries as Robert Smith (of the Cure) and Robyn Hitchcock as an influence on their work.

Steve's interest in the fantastical worlds of *Narnia* and *Doctor Who* eventually led him to the source material for these stories, above all Grimm's Fairy Tales, Greek and Norse mythology, and Homer's *Iliad* and *Odyssey*. His fervent belief in a world of magic and fantasy beyond the world of the mundane spurred him on in his reading. It wasn't so much that he was alienated from his peers, it was simply that he preferred to spend most of his time in the realm of imagination.

Throughout his childhood, Steve had the vague feeling that—in addition to being from somewhere else—he had lived a number of lives before his current one. When he started learning Latin in grade school, he didn't feel that he was learning new concepts, more that he was re-learning ancient knowledge he had first acquired long ago. Every time he learned a new word, he thought, "Of course this is the right word for this concept. I remember!" When he discovered the Eastern belief in reincarnation, it seemed to explain these impressions perfectly. To him, it made more sense than the idea of one life followed by an afterlife in eternity.

Ancient history was another subject in which Steve took a keen interest. Again, the exploits of the Romans, the Greeks, the Vikings, and the Moors all seemed to have a ring of familiarity to the young boy. History served as a retreat from what he felt to be the doldrums of modern life in Australia, but with history, unlike the *Narnia* books, Steve could be certain that the events he read about had actually happened. The Aztecs really *had* built opulent cities of gold in South America. Marco Polo really *had* traveled thousands of miles, encountering the exotic peoples and cultures of the East. The Vikings really *had* sailed the oceans in search of riches, land, and women. It all seemed so much more exciting than Shepparton, Wollongong, or Canberra.

And while Steve was skeptical of Christianity from an early age, the stories of the Old Testament—filled as they were with images of divine intervention, spectacular battles, man-swallowing whales, wise and erudite philosopher-kings—intrigued him. The arbitrariness of the Old Testament God—so quick to anger, capable of wholesale destruction with the raising of a finger—fit right in with the stories of the Greek gods and all that had come before. But Steve also noted the ways in which the stories of the Bible intertwined with documented ancient history. In his imagination, the two would mix effortlessly.

According to Joyce, the family—while nominally Christian—was not overly religious. "We weren't a church-going family," she told me.

> Not good Anglicans at all! Strangely enough, though, I worked for the Anglican Registry in Canberra for about six years and most Thursdays, I made the effort to attend the early service given just for the staff. I was also confirmed whilst I was there. I thoroughly enjoyed my work there and even got to meet the Archbishop of Westminster! I sometimes wonder if my working there had anything to do with the name Steve chose [for his band]—kind of tongue-in-cheek!"

The fact that Steve was an only child for several years probably contributed both to his sense of independence and his feelings of isolation. But in 1962, when Steve was eight, Joyce gave birth to the Kilbeys' second child, Russell. Steve was thrilled to finally have a brother. He had been very protective of Joyce as she was expecting, and he was equally protective of the new baby once it arrived. He showed remarkable tolerance, considering the fact that Russell would often very quickly destroy a model car or boat his elder brother had spent hours working on.

As a baby, Russell was even quieter than Steve, but he also had a mischievous streak, and his inquisitive nature often got him into trouble. He once touched a hot iron, blistering his whole hand, and on another occasion burned his throat and face after drinking from a bottle of petrol.

In 1964 the Kilbeys made what would be their final relocation, to Canberra. Australia's capital city is today considered a marvel of landscape architecture, sporting European-style tree-lined streets and endless manicured tracts of green space. Canberra is a city that was entirely planned out before any buildings were erected. Walter Burley Griffin, the Chicago-based architect who had won the design contest, allowed for a fair amount of indigenous plant life to coexist alongside imported European vegetation, resulting in the new city being dubbed the "bush capital." Although construction on Canberra began in 1913, the city didn't really begin to flourish until the late 1940s. When the Kilbeys arrived, it still felt brand new. Some critics (including Steve) contend that all the careful planning that went into its construction resulted in a feeling of sterility. To them, the entire enterprise seemed forced and artificial. And, despite the fact that the city had a certain cosmopolitan sensibility as a result of all the foreign embassies located there, Steve's day-to-day interactions were with peers who could be described as solidly provincial. They repeatedly teased him about his British accent.

"I guess you could call it redneck," Steve says.

It was your worst nightmare if you were sort of a sensitive type. Not that I was all that sensitive. I could adapt, I could pretend I was Australian. But for the kids who couldn't do that, it was hell.

Steve's bandmate Peter Koppes has a slightly different take on Canberra, which was also his home for most of his early life. "I really liked it," he says.

> It was fascinating watching a city grow; it deconditions you from the belief that they always existed. But . . . it's true that it didn't seem like a genuine city; it seemed like everyone was pretending. Even the slums weren't real slums. Everyone had a car. But when you become a teenager, you want to get out of it and see what the (real) big city holds for you.

As a reward for Les's years of dedicated service at H.G. Palmer's, the company moved the family into an attractive brick house in a cul-de-sac at the top of a hill, where they were able to see right over the local race track. This house was set back on a third of an acre with enough space in the back to allow the Kilbeys to build their own swimming pool eventually. Canberra may have been a bit of a drag for Steve, but for Les and Joyce their comfortable standard of living represented the culmination of everything they had worked for.

★ ★ ★ ★ ★

At age twelve, Steve had his first piano lessons. His teacher, Julie Green, became almost part of the family for a time, calling every Saturday morning, teaching Steve, then having lunch with the Kilbeys and sometimes staying for dinner. Steve picked up the piano fairly quickly, helped by the fact that the sheet music had numbers under the notes corresponding to the player's fingers. From the outset, Steve longed to move on from the classical pieces his teacher favored; he wanted to play the Beatles, not Bach. Things came to a head when Steve began teaching himself Beatles songs *instead* of his weekly assignments. This went on for a few weeks until Ms. Green gave him an ultimatum: Either he would play the piece of music she had set for him, or she wouldn't be coming anymore. Steve's response was simply to say nothing and scowl at the piano keys.

Ms. Green, with tears in her eyes, gathered up her books and headed to the door, saying to Les and Joyce, "I'm only wasting your money and my time if he's not going to be obedient—and I had such high hopes for him!" It would be a few years before Steve took up an instrument again, but music had already begun to exert a hold on his imagination. In addition to the first records of the Beatles, Steve was fascinated by one of his father's records, *Frank Sinatra Sings for Only the Lonely*. This album, a 1958 collaboration between Sinatra and his arranger Nelson Riddle, could arguably be called one of the first concept albums. The songs had been carefully chosen and sequenced so that the whole record stood as a meditation on loneliness and unrequited love. This was dark stuff from an artist who had attained popularity with breezy numbers like "Jeepers Creepers" and "Get Happy." Steve was impressed by the artistic slant of the project and hypnotized by Sinatra's world-weary, cello-like voice. He sat in his room and played the record over and over, soaking up its atmosphere.

The transition from childhood to adolescence was difficult for Steve. As he told Christie Eliezer of *Juke*:

> Childhood to me was far more interesting than being sweet sixteen. It's such a special time. When I was six, I'd go out into the garden, play with the stones, it was so magical and full of wonder. I hated leaving that, and I yearn for it always. I remember at thirteen playing with my model soldiers and airplanes and one day thinking "I don't want to do this anymore," and it was time to leave childhood behind. It was very sad.
> I let it go very reluctantly.

In his early teens, Steve's desire to perform continued to grow, although the exact mode of performance continued to elude him. For a brief period, he entertained the fantasy of becoming a professional player of Australian rules football, an aggressive and dangerous sport affectionately referred to as "footy." But the teenaged Kilbey was about as stocky as a string bean, and although he was all heart, he got knocked around quite a bit by his beefier peers in games at school.

Steve fared much better as a member of his school's debating team. Following parliamentary procedure, he and his teammates took the floor and debated such topical issues as whether New Guinea should be granted independence. This experience, he recalls, "gave me this idea that if you seem to know what you're talking about, that's good enough. You'd think when I got up on stage that [the fate of New Guinea] was the most important thing in my life. We used to crush the other teams."

Steve also became interested in poetry, gravitating toward the Romantics and, even more, the 19th-century French poets Baudelaire and Rimbaud. These writers were masters of imagery who extolled the virtues of mind-altering substances such as opium and hashish. In *Letter from a Seer,* Rimbaud advocated a "complete derangement of the senses" as a means for poetic inspiration, an approach that Steve would adopt wholeheartedly in subsequent years. Interestingly, the famous picture of Rimbaud with messy hair, glassy-eyed stare, and bow-tie askew bears a striking resemblance to the young Steve Kilbey.

Steve, who felt no allegiance to traditional Christianity, was intrigued by Rimbaud's interest in gnosticism, the belief in secret knowledge passed down from generation to generation—knowledge that emphasized that life itself was inherently illusory. Baudelaire, who seemingly embraced more conventional Christian beliefs, celebrated in his verse the pleasure of giving in to sin, and seemed to place a higher value on immediate sensual gratification than on the possibility of salvation.

Steve with Lionel, circa 1969 *(Kilbey family collection)*

In *Les Fleurs du mal*, Baudelaire explored the subject of willful transgression, and merged the character of Satan with Hermes Trismegitsus, a mystical Egyptian alchemist. It was heady stuff, and Steve saw it as a logical extension of the childhood fantasy realm that had been shaped by C.S. Lewis, J.R.R. Tolkien, and *Doctor Who*. He was not yet using drugs, but he was certainly aware of the fact that drugs had featured prominently in the lives of many great poets and artists and that there definitely seemed to be a link between chemical stimulation and creativity.

Finally, into this mix tumbled that most Dionysian of all art forms: rock and roll.

One afternoon in late fall, in the middle of an average high-school day, Steve heard something in the first-floor hallway while on his way outside to play football on the oval. The sound of delicately-strummed guitar chords wafted from the half-open door of one of the classrooms, stopping the young man in his tracks. He looked in and saw that the creator of these sounds was a new boy, a dark-haired, slender-framed thirteen-year-old who had just moved to the area; the boy sat in a chair, playing a battered acoustic guitar. A coterie of the school's most beautiful girls surrounded him, enthralled.

Steve felt pangs of envy. Here was a kid three years his junior, holding these girls enraptured in a magical spell. In a quavering voice the boy sang a song by Donovan: "The continent of Atlantis was an island . . . "

Steve walked in and sat down with the girls. They paid no attention to him. The boy, however, looked over and said, "Hello."

"Is that difficult to play?" Steve asked.

"No, I'll show you. It's really easy; it's just C and D."

He gave the guitar to Steve and pointed to the positions on the fretboard. Steve's fingers fumbled for a bit, finding it difficult to press down on the frets without getting a muted sound, but he finally strummed his first chord to the approving grin of this young man, who at such an early age already possessed a power that Steve coveted. Steve thought, "I have waited too long."

AN INTERLUDE (I)

After our first interview, Steve offered to take me to his youngest brother's apartment. I was eager to observe the inner workings of Karmic Hit—the label John Kilbey ran that released many of the family's solo projects.

Temporarily talked-out, Steve and I walked a couple of blocks in silence. It was a gorgeous night—unusually warm for the Sydney winter, with just a touch of humidity. The streets were dark, lit only by the soft lights emanating from the individual homes. "You'll probably get a kick out of this, Steve," I said, breaking our silence. "I used to teach your book *Earthed* to high-school students in Georgia."

"Really?" he said, his voice lilting upward slightly. "What did you teach from it?"

"I taught the introduction—the part where you lay out your manifesto on the death of beauty and magic."

"What did they make of it?"

"Most of them didn't get it, understandably. But with a few of them, you could see the light bulbs go on in their heads. They appreciated being exposed to something so different from what they were surrounded by. I mean, it wasn't about NASCAR or deer hunting."

He seemed to ponder this for a moment. I wasn't sure how informed Steve was on the whole NASCAR phenomenon. Finally he said, "How do you like that—teaching?"

"I *love* teaching; I don't particularly like teaching teenagers."

"I need to do more of that. I need to do *something* outside of music to make a living. Because music is a tough career to rely on, financially.

Especially now."

We walked along for a bit. I thought about the fact that here was my hero, the guy who had the type of career I had always longed for, expressing a desire to get into *my* line of work!

"Well," I said, "I think you'd be a big hit in creative-writing workshops."

"Really?" he said.

"Absolutely."

"I've come to realize I'm good at getting people inspired. That is, I'm good at getting people out of writer's block—but I'm talking about songwriting. I'm not sure if it works for writing. Maybe."

"I think it might. But how do you get out of writer's block?"

"Well, I smoke marijuana."

We both laughed.

"I smoke it every day," he continued.

"Yeah," I said, "but if you were standing in a classroom, is *that* what you would tell your students?"

"Well, that's not all of it. The main thing is, you need to keep your muse on its toes. You need to make rules, then break them. For instance, if you smoke marijuana every day and you've got writer's block, then try this— *don't* smoke it. Get drunk . . . or get sober. Whatever's the opposite of what you usually do.

"Here's a rule: no *Baby, I Love You* songs. Try to write without using the word love. Then, when that gets old, write a song all *about* love, but make it different than any you've ever heard before. You know what we do in the band now? We switch up on our instruments. I might pick up a guitar, Marty plays my bass, maybe Peter sits down on the drums. We all start playing, and we sound different, because we don't exactly know what we're doing.

"Another thing you can do is write songs with a partner. Or you could write a song, cut all the words up, and rearrange them, like the old game Exquisite Corpse. Or cut up one of *my* songs, shuffle it around, and make it yours."

Our footsteps echoed through the empty street. Steve stopped at a stairway. "Here we are," he said. We walked up the steps into the foyer of a small apartment building. Steve looked down at my shoes, now visible in the hallway light.

"I was once told never to trust a man in brown shoes," he said. He gave
the slightest hint of a smile, then rapped his knuckles on the door. I heard
steps from inside, and the sound of a latch being undone. The door opened.
John Kilbey's head, sprouting a mass of hair that had the consistency of a
Brillo pad, appeared in the entryway. His was the type of hair that stood up
of its own accord; growing up, out, and *beyond*.

"I've brought Mr. Lurie," Steve said, "but he needs dinner."

"No worries," said John in his soft voice. "You can eat with me."

We followed him down a narrow hallway, into a sparsely furnished living room. A black and white cat bounded out from a bedroom and nuzzled up against my legs, its tail sticking straight up.

"This," said Steve, spreading his arms wide, "is Karmic Hit world headquarters."

John laughed. "It's also where I live," he said.

I was a bit taken aback. I guess I'd expected Karmic Hit to be housed in an austere white office somewhere in downtown Sydney, with an attractive woman behind the front desk and a long winding stairway ascending to a state-of-the-art recording studio. But here I was, staring at a threadbare couch, two scruffy guys in jean jackets, and an affectionate cat. I leaned into the doorway of an adjoining room and saw a small Macintosh computer sitting on a small desk. John pointed at the Mac and said, "There's the studio."

The two Kilbeys laughed some more, then Steve said, "Okay Brother John, I'm going home."

Later, I watched as John hunched over his stove frying chickpea patties and a pile of cabbage. "How are you getting on here, Robert?" he asked.

"Pretty well I guess," I said. "But people think I talk funny."

"I'm not surprised," he muttered.

"What's that?" I said.

"Oh, nothing." He looked back at me and smirked.

I was having difficulty figuring out John Kilbey. He had been open and enthusiastic about the project at first, but now he seemed a bit guarded. I guess it was one thing to e-mail someone to say you're writing a book, quite another to materialize in a person's home with a notepad and a tape recorder.

Robert Lurie and John Kilbey, 2003

I wondered if *I* matched *his* expectations. Had he expected a road-weary, grizzled Nick Tosches type, chainsmoking and jittering in his leather jacket? Or a pasty, stuttering sycophant? He evidently hadn't expected a baby-faced, sweater-clad grad student with an accent somewhere between Bill Clinton and the cast of *Fargo*. Or maybe he hadn't thought about it at all.

John is the youngest of the three brothers, a full fourteen years Steve's junior. Tall and soft-spoken, he's become known as "the nice one," the Kilbey most likely to shake your hand, listen to what you had to say, give you a minute or an hour of his time.

This much I knew about John: He had at one point adopted the stage name John Underwood so he wouldn't be judged against his more famous older brother. He had fronted such bands as the Bhagavad Guitars and Warp Factor Nine. In the 1990s he transformed Karmic Hit—which at first had been simply a name Steve affixed to his solo projects—into a fully functional, profit-generating record label.

Also, in Steve's darkest moments John had been a lifeline, a quiet Buddha, loving him unconditionally. When Steve had finally returned to

Australia, he made it a priority to find a home within walking distance of his little brother.

All these thoughts bounced around my mind as John spooned cabbage onto my plate.

"Do you ever forget the fact that you live in paradise?" I asked.

"How's that?"

"Living in Australia, in Bondi, do you take it for granted?"

"No," he said, sitting down across from me, "I'm still perpetually in awe."

I thought about Bainbridge Island, in Washington State, where my family now lives—the way the island glimmers as you approach it on the ferry, the sight of the Puget Sound ringed with jagged mountain peaks. It's easy to forget the magnificence of a place you've become accustomed to.

"Sydney Harbor is beautiful," John continued, "And Bondi, well, you've seen it."

I felt a brief pang of jealousy, thinking of the three brothers living so close together, creatively cross-pollinating, in one of the most gorgeous locations on earth. But then I thought of my own brother, also a songwriter, and I thought of Seattle, and Savannah, and Minneapolis, and all the other places I had been lucky enough to call home.

After dinner we had a couple of beers and sat back and listened to tracks from Steve's new collaboration with Jeffrey Cain of the American band Remy Zero. The project, called *Isidore*, had finally given John a chance to work with his older brother; John had handled all the backing vocals on the album, sometimes multi-tracking a virtual Kilbey choir—a bed of sound on which Steve's soul-weary voice could rest. As I sipped my beer and listened to the amazing melodies coming from the speakers, I felt more at ease with my surroundings. I realized that, in addition to having a geographical home, a person could have a spiritual home—not necessarily a specific religion or a church, but a place in which your spirit could wander freely. It seemed that my spiritual home was within the music that this family created. Something about the combination of the instruments, voices, and lyrics always made me feel as if I were returning from a long journey, resting again in a familiar embrace. And if this was indeed my home, it was one I could take with me wherever I went.

3
I'VE GOT A MILK-WHITE ELECTRIC GUITAR

After his school-day introduction to the hypnotic power of rock music, Steve went home with a goal fully formed: he wanted to be a songwriter. It wouldn't be enough to simply learn the guitar and play Donovan songs. No, he would play songs featuring *his* words and *his* notes. Carefully thinking through each step of his plan, Steve determined that the fastest route to a songwriting career was via the bass. He correctly reasoned that, as a bassist, he could be up and playing in bands faster than he would as a guitarist. Once established in a band, he could slowly and methodically begin to take the reins, eventually using this hypothetical group as a vehicle for his own original songs.

Les couldn't have been more thrilled with Steve's newfound interest in music-making. He bought Steve a bass and built him an amplifier out of an old radio. Day after day Steve sat in his room, plunking away for hours. It came slowly, but he had relentless drive. Eventually he saved up and bought a good amplifier, and before long he met two other classmates who played guitar.

At first they would all sit in Steve's garage playing random notes and chords. Then one day Steve said, "Hey, do you know that chord E? You play that, and then what happens if I play E on bass?" They played the chord and the bass note together, getting so excited at what they heard, you would have thought they had stumbled upon the theory of relativity. Soon they were on to playing A, C, D, G, and, when the guitarists could finally get their fingers into the awkward position, F. (At that point, B was still a pipe dream.)

The Kilbey garage became a meeting place for struggling local musicians. "We were always jamming on the weekends," Steve says. "Guys singing in my dad's garage, guys on the drums, and about nineteen guys plugged into my one amp. Guys all over the place turning up with guitars and nobody had amps."

Les and Steve attempted to play together a few times. Their next-door neighbor was an accomplished drummer, so father and son would go over, set up their gear, and play away. These sessions mainly consisted of Steve noodling around in F-sharp while his dad tickled the ivories. If Steve ever tried to do something fancy, Les would say, "Don't bloody do that!" To which Steve would snap back, "Dad, you don't know anything!"

Over the next two years, Steve continued to improve on bass, playing mainly with other musicians from his school.

Steve, circa 1970 *(Kilbey family collection)*

Even Steve's romantic life seemed to be tied to the bass guitar; in his mid-teens he began dating a girl named Patricia, whom he claims he was drawn to partly because she resembled Roger Waters, the bassist of Pink Floyd! Steve liked to tell her that she looked "exactly like Roger on the back cover of *Meddle*." To his continual bewilderment, the compliment never went over well, though one need only glance at a picture from that era to understand Patricia's discomfort. Not only was she being compared to a *man*, but to a somewhat simian-looking man at that!

The Kilbeys now had a new addition to their family: baby John. While obviously happy to have another brother, Steve could not possibly have foreseen the impact this quiet, curly-haired baby would one day have on his career.

Those were good years for Les and Joyce; they had a house full of boys, all bustling with energy. The family's prosperity continued to grow; Les and some of his former colleagues from H.G. Palmer's had gone into business for themselves and had made a great success of it. Physically, Les had filled out somewhat and wore his hair more conservatively, but he retained his striking good looks. In fact, like Paul Newman or Robert Mitchum, he had actually become *more* handsome with the years. His one regret was that he hadn't had the daughter he so wanted. Still, it was pretty hard to complain when life had bestowed so much good fortune on him and his family. The marriage, after all these years, was still strong; despite Les being a lifelong flirt, he and Joyce remained committed to each other, and with his wickedly funny sense of humor constantly on hand to diffuse any tension, it was impossible for anyone in the family to sustain any kind of anger at him—even on the occasion when he impulsively decided to paint the walls and floor of their house in garish colors.

Steve's seventeenth year was a pivotal one in several ways. It was the year in which he lost his virginity—an experience he recalls with a certain dismay, since it signaled the final nail in the coffin of his childhood.

It was also the year in which he abruptly decided to become a vegetarian, a decision he has stuck to—excepting a few brief lapses in his early twenties—ever since. The roots of his conversion are difficult to ascertain. He says simply, "I'm a vegetarian for *all* reasons. Every reason you could possibly think of."

Some of the influence may have come from his mother. She has been an animal lover since childhood. As she wrote in *The Tale of the Old Iron Pot*: "(I've) always had this affinity with animals and it still saddens me to walk past a pet shop and see the poor little puppies and kittens in tiny cages." This sentiment, combined with his own initial readings in compassion-steeped Eastern philosophy, likely formed the backdrop for Steve's vegetarianism. It became a lifelong passion—the only moral/political issue about which he has been consistently, evangelically, outspoken.

It was also during that year that Steve joined his first band. Having grown tired of the endless noodling in the garage, he began perusing the classifieds section of the Canberra newspaper. One day he came across an ad that said, "Wanted: bass player for working band."

He called the number, went down and auditioned, and didn't do a very good job. For one thing, Steve had always played by ear, but this band played off music charts. Steve's lack of musical theory and his inability to sight-read was readily apparent to them. Still, his eagerness must have impressed them. One of the guys told Steve, "If you go home and practice all weekend and come back, we might have you in the band."

Steve learned everything, practiced round the clock, went back, and impressed them enough to get the job. He was now the bass player for Saga—a "50/50 band" (they played 50 percent old covers, 50 percent the latest ones.) It was an inauspicious beginning for the future leader of the Church, but it did give him the chance to hone his bass chops and get comfortable playing live.

Most importantly, Steve found himself earning $200-300 a week playing music. Saga performed at weddings, parties, and universities. Sometimes they'd play until four in the morning, and then do it all over again the next day.

It wasn't to last, though. Despite the fact that Steve was a reliable player and showed up on time, his attitude frequently got him in trouble. The main problem was that the others wanted Saga to be a show band—with jokes— but Steve refused to fall in line. Like Miles Davis during the cool-bop era, he would hang back, playing his instrument and looking sullen. That was *his* performance. Eventually he came to loathe the material so much that he started laughing at his bandmates onstage. This was not a wise move; Steve had made the fatal error of believing himself indispensable. He received a rude awakening when Saga convened a meeting and booted him out. To add insult to injury, Patricia dumped him on the very same day. At a stroke, his entire social and professional world evaporated. Partly to console himself and partly to relieve his boredom, he delved deeper into songwriting.

At this point Steve was ingesting a steady diet of Beatles, Bowie, T. Rex, Bob Dylan, the Zombies, and (Zombies offshoot) Argent. As he entered his late teens, he became more and more obsessed with glam rock—both as a musical genre and an aesthetic. The first songs he wrote had been woeful, love-gone-bad ballads that employed a lot of minor-seventh chords, but he eventually reversed this template, developing a style that was musically direct but lyrically obscure. This streamlined approach to composition came about almost by accident. One day, in the midst of changing the strings on his guitar, Steve started playing a riff, going up and down on an E string. The limitation of only being able to play on one string strangely freed him up, allowing him to create riffs that were angular and forceful, closer to his beloved T. Rex than the material he had been writing until now. Gone were the complex chord structures he had been laboring over. From this point forward, Steve strove to write music that was subtly evocative rather than showy.

Steve's next step was to form his own band: Precious Little. Unlike his previous group, Precious Little was conceived to play Steve's original songs, along with a few well-picked covers. However, the aspiring artiste was not yet comfortable as a singer, and recruited an acquaintance to do all the vocals. But at the band's very first gig, the designated singer looked around the curtain, recoiled, and said, "I'm not going on."

Steve stared at him. "Why not?" he asked.

"Because there's all these bullies from my school out there!"

Steve rolled his eyes and said, "Man, there's a heap of bullies from *my* school, too, but you've got to go on!"

The singer's face grew red. "I'm not going on!"

Steve grabbed him by the arm. "You've got to fucking go on, man!" he pleaded.

"I'm not going on. They'll kill me." The singer shook his arm loose and walked away. Steve had no alternative but to go out and sing the songs himself. And once he had a taste of being the frontman, there was no going back.

Not too long afterwards, Steve met a young musician who would quite literally change the course of his life. Fittingly, this meeting took place in a church.

★ ★ ★ ★ ★

Steve arrived for practice that day to find that the church hall where Precious Little regularly rehearsed had been double-booked. When he entered the big, drafty space, a heavy-metal band had already set up and was playing at a deafening volume. A curly-haired singer pranced about in skintight T-shirt and bell-bottomed jeans, shrieking into the microphone. The band's drummer pounded his kit with all the subtlety and refinement of a spouse-abuser.

But just a few feet away stood a figure who seemed utterly out of place: a
tall, dark-haired young man who stared pensively at the ground as he coaxed rippling notes from a Fender Stratocaster. One minute his playing favored overdrive and heavy-metal squeal, the next it became fluid and mellifluous, with echoes of Santana. Although the band's thunderous racket was likely to give Steve a splitting headache before the day was through, this particular musician caught his attention.

It was quickly decided that the two groups would switch off throughout the day, each doing thirty-minute rehearsals. Rather than set up both of the drumsets, the bands decided to take turns at the already-assembled kit, with the guitarists rotating in and out. During one of the transitions, as various players fiddled with their amps and stringed instruments, the mystery guitarist sat down at the drum set and started playing. It was not a showy gesture, simply a means of passing the time. And yet everyone stopped, put down their instruments, and crowded around to see him play. He handled the kit with the same ease he had displayed on guitar, effortlessly executing difficult fills before returning to his main beat. The regular drummer for the metal band watched with his jaw hanging open; he had been

Steve, circa 1972 *(Kilbey family collection)*

bested at his own instrument by his taciturn bandmate who had never previously indicated any interest in the drums. But Peter Koppes remained oblivious to it all, pounding away with a serene expression on his face.

Steve watched intently, the gears in his head spinning.

Much later in the day, out of earshot from the other musicians, Steve introduced himself to Koppes, saying, "I have an offer for you—it may sound a bit odd. I've been thinking of fleshing our sound out with a second drummer. It would give us an edge, I think—make us a bit harder. The songs wouldn't be hard to learn, and who knows . . . maybe we could get you doing a little bit of guitar here and there. I've already got gigs booked, so you'd just need to show up, learn the parts, and get paid."

Koppes thought about it a moment, then said nonchalantly, "Okay. Why not?" He turned and began gathering up his gear.

At least that's how Steve tells the story (with the aid of my imagination, I should add; I don't *really* know what the singer of Koppes' heavy-metal band looked or sounded like, but I suspect I'm not too far off). Peter remembers the meeting slightly differently:

> We went to (our) rehearsal hall and met Steve. And Steve said his band needed a drummer. That's when I saw Steve for the first time—he was playing bass in this glam-rock band—Beyond Beavers. It *became* Precious Little from Beyond Beavers. But they already had a drummer. And in the middle of the rehearsal their drummer turned up. And they said, "Ah, well, we need *two* drummers." Well, my band's drummer was really crap. I don't know how it happened, but I got on his drum kit and did a drum solo. I don't know why I did that—I'm not normally a showy kind of person. And then I saw them (Precious Little) at a concert a week later and they said why don't I come and play drums in their band. I thought they were interesting because they were playing original songs.

The two-drummer setup lasted for only a few gigs. Peter Koppes may have been one of the best drummers around, but he was an even better guitarist. His level of musicianship elevated that of everyone around him. And even though Precious Little performed a type of music he had not previously played, he slipped into this new style with ease. In terms of personality he was all business; he harbored no illusions about the "brotherhood" of being in a band. While always friendly, he made it clear that he would not hesitate to take a better offer if one ever came along.

* * * * *

Peter Koppes is an enigma. Unlike Steve, whose mysteriousness is largely an affectation, Peter caries with him a perpetual cloud of otherworldly sadness—a soft melancholy whose cause is difficult to ascertain. He has the reputation of being a quiet man, but this stems more from the soft lilt of his voice than any reluctance to talk (indeed, as an Arista rep would later comment: "Once you get him talking, he will *not* shut up!") Add to that his unusual appearance—a full head of thick, curly hair; penetrating, thoughtful eyes; a slender frame; and long, spindly legs—and it's no wonder that a friend of mine once remarked, "Koppes could be Doctor Who." That being said, Peter does not possess the kind of personal magnetism that Steve has in spades, and so he tends to recede into the background. Onstage with the Church, he makes no effort to be flashy or draw attention to himself; his performances are entirely inward-looking, which can be enthralling to the dedicated musicians in the audience but means the casual concertgoer barely notices him. Ironically, of the four players he has the least trouble subsuming musically into the larger whole of the Church, a band he co-founded but only reluctantly continues to play in.

Because of his withdrawn nature, many myths have sprung up concerning Koppes. One of the most persistent, which routinely crops up in articles about the band, is that he has Greek ancestry. Not true, he says.

> My father's ancestry is Dutch, and there's southern French and Portuguese possibly. And my mother's ancestry is northern German but she says there's a Danish ancestor. The problem is she's got brown eyes and my grandmother had brown eyes and that's just not a Teutonic thing. Once she said we might have Gypsy blood and she never went into it again. I've come to think I've got that spirit though.

It's also not often reported that Koppes came to the guitar fairly late in the game. Even though he had been around stringed instruments his whole life (his father played guitar and bass in addition to being a talented singer and pianist), Peter's first stab at playing music was from behind a drum kit. "I was taught drums military style. Military grip. I still play like that now," he says. He played in a number of bands as a teenager and, due to his restless nature, began learning guitar by watching and imitating the various guitarists he worked with. He was a quick learner—probably due to his family's musical pedigree—and before long he was playing better than the guitarists who had initially taught him.

Unlike Steve, who generally dislikes showy guitarists, Peter was drawn to virtuoso players like Jimi Hendrix and Jimmy Page. One thing he *did* share with Steve was an appreciation for Pink Floyd. The two found plenty to admire in the seminal psychedelic quartet; Steve was drawn to the atmosphere and surrealism of early Syd Barrett-era Floyd, Peter to the melodic, inventive guitar work of Barrett replacement David Gilmour.

Looking back on his first meeting with Steve, Peter reflects on the two musicians' differing tastes:

> Probably my favorite artist is Jimi Hendrix—as a human being. Just in his spirituality and his ability to soulfully express himself through his guitar. He was just amazing. See, Steve was totally into the glam-rock Bowie/Bolan thing, and I was into the Hendrix, Santana, Floyd thing. I was into guitar. I like AC/DC. I think all guitarists do. I teach guitar, and all these young kids love that stuff. It's like driving a V-8. You plug your Gibson into a couple Marshalls and turn the amp up with your pants flapping on your legs and play "Highway to Hell." You know, Steve doesn't like that kind of stuff. And interestingly, he likes Mark Bolan which is kind of boogie. Steve plays really great blues and boogie, but he's always got a grin on his face, laughing at himself doing it. But he's really a great blues player. But the Church, as I've always described it, is the whitest band on the planet.

In Precious Little, these differences proved complementary. Peter's majestic guitar playing enabled the songs to be something more than mere glam pastiche. Steve spiked the new mixture with his increasingly off-the-wall lyrics. It was a winning combination.

Having recently graduated from high school, Steve settled into an apartment of his own and began devoting all his free time to playing in Precious Little. He began smoking pot casually as well, finding it a useful catalyst for creative composition. In drug terms he could be termed a late bloomer; it would be a number of years before he began using anything heavily.

Like so many aspiring artists coming face to face with reality for the first time, Steve very quickly realized he needed a day job. He got a low-grade position in the civil service, programming computers, but his heart was never really in it. Instead of thinking about the endless stream of punch cards he handled and the dizzying sequences of binary numbers with which the bulky machines communicated (this was the early 1970s, well before the advent of the microchip and the PC), his thoughts wandered to the music and melodies that constantly streamed from his unconscious. Those early songs were by no means lyrical masterpieces. "Jet Fin Rock" featured the chorus "How come you never do the Jet Fin Rock?/How come you never give me a shock?" And "The Igloo Blues," in terms of literary technique, was more along the lines of Jerry Lewis than P.G. Wodehouse: "I've got the Igloo Blues/because there's no room for my harpoon." The music to back up these words consisted of swaggering glam riffs heavily influenced by Marc Bolan. The mascara-smeared rocker had quickly become Steve's primary musical idol. With his blues-based riffs and fantasy-inspired word-play, Bolan epitomized Steve's rock-and-roll ideal: highbrow erudition mixed with swagger and sex.

Steve had already adopted the glam look onstage—caking his face with makeup and wearing flamboyant clothes—and he showed a willingness to experiment with drugs, too. But the third component of glam rock—the glorification of alternative sexuality— was a bridge Steve was not willing to cross. He had no problem flirting with the image of bisexuality as a compo- nent of his stage persona, but never felt any desire to actually engage in a homosexual act. He muses now that, in a lifetime of sensory indulgence, ho- mosexuality is one of the few things he hasn't tried.

Baby Grande live, L-R: Joe Lee, Peter Koppes, Steve Kilbey
(Barry McCulloch)

Steve's first stab at "respectable" songwriting coincided with the metamorphosis of Precious Little into the leaner, meaner animal that was Baby Grande. In this new band, Steve ditched the bass entirely, opting instead to prance around the stage in the style of Mick Jagger. Peter's tasteful lead playing moved to the forefront, and the band (with a new bassist in tow) left the covers behind and now performed Steve's songs exclusively. Of these early songs, two stood out: "As Above/ So Below" and "Bel-Air." Both blended lyrical sophistication with sublime melodies.

Despite the improved quality of the material, however, Baby Grande failed to gain much of a foothold in the Canberra scene. Steve blames this on a phenomenon called "cultural cringe" (a term coined by Australian writer A. A. Phillips):

You rarely hear that expression in Australia anymore, but it was very much around in the seventies: this idea that anything that happened in Australia couldn't be good. It had to be from America or England or Europe. But anything from Australia was kind of second-rate, kind of local, parochial. Canberra was like a fucking microcosm of all that, so anything from Sydney was always better than anything in Canberra . . . In Canberra no one liked [us]. In Canberra at that stage, everyone was into funk—you know, like the Average White Band—or heavy metal. The paradigm was Black Sabbath or Deep Purple. It's very kind of bland or ordinary music and it seemed like the one thing it all had in common was it had all the mystery filtered out of it. The people that surrounded me—I didn't really have any friends—the people I worked with were all so achingly ordinary and just wanted ordinary things from their life and from their music and from their art. They weren't even fucking interested in discussing these other things.

Australian music historian David Nichols offers a rather broader view of the local music scene in those years, noting that "the 1970s saw an increasing patriotic fervor—and greater industry interest—in the production and con-

Opening for AC/DC, November 7, 1975 *(Barry McCulloch)*

sumption of locally made music." He points to the band Hush as an Australian glam outfit that had considerable chart success in the early to mid-'70s, alongside other home-grown bands such as Skyhooks, Sherbet, and Daddy Cool. Nichols observes that, in theory, Canberra would have been quite receptive to the type of music Steve was making: "Glam rock would have gone down well in Canberra in the era of glam rock—say, 1972 to 1975 . . . There seem to have been quite a few venues [where Baby Grande could have played], and a small local scene."

No doubt Steve's feelings were valid ones, however. Amongst his circle of acquaintances—which he admits was very small—glam rock was apparently not popular, and this impression was evidently reinforced by the uninterested audiences he encountered at Baby Grande's shows. But there are

probably a number of other reasons for Baby Grande's failure in addition
to—or instead of—cultural cringe. For one thing, Steve hadn't yet found
his style as a frontman. His onstage antics may well have come across as
awkward and affected rather than bold and electrifying. And the ability to
sing on key still proved elusive; as the few Baby Grande recordings I've heard
make clear, Steve's vocal stylings at the time were very different from the relaxed croon that would later win audiences over. Back then, he explains, he
had several singing personas, which he summarizes as follows: there was the
New York Dolls-inspired "screamer"; the Lou Reed-esque "street poet"; and
his favorite, the Bolan/Bowie glam hybrid, crooning and purring one moment, then escalating (without warning) to histrionic yelps. As a performer
and as a person, Steve tended to drive people away, and yet he kept pushing
forward. He lived in an enjoyable alternate universe that existed in complete
opposition to reality. The fact that he could sustain his glam utopia for as
long as he did—in the face of almost universal indifference—is a testament
both to his tenacity and the power of his imagination (some would say delu-
sion).

Nevertheless, he soon found that his carefully-constructed artistic cocoon was by no means immune to the bitter intrusions of real life. For just
as Steve began, tentatively, to stand on his own two legs as a musician, he
lost the one hero who loomed larger than all of his glam idols combined.

4
YOU'RE VANISHING AGAIN, AFTER EVERYTHING WE'VE SAID

In many ways my father remains a real enigma to me: a father who, as the benchmark of a father, was about the best you could have; a father who very rarely raised his voice; a father who very rarely—and only when sorely pushed—would physically discipline. A very contented man, content with his lot. Very popular, far more popular with his friends than I am. He was always very welcome and fitted in effortlessly wherever he went. And even right now at this advanced age, I'm trying to put some of my father's principles into action. If I go round someone's house, what's the major impression I want them to have of me—that I'm a difficult artist? Or that I'm a nice bloke? At this advanced stage I'm going, "I just want to be a nice bloke." When I go somewhere, I want people to feel soothed and happy and reassured. I don't want to be this fucking tornado of things.

—Steve Kilbey, July 2004

Heart trouble had been a constant in Les's life throughout the 1960s and '70s. He suffered from angina pectoris, which is characterized by episodes of extreme chest pain and usually caused by coronary artery disease. As with everything else, Les took his illness in the best of humor, often personifying his angina as a human companion. He enjoyed calling Steve up and saying, "I'm coming over. It's just the two of us: me and Angina." This breezy attitude had the unfortunate effect of lulling the family into assuming that he had the problem under control through drugs, diet, and exercise.

Steve got an inkling of the true seriousness of the malady one night when he drove over to his parents' house for dinner. Les, the amateur mechanic, noticed there was something wrong with one of the wheels on Steve's car and got down on his knees to have a look at it. As Steve watched, Les's face went gray and he began to gasp, his eyes wide. Steve cried out, "Dad, what's wrong?" to which Les replied, "Oh it's all right; it's just my angina." He managed to breathe deeply and smile. The moment passed.

Les had always wanted to own a holiday home on the coast; for him, this signified true success and prosperity. Shortly before his death, he had finally saved up enough money to buy one. He rang Steve on a Friday and asked, "Are you coming down to the new place this weekend?"

Steve replied, "Ah, I can't come down this weekend, Dad. I've got a gig at the Captain Cook."

Les said, "All right," and father and son had a mundane conversation, a parting joke, and rang off.

Steve and Les Kilbey, circa 1972 (Kilbey family collection)

That weekend Les, Joyce, Russell, and John met up at the coast house with one of Les's war buddies from England. They ate a large lunch and Les stood up, stretched and said, "I'm gonna go down and paint the wall underneath."

Joyce slapped his leg lightly and said, "Don't, you silly old devil. Don't do that now; you've just had a big lunch."

Les was adamant. "I want to get it finished," he said. He went downstairs and started working. A few minutes later the family heard a loud bang. Joyce laughed and said, "Silly devil's fallen off the stool."

Joyce and Russell went down the stairs and found Les lying on his back. He had no pulse. Russell gave him mouth-to-mouth, worked on his heart, gave him everything he knew, to no avail. As they waited for the ambulance to arrive, John hid under the table and everyone else cycled through varying degrees of panic and shock. The medics arrived and attempted to give Les oxygen. As Joyce recounted in her autobiography:

> After a few minutes, they stopped and I cried out, "Carry on, I saw him move!" One of the ambulance men came over to me and said softly, "Your husband was dead when we arrived; we only tried with the oxygen because that young son of yours was putting in such a gallant effort to save his dad. It was a massive heart attack and nothing could have saved him."

In the space of half an hour, everything changed for the Kilbey family. The prosperous, happy life that Les had carefully built for himself, his wife, and his children was shattered.

That evening, Steve was onstage with Baby Grande—"flouncing about," as he puts it, doing his best Jagger/Bolan/Bowie impersonation to an unappreciative crowd, when he was taken aback to see an unexpected face in the audience: Rudolph Kohlhase, a neighbor of the Kilbeys. Steve immediately knew something was drastically wrong; there was no way Rudi Kohlhase would go to a glam rock concert of his own accord. Baby Grande finished the song and Steve said, "We're going to have a break now." He walked over to Kohlhase, already knowing what the man would say.

"Steven," he said, "Your father has had a heart attack."

"Is he dead?" Steve asked.

"I'm afraid so."

"I was always shocked by the horrible suddenness of it," Steve says now.

> Once again, I'm not unlike anybody else. I kept thinking he was gonna come back. I kept thinking there would be a knock at the door or the phone would ring and I would think, "It's Dad, he's found a loophole."

Steve sighs, then goes on:

> My father never saw me get successful. He would have *loved* it. Much, much, much more than my mother. He would have been playing my records. He would have said to everyone he knew, "This is my son, have you heard his records?" He would have discussed the music with me. He didn't like rock and roll, he didn't like electric guitars and stuff, but he would have been thrilled.

"My father was fifty-two when he died," he says quietly. "About my age."

Les's death had huge repercussions for the other Kilbey siblings. For Russell, seeing his father die before his eyes instilled in him lifelong feelings of anger and fear: anger at the arbitrariness of life, and fear that he, too, would die young. These feelings intensified when he married and had children of his own; he worried he might die suddenly and leave his kids fatherless. Russell's attitude is pronounced enough that Steve has asked him a number of times why he is so full of fear about everything. Russell's response: "Listen mate, you never saw your father drop dead; you were away when it all happened. I was there, and it fucking frightened the hell out of me."

John turned inward. When Joyce got married again—to another man named Les—the youngest son did not take it well. He and his stepfather didn't get along; the boy retreated to his room and spent most of his adolescence there.

Steve's way of dealing with the tragedy was to devote all of his time and energy to Baby Grande.

Until recently, not much was known about Baby Grande, except that

Baby Grande, L-R: Steve Kilbey, Joe Lee, Dave Scotland, Ken Wylie.

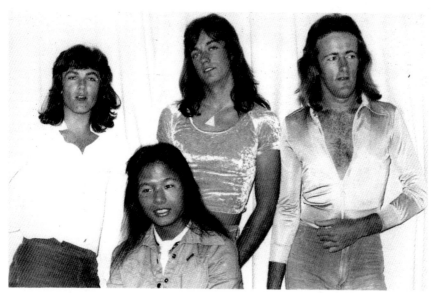

Steve and Peter both were members at one point. The most Steve has ever said about this group is that it emerged from the ashes of its predecessor, Precious Little, and that Baby Grande had a short-lived deal with EMI—the same label that would snatch up the Church a few years later.

That information vacuum disappeared, however, when Joe Lee, a former member of Baby Grande, posted a history of the band on a Canberra Musicians web site in 2004. In his essay, Lee wrote:

> Steve was a visionary who regarded music strictly as a creative platform or tool to fulfill his creative vision . . . music as a standalone concept had no relevance in his bigger picture . . . it was very much the Art of Noise and the image component that interested him.

Lee went on to state that Steve was very controlling about the group's visual appearance, insisting on certain clothes and haircuts. This is borne out

Baby Grande, L-R: Dave Scotland, Ken Wylie, Steve Kilbey, Joe Lee
(Barry McCulloch)

by the pictures accompanying the essay, which include "before and after" photos of David Scotland, the group's second guitarist. In the first photo, Scotland appears relaxed, sporting unkempt long hair, a beard, and a brown T-shirt. In the photo taken after he had been in the band for a while, Scotland looks singularly uncomfortable, his hair now carefully groomed, his natural good looks accented by eyeliner and lipstick. In this second picture he wears a tight, belly-baring, blue velvet shirt.

The other members of the band included Peter Koppes, Ken Wylie on drums, and Lee on bass, though Koppes left the band early on to explore other avenues. "I left (Baby Grande) because there wasn't a camaraderie," he says. "It's hard to describe. When I left the band, I traveled round Australia a bit but didn't get very far—the car had already been round Australia and was pretty fucked; it wasn't going to make it. So I came back to Canberra."

Later on, Peter played for a time as the lead guitarist in a less flashy band called Limazine, which brought him into contact with future Church drummer Nick Ward.

Steve affirms the accuracy of Joe Lee's assessment of Baby Grande:

A lot of it was image over content, for sure. If someone looked really good . . . it wasn't how pretty or handsome they were, it was if they had that certain *thing* that I was looking for. As you can see in those pictures, I was obviously fooling around with those ideas, but I was going a little deeper than that. I thought ideally, a la David Bowie, the music should be delivered with a kind of strong personality and image and look.

By late 1976, Steve's ambition and focus finally appeared to have paid off. A friend of Joe's, Sue Knight, had begun dating Chris Baynes, A&R director for EMI Australia. Baby Grande quickly cut two demo tracks and passed the tape to Sue, who played it to her boyfriend in the car after a dinner date. His interest was immediately piqued.

It may have helped that EMI UK had recently directed their Australian subsidiary to sign the Saints (after they were raved about in the UK press), and that EMI Australia therefore felt they could now pursue more independent bands. In any case, Joe Lee was summoned to discuss a deal with EMI, and a demo deal was quickly signed. By January 1977, the band was in EMI Studio B working on five new recordings.

Unheard by the public for nearly thirty years, some of these tracks have recently surfaced on the Internet, over Kilbey's strong objections. I have in my possession a CD that contains two of the songs from the Studio B sessions, as well as the two original demos that landed the band their deal. These tracks find Baby Grande sounding surprisingly self-assured. Steve sings in a higher range than he would later employ, projecting loudly and confidently, if not always on key.

On one track, he sings of his fascination with a pin-up girl: "Got you on my wall/make sure you never fall." There are sly nods to venial sin: "If I don't get to heaven/you're the reason I can't." The fixation on the girl becomes steadily creepier as the song progresses, the narrator's line between fantasy and reality blurring.

Musically, the band strives for a hybrid of T. Rex, Ziggy and the Spiders–era Bowie, and the New York Dolls. The rhythm section also reflects the influence of undiluted hard rock—Wylie's drumming seems the result of a steady diet of John Bonham and Keith Moon, while Lee's bass playing channels John Paul Jones's more aggressive tendencies. Although the overall sound is derivative, the Baby Grande tracks have a style and an attitude that probably would have gone over quite well with mainstream audiences in the mid-to-late '70s.

The final track—"Madame Lash"—bears mention if only because it features a protagonist who would resurface in the Church's "Welcome" twenty years later. The song itself is an S&M fantasy, with Madame Lash as the all-powerful dominatrix. Kitschy? Yes, but the songwriter seems aware of this.

The hard work in the studio turned out to be to no avail. In March 1977, the anxious musicians received a letter from EMI stating that the label had decided to cut Baby Grande loose; the recordings were apparently not up to EMI standards. Steve's voice was cited as the primary factor that had put off the marketing department and caused the label to pass. Shortly thereafter, the other members of Baby Grande convened an emergency meeting and decided to kick Steve out. They blamed their EMI dismissal on a combination of Steve's sometimes flat singing and his domineering attitude, and figured they had a better chance of "making it" without him.

Steve fell back on his original plan and made one final attempt to join and influence someone else's band. And once again, his stubbornness and arrogance got in the way. Accounts vary, but it can reasonably be ascertained that Steve's tenure in the group Tactics lasted for not much longer than a month; the band's singer and songwriter, Dave Studdert, was—not unnaturally—unwilling to cede the reins to an upstart.

When Steve originally talked to me (in 2003) about his involvement with Tactics, he implied that his departure from the band had been of his own choosing:

> On paper it seemed like (Studdert) and I were made for each other, but in reality it didn't work out and . . . we just didn't like each other. I didn't like his music . . . He was trying to be Neil Young. He had the annoying high-pitched voice but he didn't have the emotion.
>
> I remember he had some good ideas. He had this one song: "The Anniversary of Madame X" which appealed to me, and he had another song called "Careful, Superman." I liked the idea that Superman had to

be careful because that's the last thing you'd expect him to be. He used to have some good little bits and pieces, but I didn't get on so well with him.

He came over one day and we tried to record some of his songs, and he was so uncooperative and abusive and I thought, "Fuck this. Why do I want to record your stupid songs?" . . . I went to a few rehearsals, and then I snuck off.

Afterwards, when I became famous, this guy came out of the woodwork and dined out on telling stories about me.

However, Steve seemed to make an about-face in 2006—admitting on his blog that he'd actually been fired from the band:

> im sorry to all the guitarists
> bass players
> drummers
> singers
> who i criticised
> rudely loudly obnoxiously
> yes dave studdert kicked me outta his group
> hell baby grande kicked me outta my own group
> im sure the church have entertained the thought

Studdert himself recently offered a less-than-flattering account of Steve's brief tenure in the band:

At that stage Steve was very unhappy. His first band had collapsed and he was rather bitter, to say the least. He was working as a computer programmer —rather childishly, I used to wind him up by calling him a computer operator, which used to send him ballistic—and he kinda felt the world had passed him by.

If I recall, his songs were literally fourths, i.e. barre chords with the fourth and third strings held down two frets higher and then he'd move them up another two frets or down, whatever—one of the songs was definitely barre on G up 2 to barre on fifth. For various reasons, I couldn't play them very well and certainly the rest of the band lacked enthusiasm and confidence about playing them as well.

Steve played about four gigs with us—he was always moaning and eventually he suggested that we do a Jonathan Richman medley, which was the final straw and I threw him out. It is true that my songs were more sophisticated—I recall once Steve said about one of my songs that it wasn't a song, it was just a collection of chords.

Tactics went on to achieve considerable critical acclaim, if only modest sales. In *The Encyclopedia of Australian Rock and Pop*, author Ian McFarlane describes the band as "(close) in spirit to the art-punk of the likes of New York band Talking Heads, and UK outfits like Wire and Gang of Four" and quips, "Studdert's spiky 'strangled cat' vocal style was definitely unusual."

Being rejected by Saga had been a major blow to Steve, but this triple rejection—by EMI; then by his own band, Baby Grande; and shortly afterward by Tactics—devastated him. Nevertheless, he had no intention of giving up on his musical ambitions. Once again he retreated to his bedroom and his guitar.

5
CAMEL DUST HERALDS OUR ARRIVAL

Many songwriters seem to emerge into public view fully formed, giving the impression that their talents are innate. The reality is that these artists have usually spent years holed up in their bedrooms, learning their instruments and honing their skills. There is almost always a cocoon phase during which a musician practices in isolation before mustering the strength to perform in public. But much of Steve Kilbey's artistic development took place in front of an audience. Time and time again he lunged for the spotlight too early and failed.

Still, some good always came from the bad. After the demise of Baby Grande, Steve found a new tool to help with his composition process. Although he had become adept at synthesizing his disparate influences into a sound that was increasingly unique and melodic, there was still a gap between the way the songs sounded in his head and the way they came out when he played them on guitar for other musicians. He needed something that would enable him to arrange the songs exactly as he wanted: something that could make it possible for him to present that finished product to the musicians he played with. He needed, in short, a multi-track recorder.

Steve had often talked with other musicians about his desire to buy a four-track machine. The response was always, "Do you know how much they cost?" Most musicians only knew of the bulky reel-to-reel recording decks and mixing boards found in professional studios. Such equipment did not come cheap. By a nice quirk of timing, however, technology caught up with Steve's ambitions. In the late 1970s, the TEAC Corporation (who would later dominate the multi-track market under the name Tascam) released their first portable four-track recorder. This unit, quite large by today's standards, could fit on a desk or in the corner of a bedroom and recorded on large half-inch open reels. The portability allowed fledgling musicians to record in their homes, sparing them the cost and headache of professional recording.

Steve had heard about the new TEAC unit, and had been asking around for it at the local hi-fi shops. Finally, after much searching, he found one. It was pricey—$1500—but Steve considered this investment in his songwriting career an essential one. He got a bank loan and bought the unit.

It's hard to overstate the importance of the four-track in Steve's development. It was quite literally the missing link—the breakthrough that would enable Steve to become a sonic architect. He quickly built up a home studio in the bedroom of his apartment. In addition to his four-track and bass he had an acoustic guitar, an electric guitar, a microphone, and a synthesizer/drum machine combo that had belonged to his dad. Now Steve could arrange and record his songs exactly as he wanted. The fact that he was operating on a budget—with limited equipment—merely forced him to be more creative. For example, since there were no echo or reverb units commercially available at the time, Steve created an echo effect by putting the machine out of sync with itself. Also, the synthesizer was monophonic—it only played one note at a time—so Steve created chords by playing the individual notes on separate tracks and then bouncing them down to a single track. From 1977 through early 1980, Steve spent most of his time in this home studio. During this period he composed and set down literally hundreds of songs, many of them ambient instrumentals inspired by Brian Eno's *Another Green World* and *Music for Airports*. Steve worked primarily in isolation; only his brothers knew of, and were supportive of, his experiments.

"A lot of this music was electronic," he says.

Experiments with tape recorders. Blips. I took it in to work once and played it for them and they all laughed at it; they didn't think it was music at all. I'd just be doing things with white noise and feedback and loops, saturating the tape recorder. Doing whatever I could think of—playing guitar with a hair-dryer and things. Brian Eno was a huge influence on

me—the idea of having music that was both instrumental and there
would be little songs with cryptic lyrics.

Shortly after moving out of his parents' house, Steve married—seemingly
on impulse—his girlfriend Michelle Parker. The marriage was short-lived.
Steve has to be prodded now to speak of this relationship at all, and he is
loathe to give many details. He says simply, "She allowed me to do whatever
I was trying to do. She was neither an influence nor a hazard. I used to always be in my room writing songs and she would say, 'Yeah, that's nice.' She
wasn't very enthusiastic. I remember saying sometimes, 'Come in and listen
to what I've done,' and she would stand in the door kind of half-listening
with one eye on the TV."

Virtually the only mention Steve ever made to the press concerning this
marriage was during an unusually candid interview with Michelle Andre in
1988:

> [The] girl I got married to, I'm sure she didn't want to get married, it was
> like, all her life someone had been saying, "You should get married . . .
> you should get married . . ." And eventually the first eligible, sort of
> vaguely all right idiot that came walking along, she latched onto, and it
> was like, "We're going out together, ok, steady—well, people in Australia
> don't say that, but the equivalent—and then it was like, "Let's move in
> together," and it's like me going, "All right." "Let's get engaged" "All
> right." "Let's get married." "All right." So before I knew it, it was like . . .
> *This is not my beautiful house, this is not my beautiful wife!* And she *was*
> beautiful!

Peter Koppes—in typically understated fashion—drops the bombshell:

> I was with Michelle before Steve. I'd shared a flat with her and a bass
> player friend of mine, and when I moved out, Steve moved in, and he
> ended up with her as well. We'd already split up, I went off traveling for a
> while, and when I came back they were living together! I never got upset
> about that; she and I hadn't been getting along.

Notwithstanding Steve's tendency to shrug off Michelle's importance,
it cannot be denied that she was present at, and sometimes participated
in, pivotal moments in the young songwriter's development. For instance,

Michelle accompanied Steve on a three-month trip to London in 1978 that solidified his desire to become a professional musician. The main purpose of this trip was for Steve to see some bands that he knew were never going to come to Australia: two highlights being the Doctors of Madness, who had quickly become one of his favorites, and Japan, who became a key influence on Steve's composition process. "One thing that I took note of," he says, "was the idea of a bass line remaining the same and everything else changing around it. (Japan) did the song 'Obscure Alternatives' last, and the bass line was just pumping the same thing, but the chords were ascending and descending around it, and I was just riveted."

Michelle was equally inspired, but not by the music. She had her eye on the fashions of swinging London. Looking at the clothes in the department-store windows, she thought, "I can do this; I can design clothes like this."

When they returned to Australia, the couple understood that if they were to realize their ambitions, they had to leave Canberra. It was time to set their sights higher. In late 1978, they pooled their resources (including money left to Steve by his dad), moved to Sydney, and bought a house in the suburb of Rozelle. To make ends meet in the short term, Steve taught himself how to silkscreen T-shirts and began selling custom designs on the street. Money was scarce, but Steve remained convinced he could make it as a musician.

The couple had two reasons for picking Rozelle as a place to live: first, it was cheap and second, it was reasonably close to the city. As Steve describes it, Rozelle was a "real down-at-the mouth, working-class kind of suburb." During one of his first weekends there, he stood on the front porch of his new house and overheard a conversation from nearby: a man's gruff voice was saying, "Go on, you tell him how you got out of jail, and you tell him how when we robbed that bank, you weren't fucking holding the gun, now, were you?" The still relatively sheltered young man from Canberra worried that perhaps he had bitten off more than he could chew.

The house itself was a small, terraced home with three bedrooms, one of which Steve converted into a studio. Cockroaches routinely infested the place, and even when the Kilbeys got rid of theirs, reinforcements quickly invaded from the neighboring homes. Outside, dogs roamed freely, doing their business in Steve's front yard.

Steve continued to work on his home recordings. He was now combining his early glam influences with the more experimental, Eno-based structures he had recently discovered. In so doing, he developed a process that would become his preferred mode of composition for the next twenty-eight years: he built the songs from the ground up, music first, and then added the lyrics. He would usually start with a beat or a motif and shape the song around that—often improvising until he found something that worked. As for the lyrics, he adopted a "sprint" method that holds to this day: "If it takes longer than a half hour to write the words, there's something wrong," he says. And he rarely, if ever, edited the lyrics later. This would prove to be both a blessing and a curse: on the one hand, this rapid-fire, free-association approach lent his lyrics a noticeable freshness and spontaneity. But, more often than not, the words could also seem rough and nonsensical: impressive but underdeveloped.

Not all of his songs were written this way. When the recording process became tiresome, Steve would switch gears and compose the old-fashioned way: strumming out chords on an acoustic guitar and writing words and music together. These songs were usually more conventional and "poppy" than those created with the aid of the multi-track. In general, his work during this period could best be described as avant-garde pop (some of these early compositions finally surfaced on Steve's 2002 release *Freaky Conclusions*).

In 1979, Steve became reacquainted with Peter Koppes, who also now lived in Sydney and was playing in Limazine. Slowly, piece by piece, the Church began to materialize, fading into reality with a wheezing and groaning akin to that of Doctor Who's time machine.

Peter was impressed with Steve's new songs, although, being something of a perfectionist, he was quick to note that the material was still quite rough; things like tuning and pitch were touch-and-go. "I can't really tell you why I was drawn to those songs," Peter says now.

> It's just like when you meet someone for the first time, there's something you like about them. [The songs] weren't necessarily my style. But I always respected Steve's taste in music. We were into the same kinds of things: Roxy Music and Television. He taught me about Television and the Only Ones before I even left Australia. He always had good taste in music. And when I heard his songs, I heard something I respected in them.

Limazine, L to R: Mike Hamer, Peter Koppes, Dave Nicholas, Nick Ward, Tony Harvey *(Courtesy, Nic Ward)*

Peter quickly assumed the role of producer/arranger/manager, and together he and Steve took some of the best material and hammered out a professional-sounding demo tape. Peter's clean, expressive guitar playing now served as the stately sonic cathedral in which Steve's evocative lyrics resided. It sounded quite unlike any of the music that was being played on the radio at the time.

Eventually it came time to assemble a full band for performing the material. Peter brought with him the drummer from Limazine, Nigel Murray. This immediately caused tension as Steve knew Nigel from his schooldays in Canberra; in fact, Nigel had beaten Steve up pretty badly a few times.[1] Nigel had adopted "Nick Ward" as his stage name, an odd choice since the *real* Nick Ward—another boy from Steve's school—was, according to Steve, "a retarded boy [with] this great big pair of glasses and his eyes swinging around . . . he had a big oval-shaped head and used to walk like a goose."

Why Nigel had taken on an assumed name was unclear (and he refuses to discuss it to this day). Steve suspected it stemmed from trouble with the

[1] Peter provides some context for the beatings: "[Nigel] was a year above Steve and Steve had made fun of his shoes one time."

police; Peter claims the drummer was on the run from a biker gang. At any rate, Nigel's reasons for adopting the name of a boy he had allegedly hounded and bullied throughout high school remain a mystery.

Steve decided to name this new band the Church, after the enigmatic David Bowie lyric "The church of man love is such a holy place to be," from "Moonage Daydream." ("No one knew if he meant 'the church of man, love' or 'the church of man-love,'" Steve notes). Originally, the band was to be named "the Church of Man," but this was quickly truncated to the more mysterious "the Church."

In their original lineup as a trio, the Church played harder, faster, and punkier than they would on their later recorded work, which was the direct result of Ward's influence, as well as Koppes' enthusiasm for hard rock. Several songs from the Church's first album, including "For a Moment We're Strangers," "Fighter Pilot . . . Korean War," and "Chrome Injury," made their debut in the trio format.

There are apparently no audience recordings of any of their early shows, though there *is* a widely circulated tape of a 1986 show at the Fabrik in Hamburg, Germany, when the Church were forced to revert to a trio lineup after Marty Willson-Piper's temporary departure from the band. For that show, the Church essentially trotted out their 1980 set list and treated the audience to those early songs ("It's what we would have sounded like in 1980," Steve says). If the 1986 tape is any indication, the Church as a trio were a force to be reckoned with. More than anything, the recording reveals Peter Koppes' prodigious talents as a guitarist. On song after song, Koppes creates walls of sound with his instrument, breaking from the chords to soar off into outer-atmosphere-scraping leads, all the while propelled by Steve's insistent bass playing and drummer Richard Ploog's frenzied, Keith Moon-inspired thrashing. Of all the Church bootlegs in circulation, this German recording is perhaps the most exciting.

The Church of 1980 were certainly not as tight, polished, and road-tested as the Church of 1986 would be; nevertheless, Kilbey and Koppes already had several years of experience; both were seasoned live performers, and Ward and Koppes had developed a rapport while playing together in Limazine. Ward's efforts to steer the band towards a harder sound brought him in conflict with Steve from the start, but that push-and-pull initially worked in the band's favor—lending the music tension and urgency.

Pictures from this era reveal an amusing clash in fashion sensibility as well, with Steve and Peter favoring Mod haircuts and dark clothes, while Ward sports a Cheap Trick-like striped sports coat.

The new band's first practice session was held in a performance space frequently rented out to musicians and artists. On entering the building, Steve was greeted by the sight of a naked woman standing against the wall while

three fashionably disheveled men sketched her. He took this as a sign that he was one step closer to the bohemian lifestyle he had dreamed of ever since his teen years in Canberra.

As the band began rehearsing, it quickly became clear to Steve that he was part of something special. Peter had developed from a heavy-metal guitarist into an evocative, melody-driven player. The electronic devices so crucial to the classic Church sound—a frequently used Boss CE-1 chorus pedal and echo unit—were already in place. And Steve had recently acquired a fret-

Back in the day (Courtesy, Nic Ward)

less bass, the sound of which set his already unorthodox playing style further apart from that of his contemporaries.

After the trio ran through "Chrome Injury" and "Is This Where You Live?", Steve thought, "This is it. We're on to something." In his years of playing in Baby Grande and its preceding configurations, he had never felt this way, never felt this kind of spark. Now he had finally reached that higher level of musical synergy he had long fantasized about but never actually allowed himself to believe in.

These days, Ward is back in Canberra, where he runs a custom guitar and music gear business called Ward Sound. He has changed the spelling of his first name to Nic[2], and his feelings about his old band are decidedly mixed. But he echoes what Steve told me regarding the palpable excitement of those early rehearsals:

---

[2] From now on, I'll refer to him as "Nick" when his name crops up in the context of his time in the Church, and otherwise as "Nic."

When we got together as a three-piece, the chemistry was magic, and for those who are not aware, or who have never enjoyed it, chemistry is what sets the better bands apart and is absolutely, incredibly rare. We were a rockin' band with something wonderfully new. Along with Kilbey's influence, you cannot overstate the wonderful work Koppes applied. Add to this my arrangement ideas and you have one very special band. I just loved the band when we were a three-piece rockin' outfit, as rockin' as you could be with Kilbey's drawling vocals.

Around the time of their first shows, the trio also began recording demos. Steve and Nick had identical four-tracks, so recording would often be split between their two houses, with the initial tracks of material being recorded on Steve's machine, then bounced down to one track on Nick's recorder. In addition to "Fighter Pilot" and "Chrome Injury," Steve introduced three new songs: "You've Got to Go," "Fall Away" and "Insect World." The recordings were rough, but the spark that Steve had first noticed during rehearsal was unmistakable.

Even at this very early stage, though, tempers began to fray between Nick and the other two (particularly Steve). "Right from the start, there seemed to be a lot of bitching going on in this band," Ward recalls.

> We had only done a few one-dollar gigs when we decided to record a demo on four-track tape. There was a fair bit of bickering during the whole process (Piper was not on the scene [for most of the recording], though he must have come along right at the end because he played on "Insect World") and after all the overdubs were done, I told them to shove off; I'd had enough of the *Days of Our Lives*. I actually quit the band and told them to piss right off.
>
> So off they went with tape in hand to mix it down onto cassette at Kilbey's place. I figured I was rid of them. The next day [Peter and Steve] rolled up to my door, tape in hand again. They said they couldn't mix it because it was all just hiss and noise and would I give it a go, so I mixed it as best I could and gave it back to them. Two days later, back they came. They said, we can sign a record deal but I have to stay in the band. The dream of making a record was the only reason I consented and so we signed with ATV Northern Songs. In any other band, that should have

been an event to celebrate, as if we had just won the grand final—but in this case, it was all very low key, as usual.

Steve has said more than once that the Church's fortuitous publishing deal with EMI came about after Peter Koppes sent the demo tape to Chris Gilbey, but that is only half the story. Actually, the initial meeting between Gilbey and Koppes was arranged by none other than Joe Lee, former member of Baby Grande. Joe had met Gilbey a few years earlier, during the initial stages of the failed Baby Grande EMI deal, when Gilbey was the Saints' manager. Though that deal fell through, the two remained friendly. And Joe felt considerable guilt after the demise of Baby Grande, because he had been the one who delivered the difficult news to Steve that not only was EMI dropping them, but the other members of the band had decided to kick Steve out. Lee's role as the bearer of bad tidings had made him persona non grata in Kilbey's world.

A few years later, Lee saw an opportunity to make things right when Peter Koppes (with whom Lee had stayed in contact) played him the first homemade Church demo. Lee offered to put the band in touch with Chris Gilbey, who was now working as an A&R rep with EMI. A meeting was set up and, after he'd heard the tape, Gilbey set in motion a publishing deal with ATV/Northern Songs and a recording contract with EMI/Parlophone. The irony that the very label that had earlier branded Steve's voice a commercial liability was now giving his new band the royal treatment was not lost on the young songwriter. He began to think that the music business was an industry predicated on absurdity. Future experiences would only confirm him in this view.

In spite of this positive development, the animosity between Ward and Kilbey continued to intensify. They had carried the tensions from their school days into the new band (in fact, those issues remain unresolved to this day). "I went to school with Kilbey," Ward says. "He was a year lower than me. He had a smart mouth back then and nothing to back it up with. Nothing had changed by 1980."

According to Steve, Ward became increasingly unpredictable in the live setting. During one gig, Steve announced to the audience, "This is a song called 'Fighter Pilot.'" The words had barely left his mouth when Nick yelled out, "As if we fucking care!" On more than one occasion, Nick burped

loudly into his microphone during a quiet moment in the set. Ward now at-
tributes some of his frustration to his bandmates' low-key attitude toward performing. "I remember when we would be in the back room at gigs, waiting to go on," he recalls.

> I'd be pacing the room jumping out of my skin, getting psyched to deliver another killer performance. *They'd* be sitting in chairs reading! No joke, I've got a photo. I was just never right for that band. Watch 'em gig these days and you can see what I mean. Who's got the valium?

Offstage it was worse. Ward saw himself as an equal partner with Steve, and as such he felt that some of his own songs should be considered for inclusion in the band's repertoire. He also did not hesitate to comment on the quality of Steve's material (a favorite bit of constructive criticism: "This song is fucked"). Looking back, Ward concedes his role in the tension. "I was not easy to get along with," he says. "I had stomach ulcers and was suffering from depression at the time; I only found out years later that it was depression." Peter refused to take sides. He performed his duties as guitarist and arranger to a tee, while remaining aloof in other matters, turning a blind eye to conflicts within the band.

It was after a Church gig in early 1980, supporting a band called Moving Parts, that a young Englishman named Marty Willson-Piper blundered quite accidentally into this volatile mix. Initially, he served as a lightning rod, drawing Ward's anger away from Steve. But he would overcome this inauspicious beginning and go on to become the only member of the band, apart from Steve, to appear on every Church album.

Marty, like Peter, came from a musical family. His older brother, a cabaret musician, taught him the basics of guitar, though the two had wildly different tastes—the older brother favoring the bossa nova textures of Antonio Carlos Jobim, the younger the power chords and wispy vocals of Blue Oyster Cult. In his hometown of Liverpool, Marty played in several bands, most of which also featured his childhood chum Andy Mason. Like Steve, Marty did not attend college but was nevertheless a voracious reader, enjoying history, poetry, philosophy, and literary classics from Cervantes' *Don Quixote* to the novels of Albert Camus. Inspired in part by the questing spirit of itinerant French philosopher Jean Jacques Rousseau, Marty began traveling throughout Europe in his late teens. He busked to support himself, playing a twelve-string acoustic guitar on streets and in subway tunnels all over the continent. The perpetual noise of the crowds and trains caused him to develop a loud, sometimes raspy singing voice.

Marty, like Steve, had married early. He met an Australian girl during his travels and followed her back to her home country. Not long after his arrival, he went with his wife and a friend of hers—who happened to be Peter Koppes's flatmate—to see the Church. The band impressed him considerably. As rough as the music was, Steve's songwriting stood out. The lyrics—what he could hear of them—struck him as literate and beguiling, and Peter Koppes's arrangements displayed subtlety and ambiance. At the same time, the songs themselves possessed unmistakable rock energy. This was music that hit you in the chest *and* made you think.

Still, as much as he enjoyed the show and as much as he appreciated the parallels between the Church's sound and his own musical aesthetic, Marty never could have imagined, as he stood in the audience bobbing his head to "Chrome Injury," that within a matter of hours he would be a member of the band.

6
JUST A SPARK

Backstage after the Moving Parts gig, the members of the Church commenced their individual post-performance rituals. Steve reclined on a threadbare couch, smoking a carefully rolled joint; Nick sat on the dressing-room table, his back to the mirror, a beer bottle in one hand and a cigarette in the other; and Peter crouched over his guitar case, packing up for the evening.

A quick, staccato knock came from outside. Before anyone could reach the door, in strode a tall, long-haired guy who looked barely out of his teens. He wore a black leather jacket and tight jeans, and held a smoldering cigarette in his right hand. He stood before them, bouncing from one foot to the other.

"Hey, I really liked your show," he said in a thick Liverpool accent. "It reminded me of Cream."

Steve sized him up for a moment, then asked, "Do you play guitar?"

"Uh, yeah," the visitor said. "How did . . . ?"

"Good," Steve said. "I'm Steve Kilbey."

The visitor stepped forward and shook Steve's hand. "Marty."

To Steve, this new arrival looked like every rock star rolled into one: he was extremely handsome, with an angular face vaguely reminiscent of the young Keith Richards. Marty's body practically hummed with pent-up energy, and his physical presence had something of Marc Bolan about it. Steve had visions of Marty onstage, slinging his guitar, melting women in the audience with a single offhand glance.

They talked for ten minutes about the records they loved, particularly Syd Barrett–era Pink Floyd. Marty enthused about some of his own musical favorites: Can, the Velvet Underground, King Crimson. Peter and Nick paid little attention to their passionate exchange.

After Marty excused himself and left the dressing room, Steve turned to his bandmates and said, "He's joining the band."

Nick's jaw dropped. The usually stoic Peter Koppes exhibited just a hint of surprise.

"Yeah, he's the other guy," Steve said.

Peter looked contemplative for a moment, then said, "Yeah, okay. It would be good to have another guitarist."

Nick, on the other hand, lost it. "Fuck that," he said, "I'm not having him onstage. You don't even know if he can play."

"He can play."

"This is fucked. You're a fucking idiot!" He stormed out and slammed the door behind him.

The preceding account is based on Steve's memories of that first meeting, in which the hiring of Marty is portrayed as a unilateral decision on his part. Peter's version of the story matches Steve's in most respects, but with one crucial difference: Koppes insists that *he* was the one who had been pushing for a second guitarist:

> I was into Roxy Music and bands like that, Television. As much as I loved Hendrix and all the rest of them, it's only with that blues idiom that you can get away with playing solo guitar. With what we were doing, we needed two. Led Zeppelin always sounded weak in the live setting without the extra guitar. I never bothered seeing them because I'd heard a bootleg and I thought it sounded weak—Jimmy Page playing by himself. I just knew that we would be stymied in our development if we didn't have another guitarist. Marty turned up at our fourth gig, he looked good, and he seemed like a nice guy, so we basically invited him to join the band without even hearing him play.

One thing everyone agrees on is that Nick Ward was never consulted on this decision.

Marty Willson Piper, early 1980s (*Debra Mineely*)

Nothing against [Marty] really, but the ever so rare *chemistry* was gone once he came along.

Of course, I was never asked if I wanted to be in a four-piece band; he was just in. From that moment on, the band was completely different. Koppes obviously didn't have the confidence and/or the desire to be a guitar player in a three-piece band. I can see now how he must have felt, but the kind of new band that we were, I thought—and still do—that he was doing a fantastic job of it. One has to wonder if Chris Gilbey, who signed us, would have had the same gusto if he'd heard a demo for one of the other albums.

There was tension in the air from the moment Marty first attended rehearsals. Compared to Koppes, Marty was a novice, and according to Steve, Peter refused to teach Marty the chords to the songs, saying, "I had to find out what the chords were myself. You have to find out yourself. Work it out."

Thus began the Church tradition of each guitarist playing an entirely different, but complementary, guitar part. Neither knew what the other was doing. It is fitting that this famously intuitive band's most distinctive musical trait came about not as the result of some grand musical directive, but rather because of the recalcitrance of the lead guitarist.

These days, Peter spins the story in a "tough love" direction; he claims he was acting almost as a coach, pushing Marty out of his safety zone with the expectation that the young guitarist would deliver. Whether or not this is true, his lack of coddling certainly pushed Marty to develop at an accelerated pace.

Peter, like Ward, acknowledges that the addition of Marty created new conflicts, though he continues to believe that the end result justified any growing pains:

> It's an interesting thing. In the best songwriting partnerships—like Roger Waters and David Gilmour, Lennon and McCartney, Jagger/Richards—there was a tension and rivalry in the partnership. It's worse when you get three people involved . . . Steve and I probably would have been able to sort through things when it was just the two of us, but when Marty got involved, that triumvirate was incredibly volatile. Same with Nick Ward: that was a triumvirate before Marty arrived. So we had a situation where people were in conflict with one another, had a mistrust of one another.

Young John Kilbey experienced this tension firsthand during a visit to his older brother's house in Rozelle. Many years later, he described those early band dynamics on his blog:

> I remember lying in Steven's lounge, where I slept, trying to be inconspicuous while the band argued around me. They were weird and had strange jargon and hand signals, one being a sort of pistol action finger shot accompanied by a ricochet verbal effect. Peter and Marty scared me but not as much as the drummer, Nick Ward. Actually, he was the one with the pistol thing going on, now that I recall. I remember hiding under my sheet thinking, "What a dickhead!" Pete's cig was burning down near the end, the ash hanging long and precariously while he was deep in argument about something. I dared to interrupt to save Steven's carpet but he wasn't at all happy about losing his flow to a kid under a sheet in the middle of a tempest. Sheesh! I guess they hadn't even invented [the concept of] secondhand smoke in those days.
>
> I didn't understand why you would want to be in a band with these loonies—when all they did was sit around arguing.

Marty made an inauspicious onstage debut with the Church; the would-be

rock god appeared unsure of himself and spent most of the show with his
head down, playing clunky barre chords while Peter took off on echoey flights
of fancy. It *did* fill out the sound, though. And Marty definitely had the look.

★ ★ ★ ★ ★

Perhaps it was the quick courtship by a major label that caused the Church
to be resented by a vocal contingent of musicians and critics in the Australian
music scene. There was, rightly or wrongly, a perception that the Church had
not paid their dues (few knew that Steve and Peter had spent the past decade
slaving away in Canberra), and that their primary goal was to make money.
In his account of Australian independent music, *Stranded,* Clinton Walker
quoted the influential promoter/manager Roger Grierson as saying, "The
Church weren't a D-I-Y outfit, they were, 'We want to be pop stars.' That
was their schtick—and they did it well." For their part, the Church made no
real effort to ingratiate themselves with either the critics or the players in the
growing Australian independent scene, which merely reinforced the perception that they were, or wanted to be, part of the mainstream.

The divide between "independent" and "mainstream" held little interest for Steve. If the critical prestige of being independent came with the
prospect of endless low-paying pub gigs and no larger outlet for his music, then he was quite happy to throw his lot in with the big labels and go
the mainstream route. He had already been an independent artist (not by
choice) during his time in Canberra.

For the band as a whole, the ATV/EMI deal brought legitimacy to their
enterprise. The label put the band on a salary, bought the struggling musicians new gear, paid for their rehearsal space, and pulled strings to get them
higher-profile gigs. Chris Gilbey swooped in as a sort of Svengali, hoping to
shape his new discovery into a hit-making machine.

The band piled into Studio 301 in Sydney and began cutting the tracks
that would comprise their debut album, *Of Skins and Heart*. The mysterious
"Insect World" was briefly considered for inclusion, as was a hard rocking
number called "Busdriver," a song that would eventually be released as the
B-side to "The Unguarded Moment."

"'Busdriver' is just a loathsome little song I wrote," Steve says.

I remember once as a kid I'd gotten on a bus and I was too frightened to push the button that signaled it was my stop. My mother had told the bus driver where to stop and he didn't; he kept on going. I ended up miles from where I was supposed to be. With that song I wanted to get this *Twilight Zone* idea of getting on a bus and ending up somewhere where you didn't really want to be.

Another early track was a sluggish version of "She Never Said," replete with annoying vocal effects ("The chorus had a high, speeded-up vocal a la David Bowie's 'Laughing Gnome,'" John Kilbey recalls.) This track was quickly mixed, mastered, and released as a single. The public greeted it with total indifference. It would later be tightened up and re-recorded for the album.

To co-produce the LP, Chris Gilbey enlisted the aid of American Bob Clearmountain, who was then in the early stages of a career that would establish him as a legendary recording engineer and mixer, renowned in particular for his work with Bruce Springsteen. Realizing that the band were novices in the studio, the two took a very hands-on approach, and the album's hard-driving sound owes more to Clearmountain's involvement (along with Ward's influence) than it does to any vision of Steve's.

Regardless of who was ultimately at the helm, *Of Skins and Heart* is a striking debut. All nine tracks exude confidence and energy. Nick Ward's drumming is solid—belying Steve's subsequent negative assessment—and his distinctive backing vocals beautifully punctuate "Chrome Injury" and "The Unguarded Moment." As for the rest of the instrumentation, Steve's bass playing may not be ambitious rhythmically, but it is aggressive and melodically inventive.[3] Peter's lead guitar playing is a revelation; his quick, clean solos are mini-lessons in emotion and economy, piercing through the surrounding music without overpowering it. Aspiring guitarists could benefit greatly from a close listen to his work on this album.

But the most impressive thing about *Of Skins and Heart* is the lyrics. Steve had already been writing poetry and song lyrics for a good ten years, and the experience shows. The album contains some of his best writing, sung in his "drawling" voice amidst the insistent bass and chunking guitars.

---

[3] Australian singer/songwriter "Ross" comments: "Kilbey's bass on the debut album is stunning, virtuosic and propulsive, he's obviously feeding off Ward and he never played like that again on record."

Early promo shot of the Church, circa 1981. L-R: Ward, Koppes, Kilbey, Willson-Piper *(Courtesy, Nic Ward)*

Ward acknowledges this:

> I think Kilbey should have been a poet and not applied those magnificent words to music. Yes, there, I said it. I think he's a magician with words.

Most of the songs require multiple listenings before any meaning can be discerned; even the requisite ballad, "Don't Open the Door to Strangers," is suitably obscure, featuring such opaque lyrics as "Don't leave your thoughts unguarded / Don't let them float where they will / They never tell me what I want to know / Don't open the door tonight."

Almost from its inception, Steve referred to "The Unguarded Moment," the album's best-known track, as an "albatross" around his neck.

Nevertheless, it is a great track, featuring catchy melodies, fine musicianship, and lyrics tinged with Orwellian paranoia. The song's narrator describes the psychic wounds inflicted by indifference and casual cruelty, wounds that cause the narrator to "feel like dying in an unguarded moment." It's a display of unabashed sensitivity on an otherwise emotionally veiled album, and even clunky lines about "men with horses for hearts" cannot derail the momentum of the song. Additionally, the lead line of each verse provides a tantalizing glimpses of Steve's creative struggles: "So hard finding inspiration," "So long between mirages," "So deep without a meaning." This last line could be a rare instance of Steve displaying public insecurity about his lyrics. Are they truly "deep without a meaning," or is the meaning simply unknown to the songwriter himself? Critics and listeners would be split on this point. At any rate, the emotional honesty of "The Unguarded Moment" is a welcome grounding force on the album. It provides a counterpoint to the lyrical opaqueness of the other songs.

"The Unguarded Moment" is by no means the only highlight of the album, though. The opening track, "For a Moment We're Strangers," sets the general tone that will be followed throughout. The main theme of the song is that physical intimacy is not a cure for spiritual and emotional emptiness. It's not clear whether the two characters are married or simply casual lovers, but it doesn't matter. Kilbey's writing often remains open-ended enough as to be applicable to multiple scenarios. The chorus "For a moment we're strangers / For a minute you look away" applies just as easily to the furtive moments following a clandestine sexual liaison as it does to the unguarded moments of a couple who have been together for forty years. Virtually everyone has glimpsed the unfamiliar, the unknowable in a lover's eyes.

This track displays another standard trait of Steve's writing: his cynicism. The war between his pervasive cynicism and his idealism—his sometimes naïve faith in a deeper meaning, a deeper existence—creates a fascinating tension in his work. Here the cynicism comes through in the bridge—"Just one me one you / This world contains a few"—which pokes fun at the narcissism of the young lovers; after all, there is nothing unique about their situation.

In contrast to the stylistic unity of that first track, "Chrome Injury" is a disconnected series of images evoking the futuristic paranoia of J.G. Ballard and Philip K. Dick. What starts out as a fast-paced driving narrative ("Take your place behind the wheel") inexplicably segues into an empty train setting and then, in the chorus, switches gears yet again to describe a robotic monster straight out of *Doctor Who*: "Poor tormented automan/Giant pincers for a hand." Then, just before a blistering Koppes guitar solo, the song takes a hackneyed *Wizard of Oz* Tin Man tack: "If only I could feel/If I only wasn't steel." Despite the narrative incoherence, "Chrome Injury" remains one of the catchiest songs on the album and is always welcomed enthusiastically on the rare occasions it is performed live.

The other two standout tracks on *Of Skins and Heart* are "Bel-Air" and "Is This Where You Live?" "Bel-Air" features some of Peter Koppes' most melodic playing: here he forgoes the echo box in favor of a clean, Clapton-like tone. Steve's narrative in the song consists of a string of seaside tourist images, peppered with personification: "A palm tree nodded at me last night/He said, 'Hey you look so pale'"; "The sand whispered heat"; "Pain sprawled on the chair/He's always there"; and the waitress who is a "dolphin in disguise."

In the last verse, the lyric takes a turn into "Eleanor Rigby" territory, describing a lonely woman who "puts on her face in the morning space/She doesn't know she's dead" and the "sunburnt landlord" who "glares for all the people he can never be."

"Bel-Air" is a singular lyrical accomplishment, representing Steve's first truly successful blending of surrealistic imagery with linear narrative. As a commentary on loneliness, materialism, and superficiality, the song stands up quite well to "Rigby" and other more famous peers.

"Is This Where You Live," clocking in at seven minutes and thirty-eight seconds, is the first Church epic. Starting with an eerie, sustained synthesizer D note and bass harmonics, the song moves from a slowly-building funereal march to a propulsive rocker replete with a frenetic backwards guitar solo (courtesy of Koppes). Most of the album lacks what would come to be known as the classic Church sound, but "Is This Where You Live" is a harbinger of things to come. The fact that the band could build a full-blown rock anthem out of a song that features such preposterous lines as "We raise our traffic flares to him" and "Electric lights don't help my youth" is only further testament to the Church's skills.

* * * * *

Live, the Church were not nearly as polished or impressive as they sounded on *Of Skins and Heart*, but in the months preceding the album's release, the four-piece gradually began to find its footing. The newfound cohesion became apparent during a gig supporting the New Zealand band Mi-Sex, who were enjoying considerable chart success at the time. In the middle of "Is This Where You Live," Steve looked up and realized the crowd had stopped talking. It was a major breakthrough: after almost ten years of playing in bars filled with chattering patrons, after being relegated to the role of background music for so long, Steve Kilbey was suddenly being listened to. At first the shift was almost imperceptible; one or two denizens broke off from the comfort of their social groups and gravitated toward the stage. Then, one by one, heads began to turn, eyes focusing on the hitherto-ignored opening band. Like a game of Telephone, the question made its way around the room: Who *is* this? The competing voices trickled away. All that was left was the Church.

AN INTERLUDE (II)

On my third day in Australia, I caught the train to downtown Sydney and walked around, trying to imagine the city the way Steve would have seen it when he first arrived from Canberra in the late 1970s.

Quite possibly Steve considered Sydney something of a cultural let-down after his recent trip to London, but the bustling Australian metropolis had a lot going for it in the late 1970s. For one thing, Sydney was a truly cosmopolitan city. And a distinct music and literary scene had emerged there, so that Sydney could now hold its own against Melbourne (which in the past had always been considered the more bohemian of the two). Although Steve had claimed not to be interested in or influenced by his Australian contemporaries, the very existence of a substantial local music scene ensured there were venues at which the Church could play and other bands they could play with. Then there was the weather—certainly an edge Sydney had on London. Steve told me that, during those early years in Rozelle, he made a point of taking the bus out to Bondi Beach nearly every afternoon for a swim.

Sydney had grown considerably in the years since Steve arrived, but it was still possible to catch the sense of excitement that had greeted him back then. Having traveled to this large, vibrant place after spending the previous couple of years in the small town of Wilmington, North Carolina, I sensed a parallel in our experiences; I saw my own horizons expanding before me.

Mae Moore, a Canadian songwriter who collaborated with Steve in the 1990s, articulated similar feelings about Sydney in her song "Bohemia":

Elevated visions when I close my eyes
Stretched out under these amaranth skies
Make me feel . . .
Closer than I've ever been
To being alive
Since I've arrived
In Bohemia

This tune played over and over in my head as I wandered.

At sunset, I returned to my rented flat (which Stuart Coupe had found for me) in the suburb of Lewisham, a ten-minute train ride from the city center. My landlord/roommate Janet was busy preparing a roast beef dinner.

"Hello, Robert. You got some sun today, I see."

"Yeah, I walked around a bit, went out to the harbor."

"A good day for it." She bent over the stove, pulled out a tray of steaming meat. "You know," she said, straightening up, "when I first heard about your project, I thought you were some kind of *religious* researcher. I thought you'd arrive here wearing a priest's collar!"

I laughed.

"Then I realized you were writing about the *band* the Church and I thought, 'Who would want to write about *them?*'"

My spirits fell.

"I mean, I guess if you're into mainstream music . . ." she continued, oblivious to my crestfallen look. "But no one really cares about them anymore."

This was still a bit of a shock—not the idea that they were washed up; I had heard that from other people. But the notion that the Church were a *mainstream* band. I could not get my head around the idea that the authors of *Priest=Aura*, the purveyors of that album's aural surrealism, were anything other than ultra avant-garde.

But Janet, an independent film director, was part of a key population of the Church's contemporaries—the fellow artists, musicians, and filmmakers who reached their cultural independence in the late 1970s, at a time when the established musical order was being challenged. The Sex Pistols, the Ramones, the Saints, and the whole punk explosion emerged as an alternative to the slickly produced rock (the Eagles, Queen, Little River Band, for example) that dominated the charts and the airwaves. Janet and her peers wanted their music to sound different, be more challenging, and for many of them the punk and early new-wave bands they discovered in the wake of the pioneers delivered exactly that. The spare, angular melodies of the Go-Betweens, the horn-driven blare of the Laughing Clowns, the frantic crash and thump of the Birthday Party—all recorded quickly, with scant regard for high production values—that was how they wanted their music to sound. It certified its authenticity.

So when the multinational record labels began to sign "new" bands, put them in the studio with substantial recording budgets, and market these bands as the next thing, Janet and others saw this as the mainstream's attempt to re-assert its control, and they rejected those bands. Even if they were musically more adventurous than most commercial bands, their radio-friendly produc-tion values meant they *sounded* mainstream. When the Church came along, they sounded too produced, too tight, to have much appeal to this audience. They seemed to personify the mainstream striking back.

This made me wonder about the Church's place in the grand scheme of things. To me, they were an under-appreciated yet subtly influential cult band, a sort of latter-day Velvet Underground: a band that had inspired quite a few musicians, myself included, to pick up guitars and start bands of their own. I had come to understand, though, that my view of the Church was colored by the manner in which the band had been marketed in America. In the US, the Church had first made their mark in the "college rock" genre alongside XTC, Robyn Hitchcock, the Replacements, and R.E.M. Throughout the mid to late '80s they were played almost exclusively on in-dependent, campus-run radio stations. When "Under the Milky Way" broke on mainstream radio in 1988, the band was perceived as having slowly risen through those college channels to finally attain popular status, in much the same way as the highly respected R.E.M. had done. It was only beginning to dawn on me that in Australia they had roared right out of the starting gate as a major label act, with a popular radio hit ("The Unguarded Moment"). Wrapping my head around that idea required a real shift in perspective.

"And that Steve Kilbey, he's a bit of a nutter," Janet continued, breaking me out of my reverie. "I have a friend who did some piano playing on one of his albums. He said Steve would just sort of float around the studio in a silk bathrobe, drinking from a carton of chocolate milk!"

My ears pricked up. This was the kind of material I could use: Steve Kilbey as eccentric, self-indulgent composer; a sort of new-wave Brian Wilson.

But was he a genius? Was he worth all the effort I was putting forth in my pursuit of him? There were no easy answers to these questions.

That night I lay in bed, listening to the blips and bleeps of Janet's Radiohead CD throbbing through the floorboards. I remained convinced that there was a clear line that led from *Priest=Aura* straight through to the experimental pop that a band like Radiohead now cranked out to great acclaim. But how could I prove it? Thom Yorke was not on hand to attest to his reverence for the Church (though he was quoted in 2001 to the effect that the Church had been his "musical roadmap"[4]). The only reason I even had access to Kilbey was the fact that, because his star had faded, he was essentially a non-celebrity now, someone who could be tracked down.

Still, in my mind he loomed larger than Thom Yorke, or Robert Smith, or any of the other more recognized purveyors of this type of music. For me, Steve occupied a pedestal just below Leonard Cohen and Bob Dylan. It wasn't so much the lyrics on their own—like most pop lyrics, they didn't stand up as serious poetry—but the way the words and melodies and voice intertwined to produce music that was profoundly beautiful and melancholy.

I shut the Radiohead out of my mind.

---

[4] http://homepage.mac.com/fipster/church/compilations/cv-delicatessen-3.html

7
YOU'VE GOT TO GO

There was still one huge factor holding the Church back, despite the upswing in the quality of their gigs: the feuding between Nick Ward and the other members of the group, which had escalated during the recording of *Of Skins and Heart* with Ward often demanding to play guitar and bass parts himself. Steve says that rather than being a supporting part of the proceedings, Ward continually disparaged Steve's singing and Marty's guitar playing.

But the drummer had backed himself into a corner. Other than his backing vocals, there was nothing that couldn't be replaced if Ward were to suddenly disappear from the Church. The band understood this, and so did their management. It was simply a matter of making it happen.

Ward made it easy. The escalating problems between him and Marty led to an altercation. Ward elaborates:

> We were to do a gig in Bomaderry, about two hours drive. As usual, I was the chump who drove the band to the gig in my car. I went to pick Piper up first as he lived just around the corner. When I got there he came out with wifey in tow. I said she couldn't come because there just wasn't room, and that's a fact. He said "No worries, we'll get the train." "Oh great," I said and drove off, knowing too well that there would be no train to Bomaderry especially when it was a Sunday. What a wanker.
>
> So we did the gig as a three-piece; it was soooo good to be back in

the old band; it just reinforced how much (in my opinion) we had lost by adding the pommy bastard to the lineup. The energy was back, due mainly to Peter having to work harder as the only guitar.

Oh well, that was that. Next night we were back to being a four-piece. We did the gig, and afterwards when the punters had gone, all fifty of them, I was out the front where the road wreckers were packing up and I heard Piper's wife Lucy almost yelling so I could hear, "Oh we had a wonderful time last night, we did this, we did that." I'm not quite sure what Lucy [meant] exactly; probably you could say she was just shit-stirring and I bit the hook just as she had wanted; maybe she didn't figure I would be so aggro about it. I threw a line of abuse her way. She then retaliated like a mad woman; on and on she went. I remember saying to her, "Yes, rightio, that's enough now, thank you," but she went on and on. I must have said "enough" five times.

In the end I threatened to "knock her out" if she didn't shut the hell up. Well, what's a husband to do but stick up for his wife. The next thing, I had him in a head lock; he was facing me, bent over. I lifted my knee into his guts; to my surprise his feet lifted up off the ground about six inches. I was amused at this and did it four or five more times until the road wreckers intervened; the whole time this was going on, his bitch had jumped onto my back and was trying to strangle me, so I had him in a headlock lifting him with my knee repeatedly while trying to slam her in the head with my other elbow—to no avail, I might add. I think I was lucky that she didn't scratch out my eyes.

Anyway, there was nothing in it, no one got hurt and that was that. I was on the verge of leaving and after that episode, management came to me the next day to say I was sacked. That suited me fine.

That was it. No more fistfights. No more bullying. No more having to listen to Nick pitch song ideas with titles like "Cold Steel" and "Raw Steel."[5] It was time to find someone else.
Ward provides an intriguing epilogue to this part of the story:

---

[5] Ward provided me with a selection of his home demos, which alternate between cheesy (but catchy) hard-rock anthems and lovely, Mark Knopfler-tinged instrumentals. Two things became clear to me on listening to them: 1) Ward is a formidable musician, and 2) His musical sensibilities would have completely clashed with what the Church were trying to do at that time.

I remember a few months later [the Church] were playing just down
the road in Bondi so I went for a look. When they played "Unguarded
Moment," Koppes was doing my high harmony and I remember Kilbey
looked right at me and laughed. I laughed back and thought, fuck me, I
don't remember him and me ever sharing a laugh.

8
NEW CHRIST BENEATH THE DRUMKIT MOON

Steve watched dispassionately as Jim set up his drum kit. The drummer knelt down next to his snare and tuned it, pausing to strike the top with his stick, then pressed his ear to the side, listening to the sound of rattling beads. Steve stood at the lone mic, holding his bass. Peter sat on his massive tube amp, and Marty stood at Steve's side, holding his new Rickenbacker 12-string.

Steve thought about the fact that this audition was a formality, a waste of time. Jim was essentially a shoo-in—he was their mate, he shared their taste in music, and, although they hadn't yet played with him, he had the right "vibe" for the band. What a welcome change from the constant friction that came from playing with Nick Ward.

The bad thing about the audition process was that they had to waste time jamming with the riffraff, like the kid sitting in the corner, Richard: a young punk who had shown up for the audition without even bothering to bring his own kit or sticks. This is what you get when you advertise in the local press, Steve thought.

When Jim was finally ready, they launched into "The Unguarded Moment." Steve noticed at once that the beat was dragging. This was somewhat alarming, since "Unguarded Moment" was only a mid-tempo number. Also, Jim came off the roll hitting the snare twice as hard as he should. It was not a good showing. When they finished the song, Steve recalls, the kid waiting in the corner spoke up: "You're old, granddad, give it up!"—which didn't go over too well, since Jim was the same age as Steve and Peter.

The band started another song: "Fighter Pilot: Korean War." The problems persisted. This was not simply a case of nerves—Jim clearly lacked rhythm. He seemed unable to execute a decent fill, and once he was in the fill, he had a hard time transitioning back.

When the song ended, no one said anything. Steve was already trying to figure out how they would break it to their mate that he hadn't made the grade.

Richard's loud voice broke the awkward silence: "Hey, mate, I'm gonna have to use your kit!" He got up from his corner and walked over to the drum set. Jim looked down at his snare drum.

"Okay," he said.

Marty looked at Steve, his brow furrowed. Steve knew what Marty was thinking: what gall this pimply kid had—to come in, ridicule their friend, and then demand to use Jim's gear.

Richard sat down at the drum set. They didn't even bother talking to him. Marty played the opening riff of "The Unguarded Moment," and the band fell into the groove. Richard locked in effortlessly. He nailed the song. He had a manic, flailing style reminiscent of Keith Moon, yet he somehow managed to combine it with metronomic timing.

Everyone was astonished. To Steve, it felt as if the Church had been a car with a flat tire up to that point, and here was the

Richard Ploog, circa 1981 *(Debra Mineely)*

fix. They didn't need to play another song. Jim hung his head. Nothing was said, but it was clear: Richard Ploog was in.

★ ★ ★ ★ ★

On its release in May 1981, *Of Skins and Heart* did not generate the level of response the Church or EMI had been hoping for. The band slogged on anyway, playing gig after gig.

Along with the EMI contract had come the Church's first manager: Michael Chugg—a legendary mover-and-shaker in the Australian music scene. The fact that the Church were now being managed by this gregarious figure signified that EMI took the band seriously. But "Chuggie" was out of his element here, as he and EMI tried to promote the Church to a hard-rock audience. *Of Skins and Heart* may have been a relatively rocking album for the Church, but it didn't sound much like the top-selling rock bands in Australia at the time (REO Speedwagon, Cold Chisel, Styx, and AC/DC were all big then), and Chugg and others soon discovered that any attempts to promote the Church in the same vein were doomed to failure.

Russell Kilbey has quite a few memories of the shows that took place right after Richard Ploog joined the band. Russell had moved up to Rozelle when he turned eighteen, hoping to follow his older brother into the rock-and-roll life. Steve had, after all, bought Russell his first guitar and handed him his first joint. Having had that taste of adventure, Russell wanted more, and in time he would get it. But his family connections offered no privileges; he had to start at the bottom of the ladder like anyone else, which in his case meant roadying for the Church.

"The Bondi Astor was a legendary, scummy kind of place," he says now, remembering one of the early venues. "There was blood splattered all over the ceiling from people shooting up."

Russell and his fellow roadies had the thankless task of arriving at the Astor at 2:00 p.m. and hauling the band's massive amps up four flights of stairs. After setting up for the show, he was again called into action in the middle of the gig when Steve's microphone stand collapsed. Russell ended up standing onstage and holding the microphone up to Steve's face for the remainder of the performance. Then, when it was all over, it was time to drag everything back down the stairs. By the time he finished, it was two in the morning. "It was like being a carnie, hauling stuff around," he says. "It was a hard way to live, and I'm not one for hard work."

Needless to say, Russell didn't last long. After three months he quit, correctly surmising that there are ways of making a living that don't involve breaking one's back.

Russell's decision to quit the Church road crew did not in any way diminish the bond between the two brothers. In fact, the two grew closer when Steve's marriage collapsed. Although Michelle and Steve had continued to collaborate artistically—designing the *Of Skins and Heart* cover together—their romantic relationship had been over for some time. It was the classic case of a couple having married too young. Michelle wasn't about to play the rock-and-roller's wife, sitting idly by while Steve indulged in the attendant lifestyle. Besides, she had plans of her own in the fashion industry. The two parted on relatively good terms and continued to be friends for a few years (Michelle even sang backing vocals on 1983's *Seance*). Russell quickly moved into the house in Rozelle, splitting rent with his brother and keeping him company after the separation.

* * * * *

"The Unguarded Moment" was one of those songs where, even though I'd written it and brought it along to rehearsal, it sold itself. I used to come along to rehearsals and even though I was the songwriter, it was hard to get everyone playing the song. I had to sort of do a spiel on each one. But I came along with that one, and in a break I was just playing the riff and singing it and everyone was like, "What's that?" and they all just jumped on it, and within three minutes everything was worked out and everyone knew what they were doing. I remember our manager was like, "Wow," and Chris Gilbey was like, "That's it, that's the one," and we put it on our album we were making, which I guess would have been a big flop without it. But I always had a funny relationship with that song. I was never close to it. Never liked it. Never really saw what people loved about it. I was happy that it did what it did, but I never really got my rocks off playing it. Very quickly I learned to hate it. I learned to hate the idea of all those people being there to hear one song. I really hated the idea that I was having this one song pinned on me.

—Steve Kilbey, July 2003

There is a discrepancy between Steve's and Chris Gilbey's accounts of the genesis of "The Unguarded Moment." Gilbey claims he sent Steve home with the express assignment of writing a hit when the recording sessions failed to yield an obvious single. Steve, on the other hand, downplays the song as just one of many throwaway compositions he already had in the bag. The only uncontested fact regarding this song's creation is its writer's deep ambivalence towards it from the very beginning.

The authorship of "The Unguarded Moment" is credited to both Steve Kilbey and Michelle Parker. Steve maintains, however, that Michelle's contribution consisted solely of encouragement. Why Peter Koppes didn't get a credit is something of a mystery, for the soft-spoken guitarist provided far more than encouragement. As Koppes told *Shadow Cabinet* in 1996, "I wrote the middle eight and arranged the intro and outro. I've tried not to talk about things like this, because it caused a bit of a problem in the band. You know, what is writing and what isn't writing? . . . [But] I'm at a point now where I think it's about time I started telling people what I actually did."

Koppes's contributions were not limited to "The Unguarded Moment." He wrote many of the signature riffs on the early songs, as well as a myriad of bridges and middle eights, yet never received a cent in songwriting royalties for his endeavors. His deep-rooted sense of propriety apparently prevented him from making an unseemly fuss about this oversight, though it did stick with him for some time.

Regardless of who, besides Steve, ultimately deserves credit for the creation of "The Unguarded Moment," Chris Gilbey's prediction about the song turned out to be correct: When the Church's big break came, it hinged on "The Unguarded Moment." Wide public exposure to the single came thanks to Ian "Molly" Meldrum, the lynchpin of a weekly hour-long music showcase on Australian television called *Countdown*. "It was *so* influential," says Stuart Coupe. "A youth generation shaped their weekends around *Countdown*. If you missed *Countdown*, then at school or Uni the next day the first bit of conversation was, 'Who was on *Countdown* last night?' It was that important."

Countdown combined videos, interviews, reports on local and overseas music, and studio performances. Meldrum's official title was "talent coordinator," but he held considerable sway over the show's content, as well as being its most recognizable figure. A flamboyant extrovert, he had been fortunate enough to get the final interview with one of the Beatles (John Lennon) before the band broke up—which would have been enough on its own to secure his place in music history. His unabashed love for popular

music of all stripes made him perfect for a show like *Countdown*. His exuberance was hard for audiences to resist, and many struggling bands benefited
greatly from his public support. A few months after the release of *Of Skins
and Heart*, Meldrum invited the Church to be on the program.

Steve claims now to have been ambivalent about going on *Countdown*.
This seems unlikely. At that early stage the Church needed every break they
could get. It was clear that, if *Of Skins and Heart* stiffed, their career could be
over even before it started. And getting asked on to *Countdown* was a *major*
break.

To just about everybody's surprise, the Church caused a sensation.
Their makeup and longish hair—and the sound of Marty's Rickenbacker—
ensured they stood out, aided by an almost psychedelic stained-glass-like
backdrop. And crucially, beneath the band's new-wave gloss there seethed a
palpable defiance. Looking back at the footage now, Steve says, "I look incredibly disdainful. I look like I own the place, and I'm so bored being [there]
playing this song."

The television appearance generated instant results. "The Unguarded
Moment" moved up the charts, and Steve became an celebrity overnight.
"That morning I woke up Joe Blow," he says, "and that night I went to bed
Joe Rock Star. That was *it*. The next morning it was on."

The band was besieged with booking offers and interview requests.
And, two weeks after the Church's initial appearance, Steve triumphantly
returned to *Countdown* as the guest host.

One unintended consequence of the *Countdown* appearance was John
Kilbey's humiliation on the school playground. Many years later, the youngest Kilbey recounted this trauma on his MySpace blog:

> It was over in a flash but there he was on Australia's biggest TV show,
> beamed out live into every set in the whole country it seemed. And then
> an afterthought—was he wearing eye make-up? How could he do that to
> me? Didn't he realise that spelled my doom back at school on Monday?
>
> And so I slunk to school Monday morning dreading the other kids'
> reaction.
>
> "Hey Kilbey—is your brother a pooftah?" came the opening salvo.
> "Ask his wife." My speedy retort.
>
> Two weeks later and Steven was hosting *Countdown*—an unheard

of event because this honour was normally bestowed on "real" rock stars—normally from overseas. It was surreal to see him sitting there in his paisley shirt—a much more subdued and nervous SK from the funny bugger I knew—he was really into portraying a mysterious, aloof persona in those days, I think. Excited as I was, at the back of my mind all I could think was that he was wearing that bloody make-up again and that his belly button was on display for the whole show as his paisley shirt had become untucked.

Playground tormentors aside, the rest of Australia's youth seemed to fall in love with the band. The days of opening for other bands were largely over; from that moment forward the top slot on the marquee would belong to the Church.

9
A FIRE BURNS INSIDE ME

Their appearance on *Countdown* put the Church on the Australian musical map. "The Unguarded Moment" reached number 22 on the singles chart, and *Of Skins and Heart* peaked at number 30. In a belated review for *RAM*, Kent Goddard wrote:

> The Church are the dark horses of Oz rock. Until the recent success of their single "The Unguarded Moment," hardly anybody outside Sydney (and not many there either) had heard of them. For a band who were formed less than a year ago, they will now surprise many people with this very assured album.

Not a bad start at all. With the success came a devoted group of fans—disproportionately young and female—who now followed the band from show to show. Conveniently, the Church's live performances were improving. Marty, in particular, had come into his own. Koppes continued to coax otherworldly sounds out of his Stratocaster, but more and more the eyes of the audience turned to the newly flamboyant Willson-Piper, who had made the Rickenbacker twelve-string his trademark axe. This immediately raised comparisons to the Byrds, whose lead guitarist, Roger McGuinn, had used a "Ricky" prominently during that band's glory years in the 1960s. Willson-Piper denied any Byrds influence, but his "jingle-jangle" style of picking certainly sounded reminiscent of the playing on such classic Byrds tracks as "Turn, Turn, Turn" and "Mr. Tambourine Man." It's more likely, though, that the influence came from another Ricky user—George Harrison—who used a similar—albeit punchier—style of playing on the Beatles' albums *Help, Rubber Soul,* and *Revolver.*

The weak point in the Church's live performances, oddly enough, was Kilbey himself. In the studio he had learned that his voice was at its best when he sang in a relaxed, understated manner. The technical requirements

Top: Nic Ward today; Below: the custom label he made for his gold record of *Of Skins and Heart.* (Courtesy, Nic Ward)

of live performance, however, forced him to shout in order to be heard above the other instruments. He had, after all, two loud guitarists, a ferocious drummer, and his own bass to compete with. The problem of how to get his voice to be heard properly in a live setting would plague Steve for much of his career.

For Nick Ward, watching from the sidelines, the album's good fortunes (and a lack of public acknowledgment from his former bandmates) only rubbed salt in his wounds. And the hurt has lingered. He wrote to me in 2008:

I was aghast to find out that Richard Ploog had been given a gold record for something he never played on. I did receive one as well, but only because I got in touch with Chris Gilbey and told him that I'd better get mine. I have since made my own label and stuck it on the thing; for years I had it hanging in the shitter. I tried to sell it on eBay but no one wanted the bloody thing. That was when I thought to make up my own label for it. Finally, I can now look at it.

Don't tell me all I did was kick n snare. I know I put a lot of effort and musical offerings into the first record, and to be shut out and never spoken of for all this time just shows what a bunch of pricks they are—and I hope you quote me on that. I just feel like I'd like to belt the fucking lot of them. Please quote me on that too, mate.

Despite the success of *Of Skins and Heart* in Australia, the Church did not tour overseas until after the release of their second album. Nevertheless, *Of Skins and Heart* did make some international ripples. The video for "The Unguarded Moment" created a buzz when it was screened on *The Old Grey*

Whistle Test, England's influential late-night weekly music show. And in the UK's *Sounds*, David Lewis wrote:

> Somehow the Church magically manage to combine the raw individuality of their Australian background with the exotic, atmospheric sound kaleidoscope of much of mid-Sixties American West Coast music in a fresh and exciting way that has totally eluded all the other joss stick jokers around at the moment.

"The Unguarded Moment" also charted in Sweden and Canada, although in the United States the single made no impact at all—possibly due to a jarring radio edit that deleted the middle guitar solo (Peter's cherished middle eight) and one of the verses.

Capitol Records re-packaged *Of Skins and Heart* for the US market—deleting certain tracks, re-sequencing others, and adding three new songs—and released it under the title *The Church*. Like the single, it did absolutely nothing on the charts, and would be the only stateside release of Church music for the next four years. This rejigged album was also released in the UK on the Carrere label, where it did slightly better.

The new tracks for the overseas releases were taken from a double single the band had quickly recorded and released in Australia in July 1981 to follow up on their sudden success. The Church's first sessions with Richard Ploog playing drums had yielded four new songs: "Tear It All Away," "Sisters," "Fraulein," and "Too Fast For You," plus a reworking of one of the band's earliest tunes, "You've Got to Go." These tracks were notable for several reasons: "Sisters" was the first track the band wrote together in the studio—a practice that would become the norm in years to come—and "Tear it all Away" contained the earliest, clearest rendering of what would become Steve Kilbey's philosophical manifesto:

> People say to see is to believe
> But then they just believe in that they can perceive
> What they see is not the perfect view
> Filtered between the me and you
> But I'm trying so hard to open my eyes
> To see some things that tear it all away.

Gone from the new songs (with the exception of "Fraulein") was the muted guitar staccato that had dominated the first album; it was replaced here by a twelve-string jangle—a significant contribution from Marty Willson-Piper. And Ploog's drumming felt more natural, more organic than Ward's—all around a better fit for the band's sound.

The double single garnered positive reviews and more high-profile headlining shows followed. Within sections of the Australian music scene, however, there was continued grumbling about the Church. Their rapid rise following the *Countdown* performance intensified this dislike. It also didn't help one bit that EMI's full-page newspaper ads promoting *Of Skins and Heart* had proclaimed the release "Probably the most exciting debut album ever to come from an Australian act." The Roger Grierson comment cited earlier ("The Church weren't a D-I-Y outfit, they were, 'We want to be pop stars.'") dates from this period, and the prevalent view of the band at the time in the eyes of other musicians is summed up in this recollection from musician/producer Pryce Surplice:

> During the late '70s and early '80s, Australian music polarized into two distinct camps: the ones who'd ride the new wave, wipeout or not, to see where this wave Punk started would take us. And then there were the *Countdown* bands who rehashed banal audiovisual clichéd iconography for a volatile promise of fame and fortune.
>
> Australian A&R has only ever had one fallback game plan: when in doubt, re-sell last week's special with a new salad; it sold well once, it probably will again . . . no need to hire a fancy chef, we still have leftovers frozen from last week, would you like fries with that? . . . By any stretch of the imagination, "The Church" slotted firmly into this camp: unthreatening 16-year-old teeny girl pop-fluff music. "Unguarded Moment" and "Almost with You" may have had accessible melodies with a lush vocal sound, but it's basically stylistically cynical and lyrically bereft . . . Steven may believe he's the anointed antipodean successor to Syd Barrett and Mark Bolan, but he's not even Nick Cave . . . From that position any attempt to claw back a veil of credibility over history is both transparent and insulting to anyone with working memory cells.

There is some truth to the assertion that the Church's success, in the early days at least, was the result of a calculated push. Steve had made a detour away from pop music with his electronica dabblings in the late '70s, but since the forming of the Church, the end goal had clearly been commercial success—the bigger the better. Considering the fact that both he and Peter had spent the better part of a decade playing in marginal bands while working low-paying jobs, it's hard to fault them for wanting to make a decent living from their music and taking the appropriate steps to ensure that happened. But the teased hair, copious eyeliner, and contrived pouts of the *Countdown* appearance raised the hackles of many hardworking musicians in the scene, who considered themselves the "real thing" and saw the Church as "impostors."

Nowadays, Steve acknowledges his youthful fame-chasing but asserts that he sought success on *his* terms. If one can separate the image and slick sound of the Church from the songwriting itself, this assertion has some validity. True, the posturing, the hairstyles, and the fashionable clothing were all calculated to win the hearts and minds of teenagers across the land, but the band's music had real depth. It would have been easy for Steve simply to cash in and write unabashedly one-dimensional pop songs, but that is not what he chose to do. The same album that contained "The Unguarded Moment" also featured "Is This Where You Live," and one would be hard-pressed to find anything calculated or commercial in the dense surrealism of *that* track.

Pundits can spend all day arguing about the purity of an artist's intentions, but at the end of the day it's the work itself that matters. And the Church's work was —from the very beginning—impressive and ambitious; no mere rehash of Barrett and Bolan, it synthesized those and other influences into a cohesive sound that pulled off the trick of being both catchy *and* thought-provoking. Surely, one can still appreciate and even prefer the more challenging efforts of Australia's true underground heroes—the Birthday Party, the Triffids, and the Go-Betweens (to name just a few)—while conceding this point. And if Surplice's assessment of the Church's music as "16-year-old teeny-girl pop fluff" is accurate, then I can only conclude that sixteen-year-old girls in Australia have impeccable taste.

The grumbling had little effect on the Church, in any case. Their audiences continued to grow, and their singles continued to get radio play. When the band returned to EMI Studios at the end of 1981 to begin work on their second LP, expectations were high all around. Having a bona-fide hit under his belt gave Steve Kilbey new clout, and he intended to use it. He was less willing this time to defer to producers and managers. This headstrong approach allowed the band to find its own voice on the resulting album—*The Blurred Crusade*—but also came with a downside, as Steve later explained.

> I was very difficult. I've shot myself in the foot many times in my career, but in those days I was just going round the world, fucking up, offending people left, right and center. Michael Chugg didn't have any way of controlling that or seeing what was going on. It was like the blind leading the blind.

In 1981 Steve Kilbey was twenty-seven, moderately successful and, for the first time in his life, financially comfortable. This turn of events served as vindication for the years he had spent holed up in his bedroom recording hours and hours of music that no one (save his younger brothers) had heard. It was revenge on all the people who had doubted him or simply been indifferent. In Steve's mind, he had been right all along—and it was time for people to start listening to him. His ego went into overdrive, and while his arrogance didn't particularly endear him to his bandmates or others he met on a personal level, it didn't do any harm in the studio. Chris Gilbey, realizing he had lost his power to mold Kilbey into an artist of his own creation, turned the production reins fully over to Bob Clearmountain. Fortunately, the American happened to be one of the few people in the music business Steve looked up to; he was good at setting tasks and goals, encouraging Steve, gently pushing him.

Steve, in turn, found himself able to indulge all of his musical flights of fancy. If he wanted a harpsichord on a song, Clearmountain would arrange for it. If he requested it in the morning, by the afternoon a man would turn up in a truck and assemble a harpsichord and tune it up. Steve would then sit around for hours playing it on the record company's dime.

As with *Of Skins and Heart*, the recording process revolved around Steve bringing in home-recorded tapes of his new songs, with many of the guitar parts already worked out. The band would then learn the songs, rehearse and record. Rinse and repeat. There were, however, a few departures from this tried-and-true formula: On "An Interlude," which started out as a relatively short track, the band improvised an extended outro. One of the album's standouts, "You Took," took shape in a true collaborative process during an improvisational jam at a soundcheck in Victoria, according to Steve.

> I was always impressed by the bass part in the middle of [Free's] "All Right Now." I'm really into bass harmonics, and I was also very much into the idea of playing easy things—I like the idea of simplicity on bass, having a simplistic bass part and then allowing the rest of the band to do what they do around it. I was doing this bass part, and then Ploog started playing, and Marty and Peter started doing their things. It just sort of mutated and grew.

For the lead riff, Peter cannibalized one of Steve's earlier songs, "Visions of the Young." That song hadn't gone anywhere, but Peter liked the riff and set it loose in this new piece to great effect.

Anyone who has seen the Church live is quick to note that the studio version of "You Took" pales in comparison to the live, jam-based version of the song. Steve concurs. "I don't think the version on the album is by any means the best version," he says.

> Even by then, we had the thing where we take it up to this white-hot moment in the middle where it ends up just me on the bass and Ploog on the drums and then everyone really intensifying around that. I don't know why in the studio we never went for it or thought that we should. These days we would. We'd go, "Come on, we can't leave it at this."

The lyrics are another example of Steve leaving things at the halfway point. Steve often uses the stop-gap lyric-writing technique popularized by John Lennon, where you fill in gaps in the song's lyrics with nonsense phrases and then go back and fix them later. Sometimes Lennon would leave his stop-gaps in the final products, as evidenced in "Strawberry Fields Forever" and "I Am the Walrus." With "You Took," as with many of his other songs, Steve never bothered to go back and revise his words. He probably never imagined the song would become a live favorite he'd be performing onstage twenty-five years later. At any rate, he's now stuck with an imperfect song that nevertheless has flashes of genius in it. "I'm always like that," he says with a sigh. "I have something almost exact and then for some reason I'll leave a flaw in it, some sort of flaw that I learn to hate."

Steve has often lamented his band's tendency to squander success—how the Church often follow a satisfying album with a mediocre one, thereby killing their chances of greater rewards. *The Blurred Crusade*, however, is one instance where the intrepid foursome got it right. It is, by any measure, a laudable achievement: consistently solid from beginning to end and radiating confidence. For the first time, Marty Willson-Piper's guitar playing climbs fully out of Koppes' shadow, his Rickenbacker twelve-string chiming out like bells in a sunny Spanish courtyard. Also prominent is Steve's keyboard playing. The ominous sound of his Roland Vocoder, oddly reminiscent of Gregorian chant, quickly became a staple of the early Church sound.

Sonic consistency is the greatest triumph of *The Blurred Crusade*. Even though most of the songs are Kilbey compositions, the album feels very much like a group effort. In every note and every chord, one can sense the band's appreciation for the material.

If there is anything patchy about the album at all, it is the lyrics. Steve had already established himself as something of a surrealist in *Of Skins and Heart*, but *The Blurred Crusade* takes abstraction to a whole new level. Many of the themes, concepts, and images are, at best, half-baked. This tendency to wander away from the concrete and into the Twilight Zone may be partially due to Steve's increased hallucinogen intake during the period of writing and recording. Nevertheless, the songs contain enough fleeting poetic gems, character insights, and striking turns-of-phrase to compensate for the unresolved tangents and occasional linguistic clunkers.

The Blurred Crusade era marked Steve's first truly decadent phase. Now that he had minders from the record company taking care of his essential needs, he found himself free to indulge in chemical and sensory stimulation. "Marijuana and psychedelics—LSD, magic mushrooms—that was literally my breakfast," he says.

> I'd get up every morning and I'd drop a trip or drop a mushroom . . . Ploog and I, we'd go on tour and buy a pound of pot just for him and I. We'd wake up in the middle of the night and have joints rolled and smoke them, and then first thing in the morning, more joints. We'd have a joint before we had a joint! You know, I'd be like, "I'm gonna roll a joint," and

he'd be like, "Before you roll a joint, let's roll a joint so we can appreciate rolling a joint!"

Steve and Richard got into the habit of trying to outdo each other with their debauchery. They would load up on drugs before a performance and see how "out of it" they could get and still play. Consequently, the shows from this era tended not to be technically polished affairs, though the raw, hedonistic energy could sometimes work in the band's favor.

Much of the impetus for Steve's drug ambitions came from a surreal Nicolas Roeg film called *Performance* (starring, appropriately, Mick Jagger.) Steve desperately wanted to be a part of the world depicted in that film—the hedonistic world of late-'60s rock and roll. Fifteen years after the Summer of Love, the Church did their best to live out the dream, as if they were the Beatles or the Byrds or the Stones experiencing stardom and its attendant temptations for the first time. But Steve never had the intention, during this period or others, of being a drug proselytizer. His interest lay in the potential of music itself as a transporting vehicle. To him, the possibility of a fan experiencing a natural high from listening to the Church justified his actions. "Smoking pot and stuff like that definitely influenced the creation of the music and the lyrics a lot," he says, "but the music isn't about drugs."

> It's easily mixed up with that, because once again it's about that idea of getting out of the mundane plane and getting into something else, so it all becomes a big confusing thing, you know, are drugs a part of that? The references are all in there. I felt like I picked up the drug thing as something sort of inherited. It felt like it was something you were supposed to do. So originally I was acting a bit, and then one day you wake up and you realize you're really playing the part.

If Steve Kilbey had simply stuck to the path of aural transcendence, the Church might have had a smooth ride to prolonged stardom. However, with every successful performance and every new bit of coddling from his managers, Steve's ego grew. And anyone can tell you that working with a controlling egomaniac can turn even the most sublime moments of musical ecstasy into drudgery.

Compounding his need to dominate the band itself, Steve felt that he was smarter and more competent than the people who were tasked with managing the Church. During meetings with these higher-ups, it was not unusual for Steve to begin a chant of "This whole thing is totally fucked!" The others would quickly pick up on it, and soon band and managers were at each other's throats. The problem with this incitement to rebellion was that Steve rarely had any constructive suggestions as to how things *should* be done. It was all an exercise in negativity. The managers politely tolerated this behavior. Steve was, after all, making them money. For now.

10
TO BE IN YOUR EYES

The first thing I noticed on entering Stuart Coupe's flat in Lewisham was his books. Ragged volumes were crammed everywhere: on shelves, on the floor, on the stairs. Classic works of American crime fiction by Raymond Chandler, Dashiell Hammett, and James M. Cain rested comfortably next to the requisite rock-and-roll biographies. Stuart clearly had an affinity for hardboiled American prose, and his interest in dark realism no doubt explained why he had never appreciated Steve's lyrics, Steve being a student of mythology, Tolkien, the Surrealists, and the Romantic poets. Interestingly, my adult tastes matched Stuart's more closely than they did Steve's: I was more likely to curl up with the most recent James Ellroy novel than a new translation of *Beowulf*. The works of Bradbury and Tolkien had exerted a strong hold on my childhood, but they had been replaced in my late teens by the street-smart writings of Jack Kerouac and William S. Burroughs. The fantasy in those novels came not from mystical alternate universes but from drug hallucinations. Steve's music represented a bridge between these two worlds: an adult extension of the childhood myths, leavening wide-eyed innocence with the liberating yet corrupting influence of chemicals.

Stuart was no stranger to the "derangement of the senses," but *his* drug of choice was alcohol. He had the look of someone who had come out the other end of some pretty rough times: stooped and very thin—almost emaciated, with deep lines under his eyes. From his head sprouted a curly, if thinning, mass of hair, a cloud of red corkscrews that fell in his face with his every movement.

Like Steve, Stuart comes across as a larger-than-life personality, in love with the sound of his own voice. But unlike Steve, he has a knack for putting people at ease, smiling, gesturing animatedly, and filling the air with his words. And while a propensity for excessive talk can be annoying in others, Stuart at least has interesting things to say. Over multiple glasses of beer and two very tender steaks, we discussed his onetime association with Mr. K.

Stuart Coupe and Steve Kilbey were once close friends, although close is always a relative term with Steve; even at that early stage, he kept to himself and gave the impression of either being self-absorbed or possessed of a rich inner life. But the young, brooding musician at least made overtures to

Stuart Coupe in his office, 2003 *(Robert Lurie)*

Stuart that suggested friendship. He would often show up on Stuart's doorstep at two a.m. and the two would talk into the early hours, smoking marijuana and listening over and over again to Stuart's 7-inch record of Chris Bell's "I am the Cosmos." Steve would sometimes bring Richard Ploog along. The self-effacing drummer carried no pretensions whatsoever; his main goals in life were to feel good at all times, play loud rock and roll, and make the people around him laugh. He harbored no commercial ambitions and had absolutely no problem ceding Steve the spotlight, which probably explains why they got on so well.

After late nights spent recording and mixing *The Blurred Crusade*, Steve and Richard often made their way over to Stuart's house, acetates in hand. The three of them would listen to the rough mixes, and Stuart would give feedback. In those days the feedback consisted mostly of praise.

As Stuart and Steve ascended in their respective careers, it seemed only natural that the two would cross paths professionally. This happened courtesy of *RAM*, a widely read music weekly which commissioned Stuart to do a profile of Kilbey and the Church. The magazine flew him down to Melbourne for a show. During the concert, Stuart observed one of the roadies setting up lines of what he assumed was speed backstage. At certain points during the show, Steve or one of his bandmates would either lean across a speaker or go offstage, do a quick line, and come back on.

After the show, the two went off to the Prince of Wales—a hotel in the seedy Melbourne district of St. Kilda—to do the interview. Over beer and various other intoxicants, they talked for hours, eventually exhausting all four of the blank cassettes Stuart had brought with him. Finally, according to Stuart, "We went for this long, completely trashed walk along the promenade at St. Kilda beach. We were getting along like a house on fire, as two highly-charged individuals will do."

When they returned to the hotel room, the interview continued. The conversation became increasingly combative as the inebriated Kilbey declared that he was the best songwriter in Australia.

"Why?" Stuart asked him.

"Why am I the best songwriter? I think I'm the best songwriter in Australia because I enjoy what I do more than I enjoy what anybody else does. That's the only reason I can give. It's totally big-headed but I'd rather listen to one of my own records than anybody else's who's around."

This statement would come back to haunt the up-and-coming musician. There is some uncertainty as to whether Kilbey intended this and other ill-advised comments to be part of the interview at all. Stuart, on the other hand, was operating on the assumption that, since he had been paid to fly down and spend time with him, anything Steve said to Stuart was fair game for the piece. Furthermore, Steve had not at any point explicitly declared the interview over. At any rate, the ensuing negative public reaction to the article, which portrayed Steve as a pretentious egomaniac, drove a permanent wedge between Coupe and Kilbey and signaled the end of their friendship.

"At that point," Stuart says, "things went very cold." There was also the matter of a quip Kilbey had made about the host of *Countdown*. "The only reason I got on *Countdown* at all was because Meldrum fancied me," Kilbey had said."

"The shit hit the fan," Coupe recalls. "Steve was furious. Molly [Meldrum] was furious and threatening to sue because [by printing Steve's comment] I'd alluded to him being gay. Steve was totally furious because he assumed he'd never get on *Countdown* again."

Reading the piece now, it is not too difficult to see why Steve became so incensed, although the intensity and persistence of his anger are surprising.

In addition to quoting Steve's bragging and his comments about Meldrum, Stuart makes a few stinging comments of his own, though it's clear that his intention is not to write a hatchet piece. His main problem seems to be with the lyrics, as he states quite clearly that he loves the band's music. Employing the classic journalistic ploy of "some people say"—that is, quoting 'unnamed sources' that happen to give voice to the journalist's own opinions, Stuart writes, *"People might think* [italics added] that far from being the slightest bit talented, [Steve is] just efficient at selecting random images and stringing them together." Later on he quotes an anonymous friend's musings on Steve's lyrics: "Sounds like the hallucinations of an old hippie." It was this lethal combination—a negative appraisal of Steve's personality plus a dismissal of his talents as a poet—that sent the songwriter over the edge.

This notorious piece would not be the last professional encounter between Steve and Stuart. A year later, on the heels of the Nick Launay–produced *Seance* album, the Church's management got in touch with *RAM* once again about the prospect of the magazine doing a new cover piece on the band.

"Anthony O'Grady was my editor," Stuart says. "It was Anthony's idea—he kind of pulled rank and said, 'Okay, we'll give the Church a cover, but only if Kilbey agrees to talk to Stuart.' And I hadn't spoken to Kilbey since that first interview, except when he rang me up to abuse me!"

The fateful date was set up, and the two met—with chaperones—at Steve's home in Rozelle.

> I think we both went with minders in case it turned into fisticuffs. It was kind of tense and I remember being very uncomfortable walking in and going, Okay, how do I meet up with my old buddy who now hates me? Nobody likes those situations, even if you're a rock star, journalist, or whatever. We did the interview; we had the photographer come in, because the whole idea was this big encounter, which had assumed— among the audience in Australia who actually cared—somewhat mythic proportions. This was not America vs. Saddam Hussein, but in the small milieu of rock and roll this was a big fucking deal [laughs]; this was the UN meeting to improve the state of world affairs! We begrudgingly did this sort of arm-wrestling for the photo, and I went away and wrote my piece. And I honestly can't remember what Steve hated about this one, but he hated it!

Here is Steve Kilbey's response, many years later, to "Coupegate":

He got me talking about the Church, and I said some very "up" things and I said some very "down" things, but he just printed all the "up" things. And he didn't print the questions that had prompted the statements, and he didn't print the "But I might not think that tomorrow." He just printed all this "We're the best, I'm the best," and all this, and he just set me up and knocked me down. And I'd done all that because he'd been my friend. Because he'd come round and I'd really opened up to the fucker. And you know what? He tried to get me on his radio show the other night, like, after all that, he tried to get me on there. It was like, "Come on, spin any records you like." I'm like, "Fuck you, man; you were a cunt twenty-five years ago and you still are!" I wouldn't have anything to do with him after what he did to me. It was a real betrayal. It wasn't like a journalist writing an article. He was my *friend*. We used to go round his place and listen to records, me and Ploogy. We would hang out and stuff. So I really opened up to him because I thought he was my friend. With some of the comments I made in that interview, I was having a big joke at my own expense. But he just printed it verbatim and stitched me up. So I've got no interest in him or his second-rate radio show!

As I had always suspected, Steve takes the art of holding a grudge to new heights. If there's any one thing his long-standing enmity towards Stuart Coupe reveals, it's that he has grown a hard shell to protect a sensitive core. Despite all the tough talk, twenty-five years later the betrayal still hurts. Steve takes friendship very seriously; those who can truly call themselves his friends are a small but loyal number. It is relatively easy for him to suffer the slings and arrows of anonymous critics, but if a trusted friend turns on him, it opens a wellspring of deep hurt. Stuart Coupe was the first and last music writer that Steve would befriend.

Stuart's article in *RAM* seemed to be the trigger for a series of negative pieces about Steve in the Australian press, though it's unclear whether the other writers were influenced more by what Stuart wrote or by their own negative impressions of the singer. Nic Ward (who is admittedly far from being unbiased), says today, "Oh, didn't Kilbey do a great job of that! Nobody liked him, journos included. They'd interview him and then leave shit out to make him look bad. The 'I write the best songs on the planet' quote is a great example." Consciously or not, Steve had ratcheted up his level of provocativeness, making grandiose statements about his talent as well as commenting derisively on the music press itself (his favorite jab at music journalists—repeated countless times over the years—was that they were all failed musicians; they wrote because they couldn't play.)

A certain skepticism had already been apparent in the press, mirroring the general ambivalence within the music scene towards the band's rapid rise. In a piece for *Roadrunner* in 1981, John Doe had written, "It's difficult to tell just how long the Church will stay in the public eye. The band's lack of outward intensity concerning such things as 'deep meaningfulness,' for want a better cliche, gives the impression of a certain aimlessness in their approach." Nevertheless, he and others had reviewed *Of Skins and Heart* favorably. Michael Smith wrote in *Juke*, "The quality has been there from the beginning, with their debut single: "She Never Said" [through] "The Unguarded Moment" and brilliant debut LP *Of Skins and Heart*. The remarkable thing is that, in the mixture of dedication and laziness in all they do, this band of four *very* different and strong personalities can present such a strong, united front." These pieces reflect a concerted effort on the part of the press to give this new band a balanced treatment, noting but not dwelling on potential shortcomings.

The *RAM* piece, however, marked a sea change, even though the band's later characterization of the entire Australian press having turned on them is false. In fact, *The Blurred Crusade* received strong reviews and Coupe himself continued to write positively about the band's music. All the same, it became fashionable for journalists to take shots at Kilbey's earnest and sometimes ill-advised pronouncements. And in May 1982, *Roadrunner* ran a somewhat bizarre cover story on the Church entitled "Is This the Taste of Victory?" consisting entirely of past Kilbey quotes juxtaposed with grandiose sayings from Donovan, Aleister Crowley, Timothy Leary, and Mao Tse-Tung. Kilbey had apparently stopped talking to the press, and this was *Roadrunner's* response.

Looking back years later, Steve ruefully told *Juke* magazine:

Sometimes you can get away with being egotistical and sometimes you can't. I think in the very early days I was trying to be deliberately provocative—something that didn't work and which backfired and which I felt very bad about because I don't really have that high of an opinion of myself at all. I suppose if I had been reading someone else saying the things that I was saying, I would have thought, "That guy's a bit of a turkey." There are times when you can get away with being like that and I just didn't choose my moments very well.

11
SAYING SWEET LIFE IS A DOWNRIGHT DRAG, DOWN TO THE VERY LAST SEED IN THE BAG

Steve stood on the stage, swaying ever so slightly, his bass acting as an anchor as he faced the crowd. He wasn't sure how many drugs he had taken before the show; there was the usual joint or two, plus some mushrooms, a tab of acid, the indispensable coke.

He played and sang on autopilot, his right foot tapping the ground with each beat. The crowd—mostly twentysomething hipsters and some kids in their late teens—ate it up. They certainly didn't seem to mind that he shouted rather than crooned his vocals and that his phrasing was erratic. It was all part of the headlong energy of a live rock-and-roll show. He turned slightly and glanced back at Richard. Ploogsy pounded the drums ferociously, but it appeared to Steve as if he was moving in slow motion, off from the beat. Everything sounded fine, though. For a moment their eyes locked, and a look of acknowledgment passed between them. Ploog had, after all, been right there with Steve in the dressing room, snorting the lines off the table with gusto.

The two bandmates grinned at each other conspiratorially, enjoying the intimacy of their shared chemical bond. Steve turned back to face the audience, which by now had become a pulsating, multi-headed blur. For a moment he thought, *Fuck, I don't know if I can handle this.* But the moment passed, and then it was back to the performance.

The release of *The Blurred Crusade* in February 1982 solidified the Church's standing in Australia. Though it lacked a standout single to rival "The Unguarded Moment," the album sold more copies than its predecessor, easily going double-gold. And the track that *was* released as a single, "Almost with You," reached number 21 in the charts, one place higher than "The Unguarded Moment," despite being a relatively inferior offering. (Fans tend to love this track, but it has always struck this writer as a fairly lifeless, Church-by-numbers exercise. Jangly guitars? Check. Monotone delivery? Check. Lyrics about reincarnation? Check.)

Since the band had now established themselves at home, the music industry—being the capitalist enterprise it is—dictated that the Church expand ever outward and saturate new territories with their shimmering guitars and sonorous vocals. America remained out of reach still—after the first LP stiffed, the band had lost its Capitol deal—but the UK was ripe for the picking. "The Unguarded Moment" had made an impact, and *The Blurred Crusade* was getting positive reviews. *Sounds* magazine proclaimed, "The Church are no frazzled revivalists....By opening and poking among rock's rich archives, they are leaving themselves free to explore their own ideas and dreams."

In mid-1982 the Church made their live UK debut at the Venue in London. Among the audience that night were David Gilmour of Pink Floyd and—allegedly—a young guitarist named Johnny Marr. The band was in fine form and the crowd responded enthusiastically—more welcoming than the crowds in Australia, it seemed to Steve. The Church appeared poised to take the country by storm. Then came the Duran Duran tour . . .

The idea of pairing the up-and-coming Church with the hugely successful new-wave band must have seemed like a winner to EMI executives. By opening for their all-conquering labelmates, who had four UK chart hits that year, the Church would be exposing their music to thousands of new listeners every night. In reality, however, the pairing turned out to be a disaster. The paisley-clad Kilbey and Co. may have been the height of stylishness in Sydney, but they appeared hopelessly out-of-touch to the teenybopper "Durannies" who packed the shows. The audience mainly booed or ignored the Church's opening set. "The only time anyone ever clapped," Steve says, "was when Marty broke some strings on his guitar and stormed offstage. Like, 'Good, there's one gone; now the other three should go.' A very disheartening experience."

Most humiliating of all was the fact that Simon Le Bon and the other members of Duran Duran treated the Church contemptuously, slagging them off as "a bunch of Australian hippies."

Seven gigs into the tour, Steve pulled the plug.

> I said, "That's it. I'm off." And of course everyone was angry because the record company had paid 30,000 pounds to get us on that tour, and then I jumped ship.

The band sat around in England for a few weeks, doing not much of anything other than getting high, once again on EMI's dime. They did manage to regroup and headline a week's worth of club shows in England and Scotland in late November, before making it back to the Venue on December 2, 1982. This show was just as well-attended as the first; it was a good sign that the Church's audience was still there, eager to see them and buy their records. The band just needed to figure out how to take things to the next level—something that would prove harder than anyone could anticipate.

The October 1982 show at the Venue was one of the first Church shows to be bootlegged. Tapes and CDs of it are still traded by fans. Listening to the recording now, one can sense the energy of that performance. There is a feeling of imminent arrival, of a band on the verge of greatness. There is also something strangely appealing about Steve's off-key, coke-addled raving that is missing from later performances. Call it youthful exuberance. In searching for the correct notes, he casts his net wide and rarely hauls in the right one. It can elicit a cringe from the discerning music listener, but at the time, his emotive delivery probably enthralled the concertgoers. Given the aloof, laconic persona that Steve later developed (and had already assumed on record), this early recording offers a nice window to the unguarded Kilbey—perhaps not so innocent, but not entirely jaded either. It also reveals that, even at this early stage in their career, the Church were already moving into heavily improvisational territory; the set list contains no less than three extended pieces: "When You Were Mine," "You Took," and "Is This Where

Steve Kilbey at Ritchies, Melbourne, 1982 (Debra Mineely)

You Live." Unlike the shows they play these days, where the improvisation is usually confined to the encores, these songs are interspersed throughout the set. In "You Took," particularly, Koppes and Willson-Piper take their first steps towards a sort of guitar telepathy, expanding the middle section, building to that "white hot" moment that Steve describes as the song's apex. In "Is This Where You Live," Koppes—utilizing some well-chosen effects trickery—does a remarkable job of replicating the backwards guitar solo from the studio track. And, while less freewheeling than "You Took," the second half of "Is This Where You Live" showcases the band performing in complete bombastic synergy. These musical workouts represent the beginning of a serious flirtation with progressive rock—a natural step given the band's (particularly Marty's) enthusiasm for such prog-rock acts as Pink Floyd and King Crimson.

Of course there are some missteps; "Fighter Pilot: Korean War" is an absolute train wreck; Steve seems unable to figure out what key to sing the song in. Similarly, the backing vocals throughout the set are sloppy: a problem that would unfortunately not be fully addressed for two decades, until the acoustic tour of 2002.

The real historical value of the tape is the fact that it backs up Steve's description of just how enthusiastically the Church were received in the UK in 1982. The crowd is ecstatic throughout the performance, often singing along to all the songs. One could not be faulted for assuming that this is a recording of a band on the way up, not one about to hit the skids.

The Church received a decidedly cooler greeting on their return home. Australian audiences, it turned out, were becoming bored with them. Much of this was due to the reception of the *Sing-Songs* EP, a collection of five self-produced tracks released on the band's return in December, 1982. The songs themselves were not bad—the four Kilbey originals contained fine melodies and some lovely imagery—but the bare-bones production and occasionally flat vocals were perceived as a letdown after the lush harmonies and crystal-clear guitars of *The Blurred Crusade*. In many people's eyes, the Church should have been busy creating their masterwork. Instead, the tired and tinny *Sing Songs* arrived. Other than a positive review from, oddly enough, Stuart Coupe, the press was not kind. In *RAM*, "Dr." G. Taylor wrote sarcastically, "I urge you to remember that this is *serious* and *sensitive*

music, and lots of serious and sensitive people the world over—well, one
or two countries anyway—are buying it. Do not approach it with any mis-
guided levity or a puerile desire for fun."

Steve claims one critic even wrote, "Steve Kilbey writes these songs the
way other people write shopping lists, and they're about as interesting."

The members of the Church did their best to keep the fire burning by
hitting the road again. As Steve remembers, "We toured round Australia
and even New Zealand, just playing places that didn't want us, didn't like us,
didn't want our kind of music."

Michael Chugg left his office to drive the tour van, an unprecedented
move for a manager of his stature, all in an attempt to take the edge off
Steve's bitching. The gesture proved fruitless.

The tour was not a total waste; the band did manage to eke out a living—if only a meager one—and touring also kept them in shape musically.
All their hopes now rested on the reception of the next LP, which the band
recorded during breaks in their touring schedule. There was a feeling within
the Church that this upcoming album needed to be a commercial and critical success, otherwise the backslide would become irreversible.

★ ★ ★ ★ ★

Sing Songs occupies a strange position in the Church's oeuvre. Regarded as
a minor effort at the time, it later achieved collector's item status due to
its rarity. In the early days of eBay in the late 1990s, it was not unusual for
copies of the EP to sell for upwards of $500. Consequently, the songs on
this ultra-rare release achieved an exaggerated stature, especially surprising
considering the indifference with which they were initially greeted.

Lyrically, the EP does have two standouts: "A Different Man" and "The
Night is Very Soft." Both songs are more narratively complete than the typical Kilbey snapshots. "A Different Man," if taken autobiographically, could
be about the growing disparity between Steve Kilbey the persona—the rock
star—and Steve Kilbey the individual. There was definitely a gap between
the two at the time of the song's composition. As Russell Kilbey says,

I remember him just crying on the front steps, just not knowing what it
was all about. The conundrum of being famous is that you want people

to love you. It's natural for people to want people to love them, right? But then you've got all these people who love the fictionalization that is not you at all.

Sure enough, one of the lines in the song states, "But look at the dust at his feet / He's not the one she loves / It was a different man, you know he's never been found / You can be so up, you can be so down." Significantly, each verse begins with the words "Inside himself," then the song goes on to distinguish between that inner self and the outer projection—the different man.

Musically, the song features Marty Willson-Piper at his most Byrdsian, picking out a descending D pattern on his 12-string Rickenbacker. The slow break featuring Koppes' echoey solo seems, for once, strangely out of place, but the song has a lovely denouement with Marty's high pitched Ahhhhs overlapping Steve's insistent repetition of the chorus. The song is easily the catchiest of the five tracks, and it is not surprising that it was the track promoted for airplay.

"The Night is Very Soft" marks a departure for Kilbey, at least within the confines of the Church. As he states in his liner notes to the *Hindsight* collection, the song contains an element that was previously missing from Church music—sex. While this is not entirely true—"For a Moment We're Strangers" from *Of Skins and Heart* had vague allusions to a sexual liaison— "The Night is Very Soft" makes the connection more explicit, with images of "tiny drops of water" glistening "on her black fur" and a slightly ridiculous "milk-white electric guitar." Once again, the sex appears to be casual, as evinced by the lines "I sat next to nothing as she looked right through me" and "As she dresses I look to the ground." As in "For a Moment We're Strangers," post-coital shame weighs heavily on the narrator's soul, but here, for the first time, there is also pleasure and eroticism. The first line of the chorus, "Outside, the night is very soft / but where does it end?" poetically captures the duality of the impersonal sexual encounter, only to be followed by the crass "We'd pile into the Buick but you've got to have money for that."

The music mirrors the lyrics quite well, although it falls a little short of its goal; we are, after all, talking about four white guys trying to be funky. Steve, who by his own admission doesn't have a "black bone" in his body, offers a tentative, perfunctory bass line. The guitars are lush but not exactly sensual. The only band member who succeeds in getting loose is Ploog, who provides a syncopated beat that would not be out of place on an Al Green recording.

Sadly, the biggest liability of the track is Steve's voice: his flat, inflectionless vocal is woefully inadequate. An argument could be made that the woodenness of his voice is a deliberate ploy to set up tension between the sensuality of the lyrics and their mechanical delivery, but Steve's more dynamic performances on later, similarly themed songs such as "Fall in Love" and "English Kiss" would indicate that the contrast in "The Night is Very Soft" is not intentional. At the point of this recording, Steve has not yet developed into the type of singer that this material requires.

As for the other tracks, "Ancient History" is catchy but disposable, and features one of Steve's worst lines: "Some of us are white, some of us are red / Some have got these visions going round in our heads." "In This Room" is an intriguing track that hints at the darkness that lay in Kilbey's future with its chorus—"There are no windows in this room in which we've been sitting all our lives." The song features an appealing melody and innovative guitar work. The image of the windowless room is a striking one and perfectly encapsulates the overall downbeat nature of the song. Not surprisingly, "In This Room" is occasionally dredged up and reinterpreted during the Church's acoustic performances.

The EP closes on a low note with an ill-advised cover of Simon and Garfunkel's "I Am a Rock." Although the lyrics are in keeping with the standard Church theme of alienation, Steve's voice once again lets down the material. Add to this the cookie-cutter musical performances and atonal harmonies, and you have a lackluster interpretation that adds nothing to the original.

What to make of *Sing Songs* today? Lyrically, it represents a step forward—moving as it does from the dissociated LSD images of *The Blurred Crusade* into more sophisticated and literate terrain. Musically, the songs possess more quietness and subtlety than their predecessors, even if the bedroom demo production lets them down.

The EP stands now as a vital record of the painful growing period between *The Blurred Crusade* and *Seance*. At the time, it was the wrong move to make commercially, and the band would pay dearly for the misstep. One possible silver lining to the whole situation was that the failure of *Sing-Songs* to chart provided a much needed check to Steve Kilbey's ego. It was his first taste of commercial failure (notwithstanding the Duran Duran bailout, which was his own decision) after the string of successes that began with "The Unguarded Moment." If his comments in the Coupe interview were true, if he really *had* begun to think of himself as someone who could rule Australia while writing songs in his sleep, the negative reaction to the *Sing-Songs* EP must have provided a reality check. He realized that if he were to have any chance of attaining the type of success he craved, he would have to work hard for it, just like everyone else. The fact that he was undeniably talented did not mean that he wore a halo on his head. And, if he faltered, there was a host of hungry contenders ready to take his place.

12

I'LL WRITE YOU A LETTER FROM THE CYCLONE'S EYE

Steve has always had an interesting relationship with the fans who write to him. On the one hand, he claims to be uneasy with the adulation, but on the other, he clearly craves it—especially during times when the Church's prospects are in decline. For many years he saved every letter he received. When he finally moved out of his Rozelle house in 1997, he had accumulated enough to fill five large garbage bags.

In 1983 Steve spent quite a lot of time in direct contact with the fans, single-handedly running the Church's fan club. He sent out frequent mailings updating the faithful on his activities. In one letter he wrote:

> Since we last spoke . . . Marty has bought himself a small studio and
> has been writing songs, Peter has been writing too, Richard has been
> playing with the Beasts of Bourbon: a band studded with underground
> luminaries. I went for a short holiday in Sweden, hopefully to absorb
> some fresh inspirations.

He personally hawked T-shirts and other items that could generate some extra cash flow for the struggling band, rightly regarding this stoking of the fan base as an essential duty. The Church was clearly wading through turbulent waters, and it was important that all who supported Steve and the band close ranks with them.

The recording of *Seance*—the full-length follow-up to *The Blurred*

Crusade—was by all accounts a trying process. Steve, perhaps overcompensating for the lack of cohesion of *Sing-Songs*, kept his bandmates on a tight leash. It must have been particularly maddening for a musician of Koppes' caliber to be taking guitar instructions from the bass player. Nevertheless, Steve was the songwriter, and he had recorded his own demos of all of the new tracks; he wanted the band to replicate his designated guitar and keyboard lines note for note. As Steve says now, "It was an okay bunch of songs, but kind of derailed by my . . . control, by me having control over everything and not utilizing the others. I can only imagine what Peter might have put into that record, because he was so much more musically advanced than I was."

Another possible reason for Peter's diminished involvement was the tension that had developed between him and the band since the recording of *The Blurred Crusade*. As Peter explains:

> After *Blurred Crusade* I left because [management] wouldn't show me the [accounting] books and the rest of the band wouldn't back me up. And then they came to me and said the album would sink without a tour and they couldn't replace me, so would I mind coming with them on tour. And I said, "All right." So we toured for a few months and they said, "An American company wants to release the first album; why don't you go over with Steve and meet Capitol Records." And I thought, Oh well, that'd be nice. And then things just kept on going. There was never a reconnection on a personal level.

Adding to the intra-band tension, the record company brought in a new producer for the album: Englishman Nick Launay. Launay had done fine work for the hard-rocking Midnight Oil, producing their 1982 breakthrough album *10, 9, 8, 7, 6, 5, 4, 3, 2, 1 . . .*, but his up-front style was not a good fit for a band as subtle as the Church. He was particularly enamored of the "gated reverb" (essentially a filter effect that made each drum hit sound like a shotgun blast) that Phil Collins had developed and used to striking effect on "In the Air Tonight." When applied the Church's music, however, it wreaked havoc on the delicate ballads, applying the aural equivalent of a sledgehammer when a light touch would have sufficed. It *did* work to some extent on the more upbeat rock tracks "Electric Lash" and "One Day," but over the course of an entire album the effect was distracting and tedious. (Marty later commented: "We've all wondered what that record would have sounded like if it had been mixed keeping the organic sounds that we recorded the songs with. Having said that, a lot of people love that album with its stark mood and hard drum sounds.") Launay also managed to remove all of the warmth from Steve's bass playing, leaving only a trebly plunking.

"I don't think Nick Launay appreciated at all the things I was going for with the repetition and drones and things," Steve says.

> I might have put a little guitar somewhere that was supposed to be a shadow for something, and he'd fucking ditch everything else and bring that shadow out. He thought he was highlighting the things in there but it was the complete opposite of what I was trying to do.

Seance is an oddity; one can't listen to it without a sense of frustration. After all, buried inside the muddled mess of what the album actually is, there are many glimpses of the great album it could have been. Thematically, it's one of the most unified Church albums: Nearly every song addresses loss in some way, be it loss of love, loss of innocence, or loss of direction. The album starts off with the impenetrable "Fly." It's a quiet opener featuring shimmering acoustic guitar, eerie monophonic keyboard melodies, and Steve singing listlessly in his talking-voice style. Lyrically the song is a puzzle; it has no cohesive narrative, offering instead a string of unconnected—though stirring—images: the "baby" who "tossed and turned on a teardrop sea" and is "trapped inside her painted eyes." Steve signals the melancholy, introspective tone of the album with his reference to "all those dark clowns who are following me." Perhaps the word "clouds" would have been a more appropriate, less-jarring substitute for "clowns," but leave it to Kilbey to always go for the absurd over the pat.

Before "Fly" can achieve the liftoff implied in its title, however, it segues into the more sonically upbeat "One Day." This is one instance where Launay's production works: the mechanized feel of the song evokes a more guitar-based New Order. In the first verse, the classic Kilbey theme of inertia is phrased succinctly: "We run so hard and always end up in the same place." Then he breaks into the hopeful chorus, singing "One Day . . . We'll shake away the shadows of eternal night." As in "You Took," Kilbey delights in putting a dyslexic spin on popular phrases; here he declares, "It's just the storm before the calm." In the third verse he introduces an idea that he will return to later in the album: the paradoxical concept of depriving oneself of one or more of the senses in order to see more clearly: "I go back to my blindness so that I may see again." This could be a reference to childhood; Steve has on several occasions commented that children see more clearly and have more imagination because they are unencumbered by knowledge and societal rules; they are, in a sense, "blind," but they are also enlightened, beatific. Could it be that ignorance is not only bliss but in fact revelation? It's an idea Steve clearly finds appealing.

The end of "One Day" becomes self-referential as Steve revisits a line from "Bel-Air": "A palm tree nodded at me last night / He said, 'Hey you look so pale.'" Here again Steve is following in the footsteps of the Beatles, who referenced their 1962 song "She Loves You" at the end of their 1967 track "All You Need is Love."

So far so good, but with "Electric" the album hits a serious snag. It's a shame, because lyrically "Electric" is one of Steve Kilbey's most perfectly-realized songs. Unfortunately, his poignant observations on sadness and heartbreak are undermined by a maudlin vocal delivery, clunky rhythm, and that supremely annoying Launay snare effect. If one simply reads the lyrics without hearing the music, one is hard-pressed to find a better encapsulation of the end of a relationship. Lines like "I hoped that our destiny sloped / ever upwards, now it curves away and falls" might have fared better if they'd been sung by the more emotive Marty Willson-Piper. Steve gets points for trying, but his murky warble ends up sounding like a poor man's Robert Smith. Interestingly, the verses full of loss and dead feelings are buttressed by a chorus that states, "When you touch my skin the feeling is electric." Steve demonstrates here that even when a relationship is dead in the water, physical desire can still exist—which makes the breakup all the more difficult. His lover is unable to see the silver lining of the dissolution, "not understanding that you are free of me." Steve loses none of his poetic sensibility in this direct statement of love lost, but musically it's another case of ambition exceeding ability. This is an unfortunate scenario but it's better than the reverse—after all, over time ability can catch up, as the fine vocals and musicianship on later albums make clear.

"It's No Reason" finds the band exploring new terrain, creating an intriguing and strangely stirring acid lullaby. The lyrics of this track, with images of "crocodile skin water" and "marble skies" turning human, are as impenetrable as those of the Velvet Underground's "Black Angel Death Song," but there is no denying the gorgeousness of the melody. The song features the Church's first dabbling with strings, which were arranged by Steve himself. Overall, "It's No Reason" could be viewed as a gentler treatment of the landscape John Lennon visited in "Lucy in the Sky with Diamonds." This idiosyncratic track is not for everyone, but creatively it is one of the album's successes.

"Travel by Thought" is a wholly radical departure. Basically the song consists of a barely-decipherable free-verse poem intoned over an improvisational noise jam. Thrown into the mix are police sirens, the sound of engines revving, and various tape-distorted tracks played backwards. Once again Steve repeats his theme of letting go of the linear senses in order to "see," this time making the connection to drugs more explicit: "I lose my bearings but then I can see clearly." Frustratingly, lines full of beauty are often followed by lines laden with dross. For instance, verse three contains the exquisite line "Imagine the feeling before the last jump" followed by the just-plain-awful "Oh you just can't define the sad things in your mind." This is partly made up for by verse five, which contains one of the most sinister passages in Steve's oeuvre: "Don't think I've forgotten / the stranger's arms / that scare the bird that carries home dinner." Taken as a whole, this track is the crucial first glimpse on record of the Church's avant-garde tendencies.

"Disappear" juxtaposes another breakup narrative with a lullaby Steve originally composed to sing someone (presumably a girlfriend) to sleep. The first verse sets up the narrative: Our protagonist wakes up from a dream of "skipping 'cross the water / wading through the sand" to find that his lover has left him. Then Steve offers a pithy, Dylanish line: "Well I just had to smile for all the things you'll never hear me say." Then comes the lullaby: "You and me / We're as free as we can be," the positivity of these lines a marked contrast with the loss that has come before.

In the second verse he compares the failed relationship with "the fog that you walk towards but never seem to reach." Finally he crystallizes the situation with a beautiful couplet: "Awake to find you gone, a note pinned to my sleeve / Well it wasn't just the things you took, it was the things you had to leave."

"Disappear" is a lovely narrative that is again let down by the execution.

Steve's vocal delivery is flat and at some points inaudible. He sounds as if he has no emotional connection to the material whatsoever, like a stoned impostor singing Church karaoke. The band isn't up to snuff either. Koppes delivers a fine electric guitar solo, but Steve's bass clunks along gracelessly in the background. Any subtlety in Richard's drumming is destroyed by Launay's in-your-face production.

Fortunately this black hole of a track is followed by one of the album's highlights: "Electric Lash." The lyrics, while mostly disposable, do restate Steve's blindness theme: "How those eyes see me so very very clearly even when they're closed." Musically, the song is a perfect showcase for each band member's strengths: Marty and Peter's guitars mesh to create an ebullient jangling rhythm, Steve's bass and Richard's drums are tightly locked, and the singing is laid-back but not detached. The chorus of "Electric Lash" is one of the catchiest in the Church's catalog. And as if this weren't all enough to guarantee "classic" status, the song boasts an extended instrumental break in the middle: phased-out, Eastern-sounding guitars gradually coalescing back into the familiar riff. This one song reconciles infectious melodies and a breezy pop sensibility with the band's enthusiasm for atmospheric arrangements and sonic experimentation. It may not have the narrative depth of "The Unguarded Moment," but it does have a joyous spirit—something missing from that earlier single and in woefully short supply on the rest of *Seance*. If the song is a concession to commercial demands then it is a welcome one: proof positive that the Church are capable of delivering radio-friendly material that manages to be both musically inventive and catchy as hell.

What follows is the album's lyrical stunner: "Now I Wonder Why." With arpeggio guitar picking and melodic "lead bass," it's easy to see why the early Church were sometimes compared to R.E.M. The first verse of the song seems to address the specter of empty success, the paradox of fulfillment: "In a moment of triumph, I find defeat uncontrolled/In the second of honor, a despair sharp and old." Then a "she" enters the narrative, but it is unclear whether Steve is singing about a specific woman, a muse, fame, wealth, or the lure of drugs; perhaps all of the above. The chorus is both evocative and indecipherable: "Now I wonder why I thought I could ever lose/But the gain is hardly what I'd choose/Now I wonder why."

The final verse addresses the danger of becoming lost during one's
search for deeper knowledge and experience:

And after the acting, I found that I couldn't sleep
And during my drifting, I found that I was too deep
By the virtue of faith I knew that I could be lost
Beyond this dark place, unprepared to pay the cost

This narrative arc of losing one-self to dark excesses taps into classic rock-and-roll mythology. One of the Church's big creative influences, Syd Barrett of Pink Floyd, was himself lost on the road to artistic and spiritual enlightenment; the LSD he took to open "the doors of perception" (in Aldous Huxley's famous phrase) pickled his brain. There is prescience in Steve's lyrics, too; the Church would not make it through its own quest unscathed.

Steve Kilbey, circa 1985 (Kilbey family collection)

One thing that becomes clear on reading *Seance*'s lyrics is that they seem to be of a more personal nature than past offerings. Steve's oft-repeated protestation that he is not a confessional writer aside, much of his work can in fact be interpreted autobiographically. He tends to smother his personal information in surrealistic language but it is there, nonetheless.

On *Seance*, Steve sings repeatedly of a failed relationship. Is he writing about one specific person? Steve's answer is typically oblique:

That's the wonderful thing about songs, isn't it? I think it's transferable. Sometimes there's never anybody, and then later on I realize that somebody could easily slide in. And then other times it *was* somebody, and after a while it ceases to become them and is more general. Sometimes I'm not really sure."

Using a little deductive logic, it is easy to figure out who the Seance songs *could* be about. Steve had not been in a serious, long-term relationship since his divorce from Michelle Parker. Much of the language in the songs is apropos, in its seriousness, to the breakup of a marriage. Certainly the line "It wasn't just the things you took / It was the things you had to leave," with its overtones of divorce settlements, backs up this hypothesis. Still, we can't assume with one-hundred-percent certainty that these songs are for Michelle, or for *any* specific person. Steve's reliance on childhood memory opens the possibility of some of this material being about his first long-term girlfriend, Patricia. One's first love is arguably a purer and deeper and more desperately romantic love (in other words, the stuff of songs) that what Steve felt for his ex-wife. It could also very well be that Steve created a composite—combining the heart-rending passion of teenage love with the day-to-day domestic accoutrements of marriage—to vividly render the failed relationship that serves as the centerpiece of this album.

Ironically, it was just before the making of this great breakup album that Steve became involved with Karin Jansson, who would have a significant and lasting influence on his life. Karin, a Swedish musician, introduced herself to Steve after a Church concert in Stockholm in October 1982. (Interestingly, one of Karin's bandmates, Ann Carlberger, who accompanied her that night, ended up in a long-term involvement with Marty Willson-Piper.) As with all his relationships, Steve has been very protective of Karin's privacy when speaking to the press. Consequently, despite the fact that her picture graced three record sleeves (*This Asphalt Eden, Remote Luxury* and the inner sleeve of *Unearthed*) little is known about the woman who is the mother of two of Steve's children. Even the precise status of their relationship seemed nebulous to people around them, as Russell Kilbey implied when he told me, "I got on well with Steve's Swedish . . . wife . . . girlfriend . . . whatever she was."

This much *is* known: Steve Kilbey and Karin Jansson never officially married. But immediately upon meeting her, Steve felt keenly that they would have a serious and lasting connection—a connection that ran deeper than

the obvious physical chemistry that occurred between the good-looking
young rock star and the classically striking Scandinavian beauty. "As soon as
I met her . . . I felt that something important was going to happen with this
person," he says. Steve made trips to Sweden to see Karin and began to learn
the language; then Karin followed Steve back to Australia and decided to
stay. Before long, she moved into Steve's house in Rozelle. It was a creative
as well as a romantic partnership. Karin helped Steve write several songs,
and sang backup on a number of his solo recordings. A fairly proficient key-
boardist and guitarist, Karin assisted with the composition of the music as
well as the lyrics. It was by no means a John & Yoko symbiotic relationship,
but Karin complemented Steve in crucial ways. One can easily see why they
were drawn to each other.

★ ★ ★ ★ ★

Seance sold well enough initially to reach number 18 on the album charts
in June 1983, but the Church were certainly not the main attraction—their
sales lagged well behind those of such contemporaries as Midnight Oil,
INXS, and Split Enz. The band were performing a holding action at best,
trying to maintain the audience base they had built over the preceding three
years. Press reaction was lukewarm for the most part. A street-press reviewer billing himself as N.D. Plume wrote, "[*Seance*] aims at being 'haunting'
or 'atmospheric,' like the visionary Bowie of *Hunky Dory* days, but rarely
succeeds. The thickness of the sound, the repetition, the general inaudibil-
ity of the words and the expressionless delivery add up to one long dirge."
Stuart Coupe returned with his follow-up piece on Kilbey in *RAM*, alleging
that the band had run its course. The Australian *Rolling Stone*, however, was
far more charitable:

> It's as an album—as a high-volume listening experience—that *Seance*
> works. Neither overly passé nor incredibly modern, neither indulgent nor
> hit-laden, it's the sort of self-sufficient, apolitical pop/rock album record
> companies dream about. And the Church keep making them.

The Church weren't ready to fold. They dutifully spent July and August
of 1983 touring Australia once again—by all accounts maintaining a high
performance standard throughout—but there must have been a growing

sense of futility as the sales numbers for *Seance* began to trickle in. Bill Holdsworth gave a grudgingly positive review of the band's show at Her Majesty's Theatre in Melbourne in *Juke*, saying, "It was not a perfect show over the full distance, but the ultimate effect was to uplift and to energize." Many reviewers commented on the fact that the band played in virtual darkness, lit only by soft pink and blue beams that were, in Hollingsworth's words, "set up to cast intriguing shadows rather than to illuminate." It's as if the Church were playing through a filter, retreating into the recesses of a self-imposed cave and telegraphing the songs out to the audience. Not the behavior of a band on the verge of smash success, but nonetheless an interesting experience for the congregation.

When the Church returned from this tour, there was no break; they went right into the studio. A feeling of desperation had set in. That they would rescale the sonic heights of *The Blurred Crusade* was no longer a foregone conclusion. To some within the Church's world, it seemed likely that the band was nearing its end.

Two EPs of new material—*Remote Luxury* and *Persia*—were released in 1984, in March and August respectively. While the band's members were not totally satisfied with the quality of this new material, they did finally catch a break thanks to the recently inaugurated Australian Independent Charts. Previously, the only publicly available measures of a record's performance were the single and album charts funded by the Australian recording industry, which mostly tabulated sales through large retail outlets and commercial chains and therefore emphasized mainstream music to the virtual exclusion of more left-field material. The new independent charts, on the other hand, only tracked sales at the smaller but influential, independently owned record shops around the country. Somewhat surprisingly, the Church became a mainstay of these charts; the onetime "*Countdown* band" was evidently now finding favor with fans of independent Australian music. It's not so much that the Church were necessarily looked at in the same way as the indie-label bands who mostly populated these charts—they were, of course, still signed to EMI—but it suggested that many of the people who frequented those stores might well buy a Church record as well as records by, say, the Go-Betweens or the Laughing Clowns. If there was a tradeoff involved—of commercial fame for artistic credibility—it was an involuntary one, but in any case it was exactly what the Church needed. The quantity of listeners may not have been increasing, but the quality and attentiveness of the audience apparently was.

In retrospect, the tracks on the two EPs have aged quite well, with one exception. Steve Kilbey regards "Maybe These Boys" as the nadir of his songwriting career: "'Maybe These Boys' is a hopeless, horrible mess, a black stain on my soul," he says flatly. Taking a cue from their icon, the fans have, over the years, echoed this sentiment. "*Remote Luxury* contains possibly the worst song Kilbey has ever written, 'Maybe These Boys,' which has surely got to be a piss-take," wrote Trevor Boyd in his Church fanzine *North, South, East & West.*

Certainly the lyrics of this song leave a lot to be desired, but if you strip away the negativity that has built up around the track, it has some musical qualities to recommend it. For example, the intro features a nice bout of guitar dueling between Peter and Marty, each guitar in its own speaker. Here it becomes evident just how skilled both of the Church's axe men are. Additionally, the riffs are bluesier than usual—a welcome departure from their typically echoing cathedrals of major scales. The chorus of the song, while cheesy, is undeniably catchy, demonstrating again that Steve does have a knack for writing commercially viable work. And finally, the outro features a beautiful piano performance from Craig Hooper (who briefly became an auxiliary member of the Church while his band the Reels was inactive), closing out the song nicely as the other instruments fade into the background. The song caught people's attention at the time; one Australian DJ declared it his favorite track on the EP and played it on his radio show during Steve's guest appearance.

The story behind the conception of "Maybe These Boys" is an interesting one. The song was written, like many others, in Steve's house in Rozelle. Steve, being young and semi-famous, had a collection of hangers-on and freeloaders living at his place. "They were drug dealers and failed musicians and, you know, groupies and what have you," he says. "They would sit there in my studio room with me, and I would record songs while they watched. They would be marveling at everything I did, probably thinking, 'What's he doing now? Where's it all leading to?' and then, BANG, I would kind of make it all make sense."

Steve decided, one afternoon, to attempt to write a more modern-sounding song, a response to the common criticism that his music was retro or old-fashioned. He took a stab at new-wave synth-pop and the result was "Maybe These Boys." "One of the things I did was I would sort of have a go at whatever the current genre was. Of course I always got it wrong." Nevertheless, several people who heard the song, including Michael Chugg, were immediately taken with it. They convinced Steve to include it as the lead-off track on the *Remote Luxury* EP.

The other tracks from the sessions were solid. Standouts on the first EP included "Into My Hands," "10,000 Miles" (co-written by Kilbey and Willson-Piper), and "A Month of Sundays," while the *Persia* EP yielded "Constant in Opal" and "Shadow Cabinet"—two stellar tracks that the band still performs live—and the stunning pop ballad "No Explanation."

In a very positive review of *Persia* for *RAM*, Frank Brunetti wrote, "They haven't made a record which manages so well to sound both true to themselves and redolent of its time since the halcyon days of *The Blurred Crusade*."

Michael Chugg would soon be replaced, although the split was amicable. "I still have a lot of good feeling for Michael," Steve says, "but he was a fucking hopeless manager for the Church."

With the release of the two EPs and the renewed critical buzz surrounding the band, the Church began to attract American attention. There had not been a peep of interest from the US since the band had been dropped from Capitol, but now Karen Berg—responsible for signing Television, Laurie Anderson, and the B-52s—and Tom Wooly from Warner Brothers were dispatched to Australia to check them out.

Berg bristled at the prevailing trend of cashing in on one-hit wonders and was keen to sign bands that could be developed over the long run. She hoped the Church might be such a band and she was not disappointed. She and Wooly saw them perform a particularly good show in Queensland, and on her recommendation Warner Brothers signed them.

"When I think about it, we were probably pretty amazing back in '84," Steve says. "Those two (Berg and Wooly) were really interested in the artistic side of it. They were impressed with us because it seemed like we were kind of existing in a vacuum."

As part of the deal, *Remote Luxury* and *Persia* were to be compiled for release as an album in the US, with an full US tour to accompany the release. Last but not least, the Church were up for a new manager. Goodbye, Michael Chugg. Hello, John Lee—American millionaire.

13

THEY SAY IT MAKES YOU DIZZY YOUR FIRST TIME UP THERE

Steve sat in the passenger seat of John Lee's Mercedes and gazed out at the palm trees and pristine sand. Marty sat in the back, also scanning the landscape with ravenous eyes. Though Steve had persuaded himself over the past two years that he was not interested in material wealth, the opulent surroundings of his new benefactor made an impression. Lee gently turned the wheel with one hand, his other arm resting lazily on the windowsill. The evening breeze ruffled his silvery hair. He said nonchalantly, "Steve, if there is anything you'd like to have that you haven't got, what would it be?"

Steve shot back, "The new Psychedelic Furs record."

Lee laughed and rolled his eyes. "Yeah, I'm not talking about that; I'm talking about something else."

"Well then," Steve said, "I'd have to say . . . you know . . . happiness."

Lee gave a wry grin and stared ahead at the road.

Marty, who had been listening intently from the back, spoke up: "Well, I would like the new Rickenbacker twelve-string—the McGuinn signature edition—a drum machine, and a Marshall stack."

Steve laughed as Marty flopped back in his seat with a smirk on his face.

"Very good," Lee said, smiling. They drove on in silence.

Steve was the first to get up the next morning. He stumbled downstairs, rubbing the sleep from his eyes. When he reached the ground floor he stopped short. At the bottom of the stairway, arranged against the wall, were eight shining Rickenbacker guitars, stringed and ready to be played, along with a gigantic Marshall amp and a state-of-the-art drum machine. Resting against the amp was a solitary, unopened record: the new Psychedelic Furs LP.

John Lee was a wealthy American businessman who knew next to nothing about the job of managing a rock band. He already owned a car dealership, a restaurant, and many other lucrative properties, but he harbored ambitions of expanding into the entertainment industry. Managing a successful rock-and-roll band would be an attractive feather in his cap. As it happened, his dreams dovetailed nicely with the Church's ambitions for American success.

Steve enjoyed the lifestyle. Lee's willingness to fly him and Marty out to stay at his Malibu mansion and then shower them with gifts was too seductive a proposition for even the most stoic, integrity-obsessed artist to resist.

During this first visit, plans were laid for a coast-to-coast US tour, with the full backing of the entertainment giant that was Warner Brothers. This would all be on the heels of the Church's first American release since 1981.

Remote Luxury, it turned out, was not a huge success, making no impact on the mainstream, but it did garner a good amount of airplay on important college radio stations such as KCRW in Santa Monica and KCMU in Seattle. Additionally, *Rolling Stone*, which was at that point still the cultural barometer for quality rock music in the US, gave the album a respectable three stars. Debby Miller wrote in her review:

Kilbey comes up with some fascinating images. . . . The music, primarily
a mix of acoustic guitars and synthesizers, sets a consistently dark
ambience. There's a sadness, a threat or a longing at the heart of most of
the songs.

In October, 1984, the band began its first North American tour. For his part, Steve Kilbey took the humbling notion that he was almost completely unknown in the United States with extraordinarily good grace. The usually cantankerous frontman exuded warmth and graciousness during an interview with two WNUR Chicago DJs who clearly knew nothing about the band. He politely and patiently answered such scintillating questions as

"How does America compare to Australia?", "Do people go out to see bands a whole lot in Australia?" and "How did you get such a pretty sound?"

Steve understood all too well that the Church were building their reputation from the ground up once again. Having learned his lesson from the Australian backlash he'd suffered just a few years back, he took no chances with the American press—at least not during this crucial initial foray.

Not all the band's actions were so conciliatory, however. Steve worked hard to endear himself to reporters, but the band's set list during the tour made no equivalent artistic concessions. In fact, the Church did not play any *Remote Luxury* tracks until well into the set. "Constant in Opal" was usually the fifth song they played, but the first three songs were almost always from *Seance,* an album that was unavailable in the US except as a costly import. The fourth song, "Tear it all Away," may have sounded vaguely familiar to some audience members, since it had appeared on the 1981 Capitol release of the first album, but most people at these shows probably knew nothing of the Church pre-1984. After "Constant in Opal" and "Volumes," the band would usually play only two other *Remote Luxury* tracks, often much later in the set.

Packing the show with almost entirely unknown songs was an audacious and, from a commercial standpoint, foolhardy move, but the band didn't care. Steve reasoned that the audience would respond better to quality than familiarity. It was a philosophy that would guide him and the band through all future live performances.

Fortunately, in this case the risk paid off. These small-club shows were well-received. The band's aggressive live energy surprised and impressed the American audiences. Craig Hooper joined the Church on keyboards, fleshing out their sound quite nicely on such choice cuts as "The Night is Very Soft" and "A Month of Sundays."

Musically, the band was tight and focused. It's true that the players lacked the incendiary fire that had burned so brightly on the *Blurred Crusade* tour, but they also avoided many of the pitfalls of those early performances. Steve did a much better job this time around of staying on pitch. He had learned how to project his voice in such a way that he didn't feel the need to scream to be heard. Marty and Peter bounced guitar licks back and forth with aplomb and Richard was spot-on night after night. The live rendition of "Constant in Opal" proved an excellent showcase for Marty's rapid-fire

Peter Koppes, Le Rox, Adelaide, 1986 *(Rachel Armstrong/Caroline Barnes)*

lead playing. In place of the record's melodic e-bow lines, Marty ran up and down the frets, playing the notes in a lightening-fast staccato. Clearly, he had come a long way from his early days of nervous shoe-gazing.

After the sound check for the San Francisco show, Steve met a young singer and guitarist named Donnette Thayer. It was an inauspicious first meeting. The star-struck Thayer, who had heard all of the band's music via imports, clammed up and had little to say beyond some perfunctory queries about Steve's keyboard playing. Steve was friendly enough, taking the time to answer Donnette's questions and chat amiably, but the meeting did not make any significant impression on him. He certainly did not have the type of inkling that he'd had with Karin—that here was a person who would play a significant role in his life. That would only come later. For now the encounter between Steve and Donnette was brief and uneventful, although Donnette left feeling enthralled but also a little embarrassed by her timidity.

Overall, Steve judged the American tour a success, even though the band had once again lost money on the road. More important in the long term was the fact that the Church had achieved a critical foothold in the US. The American reviewers knew nothing of Steve's history of pompous statements and his combative relationship with the Australian press. As a result, Steve felt, they were more objective in how they approached the band.

It was imperative, therefore, that the next Church album build on these promising but still fragile gains. Steve was not a huge fan of the music of R.E.M., but he appreciated the fact that the members of that band were not really rock stars and yet still successful. He hoped the Church could pursue a similar path. However, rushing straight into the studio right after a grueling tour would be to no one's benefit, so the band decided at this point, at the end of November 1984, to take a much-needed break.

This hiatus would last for over six months, apart from a Melbourne show the following March. During this time, Marty left Australia for Sweden, the home of his girlfriend Ann Carlberger. He had never felt at home in Australia—the hot climate did not suit his decidedly English sensibility—so his decision to move to Sweden was not a difficult one. And now that the

Church had an international audience, it no longer seemed necessary for him to live down the street from the other guys, especially if they were not going to be playing or recording for a while.

Certainly, the Church were due a vacation. The band had been working incessantly since 1980, and it could be argued that a sense of fatigue had begun to creep into the music. If the next album was to be a good one, it was essential that the band members take some time off and recharge their batteries. Richard Ploog, for example, went off backpacking; this would become his habit after every tour.

Peter, who now had a family to support, had to go on the dole for a time. Because Steve had been the sole writer credited on nearly all the Church's recorded material, he received the lion's share of songwriting royalties, the most reliable income stream. The others had to make due with their shares of whatever the band earned from record sales, plus tour income, which is this recent case equaled zero.

Steve, meanwhile, found it impossible to quell the flow of musical ideas, even with his band on hiatus. He met with a producer and session musicians in early 1985 to record a track he had written called "This Asphalt Eden."

"What an abortion, what a tragedy," Steve says now of this one-off project. "It had a number of disastrous effects. It made me seem like I was nothing without the Church."

Steve originally intended "This Asphalt Eden" to have a lush, Nelson Riddle–style arrangement, over which he would croon in his best Scott Walker imitation. "I thought I'd written a hit," he says. "I really thought no further than, this song could be a big hit. How naive! I really thought I could hear it being played on all these radio stations, people going, *Oh boy, this is a really different side of him without the jingly guitars; it's like a big ballad.* But I was very badly deluded."

Things started off well enough: the trumpet and sax players came in and performed their lines just as Steve had instructed. Steve then laid down the guitar tracks, but at this point the drugs reared their ugly head. High on hash, Steve passed out in the studio. The producer continued twiddling the knobs as the clock ran down. By the time Steve awoke, his song had been completely altered. "Somehow I guess he thought he'd modernized it," Steve says. "I don't know what he thought he'd done. I woke up and

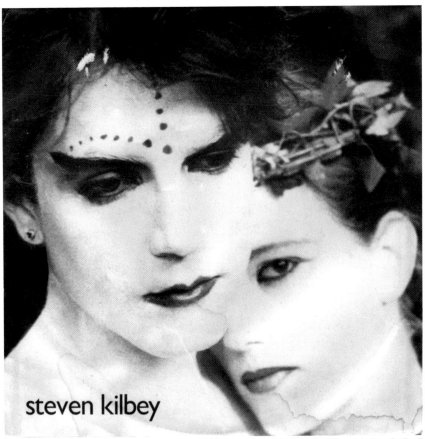

steven kilbey

Steve Kilbey and Karin Jansson, cover of "This Asphalt Eden" (1985) *(Russell Paper [aka Russell Kilbey])*

that was it. That was the end of the budget. THAT WAS IT! And I said, 'But I don't like it,' but he was like, 'Well, I'm sorry, but that's all we can do now.'"

The producer had employed a new process known as quantization. Basically, he had taken Steve's arrangement, which had been intentionally loose, and moved some of the parts around, tightening everything up. Steve's carefree big-band sound was thus replaced with a woefully mechanized, stilted, mid-'80s new-wave sound. It was a style completely inappropriate for the song. "I was horrified," Steve says. "Plus, he was telling me how great it was that everything was totally in time now. Sometimes this happens: someone blinds me with science."

Not surprisingly, "This Asphalt Eden" received no public attention whatsoever on its release. Even the independent charts remained cold to it. Credited to "Steven Kilbey," perhaps the most interesting thing about the record was its sleeve, featuring Steve in heavy makeup with Karin Jansson resting her head on his bare shoulder. The B-side of the single contained "Never Come Back," a bizarre attempt at a country song featuring Steve singing with a Southern twang, as well as a quietly mournful song called "Shell," the refrain of which seemed to capture Steve's state of mind at the conclusion of this first solo endeavor: "I'm as empty as a shell can ever be."

Perhaps due to his costly nod-off at the control console, Steve decided, for the time being, to forswear all drugs other than the occasional joint. No more cocaine, no more LSD, speed, mushrooms, or anything else. As a replacement he took up yoga and found that his mind immediately began to clear. Spending his days at home with Karin, he allowed himself to truly relax for the first time in years. Steve would later cite this period as one of the happiest of his life. "I started to lead this utterly blissful life," he told a reporter years later. "I was doing a lot of meditation, a lot of exercise; I was eating very healthy food. I'd walk down the street and feel like I could communicate with the cats and dogs."

The newfound sense of contentment and balance opened up a wellspring of creative inspiration. Steve decided to channel it into hitherto unexplored territory: he would write a book.

14
THE GOLDEN DAWN

Grey roads scar our Edens, the beautiful intelligent creatures which wandered the Earth and swam in its waters are fettered, clubbed and exterminated. Weaker or gentler peoples are conveniently deleted and replaced by stock exchanges and mortgages and space programs and prisons and great open sores that go deep into our mother planet until all her marrow is sucked out by her insane, cannibalistic offspring. The Arts have been entrusted to the brokers, to the accountants, to the media. It's all gauged in Quantity instead of Quality or stuck in Mausoleum Museums to be bled out by condescending custodians. Art tells us something priceless about ourselves; Entertainment admits nothing yet the price of that admission is so great.

—Steve Kilbey, *Earthed* introduction, 1986

Earthed, the non-linear novel Steve wrote in 1985 and published the following year, gave his fans their first opportunity to read his words unadorned by music. It offered a hitherto rare glimpse into Steve Kilbey's inner world, and a most unusual world it turned out to be. Steve had begun exploring different spiritual traditions in earnest, and his explorations took him everywhere from Buddhist sutras to Yogic aphorisms to the occult writings of nineteenth-century theosophist Madame Blavatsky. He had a keen interest in George Gurdjieff and his main follower, P.D. Ouspensky, who had synthesized various eastern and western traditions, particularly mystical and esoteric thinking, into an spiritual philosophy of self-development. This philosophy attracted a certain following throughout the twentieth century, particularly among artists and writers—Frank Lloyd Wright, Aleister Crowley, Katherine Mansfield, Keith Jarrett, Timothy Leary, and Robert Fripp, to name a few.

There is, however, a dubious undercurrent to this first generation of New Age thought: for example, Blavatsky's career was dogged by well-substantiated charges of fraud, while the charismatic Gurdjieff was regarded by non-devotees as a manipulative charlatan. Acceptance of their world view therefore requires a certain suspension of disbelief.

It is unclear how much of this New Age / occult philosophy (as opposed to established Eastern spiritual traditions such as Buddhism and Hinduism) Steve bought into; he had an inherent skepticism that his mystical cohort, Richard Ploog, wholly lacked. But the secretive characteristics of Theosophy, Rosicrucianism, and the Golden Dawn played right into Steve's childhood fantasies as well as his current elitist tendencies. Blavatsky's *Secret Doctrine*, in particular, which contained an entire underground history of civilization—from the "Golden Age" of Lemuria and Atlantis down to the current dark age of the Fifth Root Race (begun shortly after the death of Krishna)—seemed tailor-written for Steve. It was arcane and preposterous, and only a select few "got it."

Steve avoided most of the typical pop culture clichés—he did not become a fan of Aleister Crowley, for instance, though certainly he read his work—preferring instead to learn about those occultists and New Agers who approached magic and the spirit world in a more life-affirming fashion. There would be no sacrificing of black cats in Steve Kilbey's spiritual practices.[6]

Much of this esoteric reading found its way into the obtuse prose of *Earthed* (and later into the lyrics of the Church's *Heyday* album). Taken at face value, *Earthed* barely stands up as a novel. There is no central plot connecting the disparate threads, though there is a mysterious character named Neuman who pops up at regular intervals. We are only doled out small tidbits about this person: He owns a "syllable gun"; he is descended from a "beautiful man-creature" who, "like us, felt so terribly alone"; he has

---

[6] Interestingly, Steve *did* pen a Crowley apologia of sorts in a February 2006 blog entry: "I guess I think underneath it all—and some of you take things far too literally—Al (Crowley) was onto something but it ain't my path."

a horse; and the narrator sometimes refers to him as "The Parable Man." As far as the narrator himself is concerned, we are offered disjointed memories of his grandfather, his father, and his uncle. Some sections of the book employ first-person-singular narration, others first-person-plural. Structurally, the book is similar to William Burroughs' *Naked Lunch*, although *Earthed* lacks the constricting paranoia that informs that novel. Instead it is pervaded by a tone of gentle melancholy. As with Kilbey's music, the various prose poems evoke atmosphere rather than conveying literal meaning. One of the more colorful passages reads:

> I pointed to the top shelf and they climbed up and brought over a mysterious big box. We took it home and out jumped fifteen clockwork Romans who hacked each other to pieces and lay twitching on the carpet, bleeding sewing machine oil.

Like Steve's lyrics, *Earthed* is haunting, lyrical, sometimes sad, sometimes wry, often absurd, and ultimately impenetrable. Once again Steve Kilbey makes no attempt to clarify or illuminate his ideas. Even so, compared to *Tarantula*—Bob Dylan's demented first foray into prose—*Earthed* comes off as user-friendly.

Perhaps not surprisingly, the critical reaction to Steve's prose venture—which he published himself, in a limited edition of 2,000 copies, and sold mainly via mailorder—was mostly negative. One Sydney music weekly ran a review entitled "Earth to Kilbey . . . " in which the pseudonymous reviewer ("J. Wallace Grubblesnutch") commented:

> *Earthed* should be buried. I never had much truck with Shakespeare, but I bet he didn't decide to write sonnets just because some kids at the Trade Union Club told him he was "a fuckin' genius, mate. Unrool!" Steve seems to think he's on to something. I don't. Here's why . . .
>
> For one thing, no legitimate publisher wanted to touch the thing with a surgical probe. Sure, Steve decided to "self-publish his poetry rather than go through the 'straight' world of book publishing," as the press release puts it. . . . But I find it hard to picture Steve being offered twenty grand upfront by Angus & Robertson with a print run of 50,000 and total press exposure, then turning around and saying, "Naw. You're too straight for me . . . " Can't see it, myself.
>
> For another thing, he can't write.

Bad reviews notwithstanding, some readers *were* profoundly affected by the book's eccentric unpolished beauty. According to Steve, a former head of the Ancient History program at Harvard University wrote him a letter some years later, citing *Earthed's* evocation of distant times and places as her major inspiration for going into her field. Others (mainly Church fans) found much to like in the book's introduction, which laid out—somewhat heavy-handedly—an anti-materialistic manifesto. While the bulk of the book's "plot" remained impenetrable, Steve's sustained railing against mass superficiality came through loud and clear. *Earthed* itself may not have been an antidote to that, but the next Church album would represent a continuation of this concerted effort to "tear it all away."

* * * * *

When the Church gathered in Sydney in mid-1985 to begin work on their next album, it was clear at the outset that it was going to be quite different from its predecessors. The most significant change was that Steve would no longer write all of the music. Instead, the band decided to collaborate, jamming in their rehearsal space until they arrived at fully formed songs, then leaving Steve to write the words. In one sense, this was no different from Steve's previous method—he had almost always written the music first—but now the full band was in on it.

"That was kind of inspired by the success of the song 'Shadow Cabinet' (from *Remote Luxury*)," Steve says, "which we wrote as an ensemble and I later put lyrics on."

> I think we all really liked that song and we all thought, me included, that each player could write their own parts better than one player could write all the parts. What we were starting to realize was that our songs were going to be more pointillistic. Instead of a song where everyone is playing along, it was going to be more people playing different things. When you stand back you can see the whole picture, but the individual parts may have no relationship as such.

Peter and Marty had already essentially been doing this since the first album, but now Steve began using the approach as well, which led to contrapuntal songs like "Tristesse" where, in addition to the vocal line, each stringed instrument seemed to be playing its own melody.

The Church also decided to mix things up by employing a new producer. Peter Walsh—who had produced Simple Minds' *New Gold Dream* and co-produced Scott Walker's *Climate of Hunter* (one of Steve's favorite albums)—was brought on board. Walsh had a very different production style from Nick Launay, John Bee, Bob Clearmountain, or any of the other people the Church had worked with; he favored lush, atmospheric arrangements that sounded almost orchestral. In fact, Kilbey and Walsh decided to bring in a string section and brass to augment the usual lineup of two guitars, bass and drums. Both Echo & the Bunnymen and the Waterboys had recently released albums that featured string accompaniment, and the members of the Church felt it was time they created their own wall of sound. Steve explains:

> Walsh and I kind of wrote the parts together, and then we went out and met an arranger and went over things, and the guy would sit there and play things on a piano and go, "We'll have some cellos doing this," and then particularly on "Night of Light," I really took over and said, "Can't we have all these slides and things at the end?" It was very gratifying to go in there and hear the orchestra play it.

He has a few reservations about the end result, however:

> Some of the brass on the album is a bit heavy-handed and awkward-sounding. I've never really liked brass that much myself, and I've never had much of an aptitude for thinking about where it should be or what kind of lines it should be playing or even how it all works: what the trumpet and what the trombone and what the sax do. I'm not really big on that whole area. When I do hear sax, when I do hear trumpet, when I like it most is when it has that smoky, nightclubby, bluesy kind of sound— the trumpet with the mute or the sax when it's very breathy—but when they're squealing and wailing and honking and fanfaring, I kind of turn off very quickly.

In addition to his collaboration with Walsh, Steve's ongoing romantic and creative partnership with Karin Jansson yielded "Youth Worshipper." The song, a fairly topical commentary on those who use cosmetics and other means in order to prolong their fading youth, was bolstered by

The Church, circa *Heyday* (Wendy McDougall)

Jansson's buoyant melody. Although Steve did the bulk of writing on this track, Karin served as an efficient editor, helping him pare the song down to its essentials.

As the band began cutting the album at Studio 301, it became apparent that there had been a dramatic change in Steve's voice. Perhaps it was the extended break from performing, or abstaining from drugs, or the hours of yoga; in any case, Steve's singing was now much more relaxed and warm, and he possessed a wider, more dynamic range. For years, critics had pointed to Steve's sometimes dour voice as the Church's weak point. Suddenly, during these new recording sessions, his distinctive new vocals became one of the band's great strengths—its signature, in fact. In addition to singing all the leads, Steve also tracked multiple harmony parts for each song, sometimes singing an entire octave higher than his normal register.

There were other dramatic changes within the band as well. The balance of power between the guitarists had shifted, with Marty handling the bulk of the lead riffs while Peter provided their rich underpinning. The soaring Koppes leads were replaced by chiming arpeggio riffs from Marty's Rickenbacker 12-string. The traditional guitar solo had been phased out of the Church's sound.

Years later, Peter explained this shift to Thomas Irvin of *Shadow Cabinet:* "We thought it might be a bit passé, like drum solos. We probably tried to avoid songs . . . with a structure that needed a guitar solo." This new sound had shades of the Byrds and maybe even R.E.M., but the combination of these riffs with Steve's fluid bass grooves and Ploog's spot-on drumming created a sound unique to the Church. Finally, the band had awoken from its mid-'80s lethargy and was once again making energetic, celebratory music.

The Church chose *Heyday* as the title for this new body of work. They meant it ironically, a reference to the fact that critics repeatedly talked of the band's 1981-82 "heyday" and tended to dismiss the Church of the mid-'80s as creatively and emotionally spent. Of course, the title proved more prophetic than anything: the band was on the verge of a *real* heyday, a period of commercial and critical achievement that would far surpass its previous, so-called mainstream success.

When he wrote the lyrics for the album, Steve utilized the same kaleidoscopic method he had employed in the *Earthed* prose poems: a single compressed piece of writing could simultaneously refer to the life of a touring rock band and the entire history of Western civilization, as with the opening track, "Myrrh." In "Tristesse," he personified melancholia in the form of a beautiful woman, ironically pairing his sad tale with the bounciest, most joyful music the band had ever composed. "Suddenly I had figured out a way to get it all in there," he says.

You see me go from the completely stilted imagery of *Seance*—and I can just see how those songs are sort of planned and worked out—... to *Heyday*, where I had a complete lyrical breakthrough. I was starting to get references in more, dropping names and giving hints, alluding to things. I think the band had a great leap forward between those albums.

One of the great lyrical triumphs on *Heyday* is "Columbus," which features an intriguing chorus fraught with implication: "Oh Columbus, I never should have let you go." As is often the case in Kilbey's songs, the next verse contradicts the pessimism of the preceding statement, with the narrator pleading, "You don't suppose there'd be room in there somewhere for me?" Steve tells an imagined historical tale: the King of Spain expressing regret about his sponsorship of Columbus's fateful voyage. In doing so, he accurately documents the mixed feelings other nations have about the ongoing experiment called America.

In "Disenchanted," Steve seems to predict his own success and eventual disillusionment:

And I'm asking you
If you think that success is its own reward
Now then go and see where your persistence has scored
The voice is a-calling and it can't be ignored
You might be underground but you're over-insured
You used to be unknown now you're mapped and explored
You like to be untouched now you're handled and pawed
And it's never gonna end

"There were two inspirations for that song," Steve says.

On the one hand it was inspired more by my brother Russell, who had had a little bit of success with his own band [the Crystal Set], just a teeny bit. Also, I was doing a bit of a sour grapes thing in advance, saying, "Well, I don't want it. I'll probably never have it, but I don't want it anyway, because I know it's going to do all those things." Despite all that, I think very few people *really* know it's going to hit them and how it's going to affect them. On that song I'm trying to look at it on a whole lot of levels simultaneously, on loads of levels, look at everything that happens to me, and try to be honest about it. "Tantalized" was about the same thing, just from the first person rather than the second person.

Indeed, the final verse of the song "Tantalized" neatly summed up the trepidation Steve felt about his on-again, off-again pursuit of success:

> I felt the dirty streets surround me
> I let the buzzing swarm confound me
> I gave money to ghosts, I insulted my hosts
> I could never get off the stuff that spellbound me

Heyday is now remembered for its pristine sound: a refreshing ray of light after the murkiness of its predecessors. But Steve contends that the album could have sounded even better had Peter Walsh had more time to mix it:

> Peter Walsh was a meticulous, amazingly detailed producer. Every electric guitar track had five acoustic guitar tracks backing it up. And every vocal had layers and layers of other vocals all carefully folded in, and there's all kinds of other things in there. Unfortunately for him, he underestimated the time and overestimated his ability to do a good mix in a quick time. And even when he began mixing, he spent three days on the first song and two days on the second song and then he got down to mixing three in a day; he was running out of time. I can't remember what the constraint was, whether he was starting another album or whatever it was. The tragedy of (*Heyday*) was, if someone had gone, "Hang on, Peter, you need another two weeks," the album would have been an absolute stunner.

On its release in early 1986, *Heyday* received mostly favorable press, with one high-profile exception: *Melody Maker*—one of the UK's main music magazines. Its reviewer accused the Church of trying to sound like UK bands the Smiths, Big Country, and Lloyd Cole and the Commotions—although in fact the Church had been around before those bands. If anything, the influence may well have been the other way around.

Writing in *Sounds,* Richard Cook was more generous:

> Scattered through this group's prolific history—they can't stop pouring out the songs and the records, it seems—are a cluster of jewels . . . Will

they sew together the classic record that lurks inside them? *Heyday* comes decently close.

In the US, *Rolling Stone* published a glowing review in which David Fricke—who would become an important champion of the band in years to come—described the Church's sound as "stately cathedral guitar rock distinguished by a haunting resonance, a regal rhythmic bearing and an unexpected hint of menace. What you get is more like a diligently polished Television than Byrds-by-numbers."

In Australia, *Heyday* represented a significant turnaround. Suddenly, the Church were back in the spotlight and on the covers of the street music weeklies. Many critics were able to set aside their reservations about Kilbey and give the band its due for having hung in there and produced such a solid album. Clinton Walker, never a huge fan, gave the Church more than a fair shake in the Australian edition of *Rolling Stone,* declaring:

> At this stage, no one can accuse the Church either of throwing down the gauntlet, or of selling out. Kilbey's visions haven't changed . . . Taking a deliberate step back from the unfocused indulgence of its immediate predecessors, *Heyday* picks up again the clarity and drive of vintage Church. This band hasn't proffered a more coherent collection of songs since their second album, *The Blurred Crusade."*

It seemed that the long break and the shake-up in the composition process had paid off. More than a return to form, the album signified a step forward, a striking out into richer, more confident sonic terrain.

People who hadn't paid the Church any attention since 1982 returned to the fold, while new fans signed on. When the Church took the new material on the road, the very same venues that had been half-full just two years before now sold out. And, instead of dwelling on the band's past triumphs, music writers began to speculate on what the Church's future might hold.

As the band readied the new material for an international tour, their American label Warner Brothers made just one request: get rid of John Lee and get a real manager. On a personal level, this dismissal was difficult for Steve, as Lee had been so warm and generous to both him and Marty. It was hard to look such a friend in the eye and say, "You're fired."

However, in a business sense, it was obvious to everyone that Lee knew nothing about managing a rock band. Others in the music industry regarded him as a dilettante. Sure, he could throw splendid bacchanals at his Malibu mansion, but when it came to booking a tour or getting the band the radio and press coverage it needed, he was useless.

To fill the void left by Lee's departure, Warner Brothers suggested a portly Italian-American character named Michael Lembo. According to a former Arista employee, "[Lembo] was a freaky, obese guy . . . Probably not that old, he seemed older because he had a receding hairline so severe you'd call him bald, except he had this wild frizzy black hair—what was left of it—and it was *long* and wild." The loud, hyperactive Lembo was the total opposite of the polite, deferential John Lee.

"Everything was very emotional with him," Steve says of Lembo. "When he came to Australia, he stopped around and tried to convince everybody what a big shot he was, which amused us and got our backs up a little. And he was very rude to people he considered weren't useful."

Indeed, Lembo did an excellent job of alienating at least one longtime fan. According to Steve, the fan introduced himself to Lembo and said, "I'm so glad you're managing the Church now." To which Lembo's reaction was a curt, "Why should I fucking care what you think?"

Still, Lembo was definitely a better manager, both organizationally and in terms of promotion, than Lee had been. Not being a millionaire, he had a clear interest in seeing the Church sell as many records as possible. He viewed the band as his ticket to greater wealth and recognition, and that served to motivate him to do a good job.

Mike's Management, Lembo's less-than-imaginatively titled production company, quickly put together a tour. For the American leg, Lembo scored a major coup: a month's worth of package shows with the popular English band Echo & the Bunnymen. The downside of this arrangement was that, for the first time in many years, the Church would be relegated to the opening slot, but the band's management figured that the combined appeal of the two groups would draw large audiences. What's more, the two bands played a similar style of music, so it was very probable that fans of Echo and the Bunnymen would be impressed by the Church and end up buying the Warner Brothers releases. After the Bunnymen tour in April, the

Steve, backstage on the 1986 US tour *(Michael Barone/Dana Valois)*

Church would tour the UK and Europe and then swing back through the US in July, playing smaller theaters on their own.

The Bunnymen tour was the first time the Church had been paired with another major band since the Duran Duran fiasco in 1982. *This* pairing, however, worked totally in the Church's favor. While it was true that in 1986 the Bunnymen were more recognized in America than their touring companions, the Church were not far behind, especially with all the college airplay the band had been getting for *Heyday*. Additionally, both bands were at their performing peak. "Echo and the Bunnymen were really good," Steve says. "I never resented opening for them, because I think they probably had the edge on us. When they were on, they were *really* on. But Ian McCulloch (frontman for the Bunnymen) was starting to believe his own myth. He was absolutely intolerable on that tour."

The mercurial McCulloch rarely spoke to Steve or his bandmates, and more than once off-handedly dismissed them—just as Duran Duran's Simon Le Bon had—as "a bunch of Australian hippies." As a fitting rejoinder to such intimidation, the Church managed to carve out an impressive chunk of McCulloch's audience for themselves. Many Americans were turned on to the Church for the first time because of that tour and, indeed, the Church's star began to rise just as the Bunnymen's began its descent.

"It was a good pairing," Steve concludes. "It really set us up to kick the goal for 'Under the Milky Way' for sure."

The European leg of the tour started off quite well, at least musically. As recordings from the shows demonstrate, the band was clearly energized by the new material, and Marty had stepped to the forefront as a fiery lead guitarist. Richard Ploog played at his absolute peak and, most importantly, the group's performances possessed all the raucous energy of past gigs without sacrificing the beauty and melody of the new material.

Behind the scenes, things were not so rosy. Marty's increased importance in the band created an ego tug-of-war between him and Steve. Peter, ever the manifestation of Buddhist calm, refused to take sides in this personality clash.

To this day, neither Steve nor Marty has revealed the specifics of their dispute. The most Steve will say is, "Due to the process of being on the road a long time, people can start to sort of get in conflict with other members of the band, and he started to get in conflict with me." Things deteriorated until, on the night of the Hamburg gig (June 10, 1986), Marty and Steve found themselves on the verge of a fistfight.

"He probably would have made mincemeat of me," Steve says, "and luckily one of our roadies restrained him." Peter adds: "Steve threw grapes at Marty while Marty was being held back."

The immediate consequence of this confrontation was Marty's announcement that he was quitting the band. And so it came to pass that the friendliest, most easygoing member of the Church stormed out mere hours before the band was supposed to take the stage. In just a few tense moments, the band's forward momentum—the product of so much careful work—had come to an abrupt, almost violent halt.

Marty, Backstage at Le Rox, Adelaide, 1986 *(Rachel Armstrong/Caroline Barnes)*

15

FOR A MOMENT WE'RE STRANGERS

Marty has always been the one that the other members of the band want to be with. It seems wherever he is, you just know on a day off that if you don't go where Marty goes, you feel like you're missing out on something. And he's always seemed to have that, especially with Richard. Richard was always bursting his fucking britches to get Marty and be with Marty and see what Marty was doing, and I knew that if Richard was hanging with me, he felt that he was having a second-rate day, because he wasn't where the happening things were going on. And in a lot of ways, Marty was like that; it seemed like wherever he was, there were the girls. He was always bumping into somebody famous. Something groovy was always happening to him.

—Steve Kilbey, July 2004

Steve walked up to the microphone at the Fabrik in Hamburg and stared out at a sea of expectant faces. He imagined their eyes all directed to his left, at the empty space where Marty should be standing. Steve had smoked more marijuana than usual in the half hour leading up to this moment, trying to quell his nervousness and block out the questions reverberating in his head. But try as he might, they could not be silenced. Those questions were: What next? Continue on as a three-piece? Replace Marty with Craig Hooper? Hold public auditions as they had with Ploog?

Of course, disbanding the group or changing its name was not an option. There was too much riding on *Heyday*. The album had only been on record-store shelves for a month, and Lembo had booked an extensive tour from which the band could not back out now. No, the show must go on.

Backstage, Steve, Peter and Richard had hastily put together a set list heavily weighted with material from the first album. It would be nearly impossible to perform many of the "pointillist" songs from *Heyday*, as those songs relied so heavily on the interplay between Peter and Marty. Instead, the band opted for the two most chord-based songs from the new album—"Columbus" and "Myrrh"—and a string of up-tempo numbers from the past: "Chrome Injury," "For a Moment We're Strangers," "Fraulein," and "The Unguarded Moment." This approach presented its own obstacles: most of the songs had not been performed live since 1982, and Marty's hasty departure had not allowed for adequate rehearsal time. The band's solution to the quandary was to ingest more pot.

Then there was the issue of how to begin the gig. Should the band simply launch into the first number with no explanation of Marty's mysterious absence? Or should Steve attempt to explain the whole sordid mess to the audience? In the end, he opted for a compromise. After a moment's hesitation, he said into the microphone, "Hello. I'm afraid Marty is not going to be with us tonight. We've had to rearrange the set somewhat, too." He paused, then said quickly, "So here we go."

Peter started up with the opening riff of "Myrrh," playing twice as fast as on record. Steve joined in with the ascending bass line and glanced back at Richard. The diminutive drummer had his eyes fixed on his sticks, hitting the snare and tom in a steady, building pattern as his foot did the same with the bass pedal, working inexorably towards the mini-crescendo that heralded the first verse.

And so they were off. And it sounded good, really good. Richard had never played in the original trio, but he had no problem adjusting to the new format. Yep, Steve thought, leave it to Ploog to fill up the space with the crash and clatter of cymbals and furious rolls. It sounded like an octopus playing the set instead of a mere two-armed mortal.

Peter became two guitarists, effortlessly moving back and forth between chords and solos. He did all this while standing perfectly still, his head bent slightly downward, a beatific expression on his face. It was as if his heart rate barely registered the fact that he was not in his living room but was, in fact, in front of a roaring audience.

This night was Peter's vindication. Sure, Marty had the moves, the looks, the clothes, but Peter had absolute mastery of his instrument. What's more, he made it look so very easy. Peter had no stake in the quarrel between Marty and Steve. Marty could leave or stay. Peter would be happy as a clam, going on as he had always done.

Steve, too, was beginning to realize that, even if Marty remained gone, things would be okay. Certainly the crowd seemed to be pleased, and if the band was now lacking in the rock-and-roll stage moves that Marty had so ably provided, they made up for that loss with sheer speed, flying through the back catalogue, not even bothering to stop between songs.

Other than a few muffed notes here and there, the band gave little evidence of being under-rehearsed. Certainly, Steve thought, there must be something to the theory of body memory: the idea that, once the body has repeated a movement enough times, it is remembered at the cellular level. As "Columbus" segued into "Life Speeds Up," the three musicians played ferociously, fueled in equal parts by nerves, fear, anger, and the novelty of an entirely new set. It was definitely one of their most memorable nights. Beyond his terse intro, Steve felt little need to speak, only uttering the occasional "Thank you" or "This is a really old one off of our first album." It was a tight show, lean and mean, with absolutely no filler.

★ ★ ★ ★ ★

Yes, a three-man Church would have worked out. And yet, there was an undeniable added energy that Marty brought to the band—and not just to their live performances. His perpetual optimism served as an important counterbalance to Steve's cynicism. To continue on without him would disturb the delicate balance that had grown up within the Church. Most of all, they missed his physical energy. As Marty would sing a few years later, "No repairs are needed, just a spark."

Fortunately, the Hamburg show had been one of the last dates of the European tour. The band cancelled the three remaining shows, and took a two-week break to regroup, but everyone knew that canceling the imminent US dates was out of the question. Clubs had been booked, interviews had been scheduled, and this was all taking place at a make-or-break point in the band's career. So it was never a question of whether or not the band would continue, but how.

Steve did not have to face this dilemma for long. A week and a half later, he received a call in Stockholm, where he was staying with Karin. Marty was in town and wondered if Steve would join him for lunch.

Steve arrived early at the designated meeting place, a small garden cafe called the Bistro Bohème, and waited nervously for Marty to arrive. All around, he heard the clinking of glasses and the low buzz of afternoon chatter. Steve sipped his espresso, temporarily losing himself in the shapes the sunlight made on his table-top. His head, topped as it now was with a tousled, gravity-defying coif, created a wild, shape-shifting shadow—a Rorschach test ebbing and pulsing between his coffee cup and napkin.

Steve figured there were two possible reasons for Marty's summoning him here today: either the guitarist had come to his senses and wanted to rejoin the band, or he wanted to make his severance final and discuss such thorny issues as royalties, copyrights, etc. Steve obviously preferred the first scenario, but he had to be prepared to accept the second in good grace.

Marty did not immediately show his hand when he arrived. He gave a brief "Hey" and went to the front of the cafe to order his drink. After chatting briefly with the barista he came back to the table, sat down, and examined his coffee cup intently. Finally, without preamble, he looked up and said, "I've had some time to think about this." He sighed, then continued: "I want to be in the band. Let's make this work."

Looking back, Steve can be reflective about the band crisis without pointing fingers. "It would be really hard," he says, "even if Marty was here now, to say what exactly the reason for our falling out was. He just didn't dig me. I think he thought I was uncool and controlling and egotistical and selfish. All of that was true."

During the fateful reconciliation lunch, Steve and Marty did not sort out their differences, but they *did* decide to set those differences aside for the good of playing together in a band. If their personalities were truly at an impasse, then it was an impasse from which they would retreat. "It totally cleared the air," Steve continues, "and he came back and there was no more of that stuff that had been happening before. We've only really had a couple of arguments since that point."

Steve and Marty, 1986 *(Rachel Armstrong/Caroline Barnes)*

With Marty back in the fold, the Church blazed through their US club tour, playing as if each gig could be their last. Journalist Abby Weissman caught the Minneapolis show and wrote about the experience in the *Aquarian*:

> [The Church] came on—and launched into their set with a velocity that would blow away any crowd of hardcore metalheads . . . *Heyday* barely hints at what the Church is like live. These guys play like *motherfuckers*; the producer who translates their concert sound to vinyl could well make them a mega hit.

Unfortunately, despite many positive live reviews and the fact that *Heyday* had received more airplay and higher sales than its predecessor, Warner Bros. wasn't satisfied. It didn't help that the Church's biggest champion at the label—Karen Berg—was now focusing most of her energy on a rising band from Minneapolis called Hüsker Dü. And so, on the very eve of worldwide success, the Church were unceremoniously dropped from Warner Bros.—a decision the venerable label no doubt came to regret.

Perhaps even more surprising than losing the Warners deal was the fact that EMI—the label that had served as the Church's Australian home since literally the first month of the band's existence—decided not to renew their contract when it expired, leaving the Church a free agent just when momentum seemed to be building for them.

Both the Warners and EMI rejections may seem inexplicable now, but from the labels' perspective, *Heyday* had not performed up to expectations. Management had predicted a blockbuster and what they got instead was a modest critical success—a nice little gem of an album, to be sure, but one that had come with a heavy price tag. Once Peter Walsh and the orchestra had been paid, there was not much left. None of the singles had gotten any traction, and the record companies didn't make any money from the sold-out gigs. EMI had heard that thing about "momentum" before, but how long were they supposed to bankroll this band, waiting for it to kick in? Anyway, if the Church took off in the future, EMI still owned the back catalog. Time to cut their losses.

Not every label felt this way. In fact, as soon as news spread that both Warner Brothers and EMI had passed on the next Church album, the phone started ringing with offers from other companies who had been impressed by the Church's recent tour and understood that the momentum was very real this time. The road-weary band members left it up to Mike Lembo to sort it all out and, as 1986 wound down, returned to their respective homes for a much-needed break. For Steve this meant a return to Sydney, Karin, and the comfortable domestic life he had been living prior to the tour. It would be a working vacation—his plans included a solo release and the recording of a musical soundtrack to his *Earthed* book.

Both Marty and Peter worked on solo projects of their own. The two guitarists realized there was no reason why they couldn't have solo careers, independently of their roles within the Church. The timing was right; the loyal fan base the Church had built up over the years guaranteed a ready-made audience for each member's side projects.

Steve had no desire to repeat the debacle of his first solo session at EMI, especially when he had hours and hours of home recordings gathering dust. He envisioned his first solo album as a collection of the very best of these recordings, polished and remastered as necessary, and it came together very quickly.

Through Russell's band, the Crystal Set, Steve had met the passionate, charismatic John Foy, who owned a hip alternative label called Red Eye. The Red Eye label was ostensibly an extension of the popular shop Red Eye Records, located in downtown Sydney, but the two had, in Steve's words, "only a very loose affiliation." The main thing the store and label shared was the logo of a giant bloodshot eyeball. Foy's high principles appealed to Steve; his fierce dedication to musical integrity proved a welcome tonic to the greed and commercialism of the American music business. As Steve puts it,

> [Foy] made me look like Mike Lembo. He made me look like kind of an LA slacker. If he decided that red vinyl or puke-colored vinyl or triple-thickness cardboard sleeve was what he wanted for the record, he didn't care if it meant he was going to lose money or you were going to lose money. It was all about putting out beautiful-looking records.

This ethic gave Steve the confidence to showcase his more experimental musical voice, which he had somewhat de-emphasized since the founding of the Church. Using one of his favorite albums of the '70s—Brian Eno's *Another Green World*—as a template, Steve cobbled together eleven home-recorded vocal-based tracks and three ambient instrumentals from his archives. He had played all the instruments on all the songs except three, which featured backing instrumentation and vocals from Russell Kilbey and Karin Jansson. In keeping with the homemade vibe, the inner sleeve featured a Kilbey family collage, with a baby picture of Steve, photos of Karin and Russell, and candid shots of Steve as a teenager. Buyers of the LP were treated to multiple photos of Steve brooding—sometimes in full makeup and sometimes cosmetically unadorned. Self-indulgent? Absolutely. But no more so than the album art of his icons Bowie, Eno, T.Rex, and Roxy Music. Included in the sleeve notes was Steve's home mailing address. While fans of the Church had to go through various levels of management to reach Steve, anyone who picked up this little gem had direct access to the artist himself.

Appropriately, the collection was titled *Unearthed*, which was not only a proper description of the tracks' provenance but also a nice omega to the *Earthed* book's alpha.

For a project that had been undertaken with no thought toward commercial outcome, *Unearthed* turned out to be quite profitable for Steve during his vacation from the Church. Release by Red Eye at the end of 1986, the album—which had cost virtually nothing to make—generated $20,000 in royalties from Australian sales, and it was also picked up for US release. Enigma Records, a thriving, independently owned label that had played an important role in the Los Angeles-based "Paisley Underground" scene of the mid-1980s, paid Steve a tidy sum up front for the rights to release his album stateside. These royalties, on top of the steady stream of income he received from the Church catalogue, served to make 1987 a comfortable year for Steve and his family, even though the Church was largely inactive.

Unearthed became an underground hit in Australia, garnering favorable reviews and even a fair amount of TV coverage (Steve hauled out his acoustic guitar and performed for the camera on several Australian talk shows.) Interviews from this period capture Steve in a cheery mood. He had every reason to be happy; he had just come off of a very successful US tour and there was much American interest in the next Church project. Additionally, with the *Earthed* book and the *Unearthed* album, he had shown that he was

hardly just the bassist and voice of the Church. He was an artistic all-round-
er and a versatile songwriter, proficient on several instruments and able to
create quality material independently, without the aid of producers or flashy studio tricks.

Given how it was assembled, it is sur-prising how unified the *Unearthed* al-bum sounds. In fact, this homebrewed independent release contains some of the best writing, singing, and playing of Steve Kilbey's career. The lack of self-consciousness in these record-ings is their great strength. Although Steve's voice does not always hit all the right notes, he has rarely sounded so relaxed and uninhibited. He seems entirely comfortable in his own skin, and because of this the songs feel very personal. Even with titles such as 'My Birthday the Moon Festival," the ma-terial showcases Steve at his least pre-tentious.

Backstage, 1986 *(Rachel Armstrong/Caroline Barnes)*

One particular highlight of the album is the breezy, mandolin-fueled "Guilty." Once again, upbeat music—in this case, a jaunty, almost Doobie Brothers–like keyboard melody—conceals cynical, melancholy lyrics. The first-person narrative is a study in xenophobia. After each verse describ-ing the chasing, shooting, and burying of "aliens" ("those people with the strange eyes"), we are treated to a chorus of "I find them guilty / I take them away." The fact that the song is easy to hum and dance to makes it all the more insidious.

"Pretty Ugly / Pretty Sad" is a pointed self-critique that finds Steve equating himself with a performing clown—a sad clown, not surprisingly. "Pretty Ugly/Pretty Sad" is a classic Kilbey pun. "It was just the idea of the way 'pretty' can be an adjective to other adjectives," Steve explains,

> ... and you can use it with a word that would naturally be its opposite. Just in the last week, my daughter Aurora has realized that pretty has two meanings. It's a qualitative type but it's also a compliment. She's been going, "I'm pretty beautiful aren't I?" and I'll go, "No, you're pretty pretty."

In the song, Kilbey muses on the nature of God—"I wonder who designed this maze/if it's unending"—and also the fleeting nature of fame: "Now I'm pretending, extending my welcome in this town." He lapses into self-pity: "I turned around to see the clown/I should have pulled the mirror down," but also pokes fun at his self-absorption: "I pulled my useless pity on." With all its contradictions and paradoxes, "Pretty Ugly/Pretty Sad" may be the most accurate self-assessment Steve Kilbey has ever penned.

"Judgment Day" is a successful stylistic mash-up of Bob Dylan and the Byrds. It's no "Jokerman," but the song does feature one of Dylan's favorite devices: each verse is crafted to end with the same two words, in this instance "Judgment Day." The chorus is another great example of Steve's happy/sad juxtaposition, as the ominous statement "Hey some people got a lot to answer for" is sung over a cheerily jangling guitar. Each chorus ends on a note of cautious optimism: "but you keep on going." This three-minute slice of catchy, danceable, intelligent pop would not sound out of place on an R.E.M. album.

Many of the other tracks, in particular "My Birthday," are more concerned with mood and atmosphere than with literal meaning. Then, towards the end of side B, Steve tosses out a stunning pair of ballads: "Nothing Inside" and "Othertime." Neither song is significant lyrically, although both contain sporadic gems (for example, "You lied, there's nothing inside/Always at the church but never a bride") but both feature the kind of chord progressions and melodies that lead critics (myself included) to resort to hackneyed expressions like "achingly beautiful." Appearing late on the album, these two songs—with their sparse arrangements of guitar and voice, with minimal overdubbing—puncture the heavy atmosphere of the preceding tracks and bring the listening experience down to a more intimate, fireside mood.

To show his songwriting versatility, Steve follows "Othertime" with the moody, droning "Heliopolis" and closes the album with an ambient instrumental that sounds very much like a percolating coffee pot.

On the heels of the *Unearthed* release, Steve began recording his *Earthed* soundtrack, which was released on Red Eye in May, 1987. This synth-heavy record sounds dated today, but it is nevertheless a sophisticated and wide-ranging work. The credits read "Written*, played and recorded by S.K... again. *except "The Empire Mourns Her Sun Without Tears" (K. Jansson). Of the twenty tracks, the more organic pieces such as "The Dawn Poems" and "...The Reality Generators Malfunctioned" work best. The drum machine and thin synths can sometimes grate, but this is a problem of equipment rather than composition.

It's hard to come away from the *Earthed-Unearthed-Earthed* cycle without an appreciation of Steve's boundless creativity. A lack of editorial discipline permeates these projects, but the excitement of engaging in art for art's sake compensates for the rough edges. This was surely a very different experience for Steve than working with the Church. In the Church, the musical whole was often greater than the sum of its parts; there was no way a single person could replicate the Koppes/Willson-Piper interplay. But the solo projects allowed for undiluted, uncompromised personal expression. For a while, the two sides of Steve's musical career would complement each-other well, each fulfilling needs that the other could not.

16
DESTINATION STARTS TO UNFOLD

Ah, *Starfish*. That was the big one for me. It was my introduction to the Church—and to my new life. The album hit the streets in late 1988, just after I'd turned 14; I became aware of it after seeing the video for "Under the Milky Way" on MTV.

I was in eighth grade, attending a Catholic middle school in southwest Minneapolis. The school, Annunciation, was just a few blocks from where I lived, and I'd often stop at the Lyndale public library on the walk home. Virtually every day I flipped through the record and tape racks and read back issues of *Rolling Stone*. I'd only recently discovered the addictive power of rock music, so I had a lot of catching up to do.

Rolling Stone gave the Church a fair amount of press in 1988, tagging them—rightly or wrongly—as the Australian equivalent of R.E.M. The positive buzz on R.E.M. had already filtered down to me from friends' older siblings, so the comparison was, in my eyes, a favorable one. The magazine also mentioned Pink Floyd as an influence on the Church, and this intrigued me further. My friend Joe Carpenter's record collection included *Dark Side of the Moon*, and I certainly loved what I'd heard.

Eventually, I coaxed my mother to drive me out to the mall so I could buy *Starfish*. I desperately wanted to get the album on vinyl so I could play it on my new Sears turntable, but the mall store only had it on cassette. Deciding that beggars can't be choosers (especially when Mom's driving) I snatched one up. Cassette turned out to be the right choice for this album—

it did not leave my Walkman for the next six months. It became my constant companion, the soundtrack to my daily existence, and an escape capsule when life became too stressful. Something about the album just clicked with me: Steve Kilbey's whispered vocals and Koppes' and Willson-Piper's layered guitars conjured a world of wintry beauty: of tree limbs hanging heavy with snow, and bells ringing gently in the forest. It was a world that was familiar and yet alien. At nights, sledding with my brother and sister near the frozen Minnehaha creek, I caught glimpses of that world in the iced-over waters and softly moonlit sky. But during the day it was blotted out by car horns and speeding vehicles kicking up slush onto the sidewalks.

Every now and then I'll get out *Starfish* and play it for friends. Most people seem to enjoy the music, but it's obviously not possible for them to understand the album's watershed importance to me. It was not merely the album itself that altered the course of my life; it was the way the album arrived at just the right time, just as I was on the cusp of adolescence—still a child and yet no longer a child. To hear *Starfish* divested of these elements is to simply hear a good rock album. But for me, hearing it in the winter of 1988, as the Minnesota snow was just beginning to melt and the decade was drawing to a close, I had found my purpose. Within a week I would own a guitar and, before year's end, I would be in a band.[7]

* * * * *

The pattern of events leading up to the recording of *Starfish* had a lot to do with the sonic cohesiveness and creative fertility that marked that album and made a US breakthrough possible for the Church.

In 1987, while Steve was busy promoting *Unearthed*, Peter and Marty both recorded and released solo albums of their own. Peter's album, *Manchild and Myth*, was a surprise to most fans. It was keyboard-based, featuring only spare, supplemental guitar work—highlighting Peter's songwriting and arranging skills rather than his musicianship. But the album suffered somewhat from a tinny-sounding drum machine and lackluster vocals; it

---

[7] Not long afterward, I discovered that the most exciting and thriving music scene in the country existed practically in my backyard. Both Hüsker Dü and the Replacements would become very important to me in years to come, but my teens were owned by the Church.

did not have the warmth or organic sound of Steve's *Unearthed*. Its strongest moments—such as the excellent "A Drink from the Cup"—rivaled anything Steve had written, but the first-rate tracks were almost invariably followed by mediocre filler, making for an uneven listening experience.

Marty's first album, on the other hand, was a remarkable achievement. Recorded entirely on a four-track, with help from childhood friend Andy Mason and girlfriend Ann Carlberger, *In Reflection* revealed a songwriter bursting with ideas. While performing his guitar duties in the Church, Marty had never stopped working on his own material. He had absorbed the best qualities of his band's music while retaining his own style. As a result, almost every song on *In Reflection* overflowed with rich harmonies and hooks and, as with *Unearthed*, the homemade quality of the recording added to its intimacy. What's more, Marty included with the record a detailed booklet describing the writing and recording process from start to finish. It was a virtual how-to manual of home recording. This stood in marked contrast to Steve, who at that time was very private about his writing methods. Marty invited *his* listeners into the studio with him, telling them when and where and why he wrote his songs, and how he got them onto tape. One could easily see that, despite their musical bond, the difference between the guarded, self-involved Steve and open, puppy-dog enthusiastic Marty was considerable. And the fact that one band could contain two such divergent artistic personalities was unusual—tension often lurked under the surface, though the creative push and pull ultimately benefited the Church. Years later, Donnette Thayer summed up their partnership this way: "Steve and Marty have a Lennon/McCartney competitive thing going on, although, oddly, they both seem to be John."

Mike Lembo had also been busy in 1987. After shopping the band around, he had found a new American label for the Church: Arista. The home of Whitney Houston did not at first seem an obvious or even a rational choice, but the label was eager to sign a more innovative modern-rock type band to round out its eclectic roster—which at the time also included Barry Manilow and Aretha Franklin. Clive Davis, the label's president, had an impressive pedigree, having signed Donovan, Bruce Springsteen, Billy Joel, Pink Floyd, Janis Joplin and Earth, Wind & Fire during his tenure as head of CBS Records. He was certainly no stranger to musical innovation, but he did

not discriminate between the experimental and the unabashedly commercial—he appeared to love it all.

The Church had actually been in the process of finalizing a deal with Beggars Banquet, but Mitchell Cohen, a new A&R rep at Arista, called Mike Lembo and outbid Beggars. As Steve remembers it, "They rang Lembo and told him they wanted to sign the Church. He didn't think they were serious so he named a silly figure—and they said, *All right*. Though whatever happened to that silly figure I don't know; it certainly didn't go in *my* pocket."

The contract with Arista covered North and South America, the UK, Europe, South Africa, and Japan. For Australia, Lembo had worked out a deal with Mushroom Records to replace the band's lapsed EMI/Parlophone deal.

Arista had an interesting proposal for the band: record the next album in Los Angeles with producers of the label's choosing. This would represent quite a change for the band. It would be the first Church album not to be recorded in Australia at Studio 301. They would be in a foreign city, away from friends and family, and working with a completely new group of engineers and producers.

"It seemed a silly enough idea that there might be something to it," says Steve.

> Plus, I'd had a kind of premonition that this could work, and I also thought that we had taken the EMI/Sydney thing as far as we could go. We were in a real rut of going to the same restaurant every night, playing the same pinball machine, working with the same engineers. I thought it would be good to break that.

★ ★ ★ ★ ★

So it was that the Church ended up in southern California—a land of jaded beauty that held in its nonjudgmental embrace both Disneyland and the porn industry, and somehow reconciled the dizzying disparities of Malibu and Compton. Steve would find more than enough songwriting inspiration in this disorienting place.

When the band arrived, Arista had lined up Waddy Wachtel and Greg Ladanyi to produce the new album. These two had played important roles in shaping the "California Rock" sound, having between them worked the boards for the likes of the Eagles, Fleetwood Mac, and Jackson Browne. Placing them with the Church seemed a strange choice, but Steve reasoned that it just might work, as long as the band were allowed to keep their core sound.

Steve and Marty have subsequently disparaged producer/musician Wachtel in interviews, portraying him as a bit of a musical 'square' who was unable to grasp the more esoteric aspects of the Church's music, but one look at the man's discography should dispel such holier-than-thou attitudes. While it's true that he was involved in a few projects that the Church and their followers might have considered bland, he also collaborated extensively with such challenging artists as Randy Newman and Warren Zevon (co-writing the latter's enormously successful "Werewolves of London" and co-producing the album on which it appeared, *Excitable Boy*.) It's also worth noting that directly *after* his work with the Church, he contributed some truly outstanding guitar playing to Keith Richards' first solo album (and subsequent live album) and also played on Tom Waits' *Bone Machine*. Clearly, Wachtel was not some studio hack solely concerned with the top 40; he was an accomplished songwriter in his own right, and a guitarist with a distinctive style.

Ladanyi's resume may have appeared a bit more dubious to the integrity-obsessed Steve. No one can dispute the importance of Jackson Browne's *Running on Empty*, an ambitious concept album that Ladanyi midwifed into existence, but for most of his career he had seemed shamelessly enslaved to the mainstream. *Toto IV*, with its overwrought and saccharine sound, represented a real nadir for rock music, even if some of the songs were undeniably catchy. Most damning, though, was the fact that he played a pivotal role in crafting the sound of Don Henley's first two solo albums; for that onerous achievement, I believe he has earned a special place in hell.

Still, despite any misgivings that the Church may have had about their new producers' past associations, both Ladanyi and Wachtel—on balance—had a wealth of experience engineering organic, guitar-driven pop records, and that was exactly the type of sound the band was after. If done right, it *could* work.

But before any recording could begin, the band had to finish writing the material. They had arrived in LA with only three complete new songs:

"Blood Money," "Under the Milky Way," and "Hotel Womb." Arista provided the Church with a rehearsal space in downtown LA, and the band
spent most of their first month there jamming out ideas for songs. Since
Heyday had been such a creative success, the Church decided to continue
with the group composition approach. To everyone's satisfaction, the new
material had a rawness to it, a bit of angst that could probably be attributed
to the gaudy surroundings of Los Angeles. In terms of structure, it built on
the complex guitar interplay that so distinguished *Heyday*. As Peter Koppes
remembers:

> It's a strange thing—I was playing the solos at the beginning (of the
> Church's career); Marty was playing the melodic motifs, and at a point
> where I started playing more of the chord progressions, he started taking
> over playing the lead riffs and the motifs became more rocky—like on
> "North, South, East & West." There are times when we do both—like
> "Reptile," where you get these syncopated arpeggios. It's like the jingle-
> jangle but more strident, and no one really knows who's holding down
> the chords or the root notes. And that became a style that we explored.
> As electronic devices became available, I just think that's what Hendrix
> would've done too. He would've—anything that came under his nose he
> would've tried it. We're a psychedelic band. Sometimes the sounds are so
> amorphous and orchestral that people don't realize it's a guitar . . . That's
> how the songs have developed.

When Steve began writing the lyrics for the album, he found the under-
lying paranoia, claustrophobia, and greed of the giant American city fertile
terrain. Thus the band's new, aggressive music found itself wedded to the
edgiest and darkest lyrics of Steve's already prolific career.

He did not have to look far for inspiration. 1980s Los Angeles (like
much of America) had a level of crass commercialism that was almost por-
nographic. And there, too, in the slums of South Central, were the have-
nots, the desperate, and the violent, waiting for the breaking point. Tension
seethed beneath the city's gilded surface, and Steve was right in the middle
of it, driving his red rental car down what felt like the wrong side of the road
every day. It was all so alien that the members of the Church were driven to
close ranks and live out of one another's pockets.

The band's housing arrangements didn't help. Arista put them up at the Oakwood Corporate Apartments (on Sepulveda Boulevard), Steve and Richard sharing one apartment, Peter and Marty right across the hall. The set-up wasn't too far removed from the fanciful scenario in *Help*, where the Beatles live together in a big house. For four individuals as idiosyncratic as Steve, Peter, Marty, and Richard, the arrangement left little breathing room. Additionally, because the musicians didn't know many people in the area, they found little to do on their days off except sit in the apartment, smoke pot, and watch TV.

Steve's isolation was short-lived. Donnette Thayer, the young musician Steve had first met during the *Remote Luxury* tour, was now playing guitar and singing backup in a semi-successful San Francisco band called Game Theory, who were signed to Enigma—the same label that had released *Unearthed* in the United States. When she learned that Steve was in Los Angeles, she arranged to meet him during one of her frequent visits to the area.

Arriving at the Oakwood, Donnette was surprised to find Steve—the ascetic who had so often preached publicly against the trappings of material wealth—glued to the television, watching an episode of *Lifestyles of the Rich and Famous*.

She later wrote of this experience on *Shadow Cabinet*, saying, "When Robin Leach finally released his many-legged grasp of my pop hero and Steve began to pay attention to me, he played me the chords of 'Centaur' and sang the chorus which had lyrics. I thought the song was marvelous." "Centaur" would eventually make its way onto an album by Hex—Steve and Donnette's collaborative project.

Steve took a passing interest in Game Theory and began attending some of their shows. He concluded, as did some others, that Donnette was woefully underused in the band. She had a stunning, angelic voice but was most often relegated to backing vocals, playing second fiddle to boyfriend Scott Miller's unremarkable warble.[8] Miller wrote smart, hook-driven songs—indeed, Game Theory had already built up a following long before Donnette joined the band—but every time she opened her mouth to sing, the difference between her vocal abilities and Miller's was thrown into sharp relief.

After spending some time with Donnette, Steve came to realize that she

---

[8] Former Game Theory bassist Guillaume Gassuan wrote on his web site: "Scott's great talent was as a songwriter. Had he given the vocal reins away, the music would have been much more accessible and the band might have really broken out."

Game Theory, circa 1986. L-R: Scott Miller, Donnette Thayer, Shelley LaFreniere, Gui Gassuan, Gil Ray *(Robert Toren)*

was not simply an attractive fan; she had talent and intelligence to match his own. The two began an on-again, off-again romantic relationship that would span several years and yield two remarkable collaborative albums.

"During my first visit," Donnette has written,

> Steve and I talked a lot about fame and money. I unashamedly advocated seeking both. Steve said that he was a purist and was only in it for the creative fulfillment that music provides. We debated the stardom point hotly; Steve insisted that it was unimportant how much acclaim or riches are garnered in the process of creating great art. After many such conversations, Steve wrote me a postcard saying that he hoped that I would be a star, or at least a starfish. Thereafter, during that period of time, when I wrote to him, I would sign my name as Starfish.

Much to Donnette's surprise, *Starfish* became the title of the next Church LP. Furthermore, "Unsubstantiated"—a song recorded during the *Starfish* sessions but not included on the album—was written specifically about Donnette.

The beginning of this new relationship marked the establishment of two separate lives for Steve: his semi-domestic, relatively quiet life with Karin in

Rozelle, and his more glamorous life with Donnette in America. This life in America seemed to offer everything on a larger scale: more drugs, more money, more adulation. But it would do irreparable damage to his soul, and cause his already large ego to grow even larger. None of this should be pinned on Donnette, a warm and creative person who in many different ways served as a great source of inspiration. Maintaining two separate lives is bound to take its toll on anyone.

Donnette Thayer, circa 1983 *(Robert Toren)*

It is unclear how Karin felt about this arrangement. There can be little doubt that she knew about Steve's American girlfriend—he took several vacations with Donnette, even spending one Christmas with her family, and of course there were the two albums they made together. Presumably his relationship with Karin was off-and-on during this period, just as it was with Donnette. Ever since the collapse of his marriage, Steve had shied away from monogamous relationships, which he viewed as stifling. In an interview with Michelle Andre of *Ears and Mouth*, he went so far as to declare monogamy contrary to basic human nature. From these comments and others, it seems likely that, even when they lived in the same country, Steve and Karin had an open relationship, or at least a "don't ask, don't tell" arrangement.

Because Steve has always been jealously protective of his loved ones' privacy, specific details about these relationships are hard (even for the intrepid biographer) to come by, and in the end are only really relevant to those directly involved. What *is* relevant, however, is that these relationships and experiences evidently fueled the dark lyrics that Steve wrote during this period. In "Blood Money," he described an empty sexual transaction between a politician and a prostitute. In "Destination" he sang of "the space between our bodies." And, of course, "Under the Milky Way" featured his now-famous phrase, "Wish I knew what you were looking for/Might have known what you would find." More directly, the awkwardly phrased first line of the otherwise stately "Antenna" could be interpreted as a rebuttal to Karin's long-distance suspicions: "Why do you always wrongly assume/That you're so well aware of what's happening there/Right here in this room?" He goes on to sing, "You're just an antenna, you're just a wire/There's a thousand tongues wagging in your ears tonight/And you turn around and you call me a liar."

Before the band could begin recording these new compositions, however, the producers demanded that Steve get some vocal instruction. Greg Ladanyi wasn't impressed with Steve's singing and didn't like the idea of Arista shelling out thousands of dollars to record someone he perceived to be a flat vocalist. Steve dutifully signed up for lessons, and Peter, eager to improve his own singing voice, tagged along. Their teacher was a retired opera singer who told Steve exactly what he needed to hear—that he had a great voice; he just needed to learn how to relax and open up. After a few weeks of vocal and breathing exercises from this aging maestro, Steve and Peter returned to the studio and impressed their producers enough to commence the recording. Steve maintains to this day that the lessons didn't do anything for him, but even a cursory listen

Steve and Donnette Thayer, 1988
(Courtesy, Donnette Thayer)

to *Starfish* proves otherwise. The phrasing and delivery on this album are more nuanced than on previous offerings—surpassing even his fine work on *Heyday*—and stylistically Steve approaches the melancholy tones of one of his favorite albums: *Sinatra Sings for Only the Lonely*.

The recording of *Starfish* went quickly and smoothly, although the relationship between the band and producers grew increasingly strained during the process. Wachtel pushed for the musicians to abandon their echo boxes and concentrate on creating a more rhythmic groove. The Church resisted, thinking this might somehow compromise their signature sound. Marty, in particular, bristled at the fact that the producers seemed never to have heard of Tom Verlaine, Bill Nelson, or any of the other left-of-center guitarists that he used as reference points. "Under the Milky Way"—the song that would guarantee Steve Kilbey royalties for life—initially met with indifference from the producers because it showcased just the sort of swirling psychedelia that Wachtel and Ladanyi were trying to get the band to move beyond. Interestingly, both Marty and Peter were also unenthusiastic at first. Ploog, on the other hand, loved it and predicted it would be a hit.

Perhaps some of the initial reluctance from the two guitarists stemmed from the fact that "Under the Milky Way" was not a band composition—Steve had written it with Karin a few months earlier and presented it to the group as a finished song. This may have smacked too much of the old days when Steve had written everything; it certainly flew in the face of the band's new communal songwriting process.

Despite the fact that Richard Ploog had been the biggest champion of "Under the Milky Way," he didn't actually play drums on the track. None of the live, in-studio performances of the song seemed to work for the producers, so Steve, Peter, and Marty recorded their parts to a click track. Then Waddy Wachtel brought in studio legend Russ Kunkel[9] to add drums and percussion.

After the initial guitar tracks were laid down, Steve spent some time in the studio with a technician named Welles (whom Steve nicknamed Orson), tinkering with the song.

"We had the middle section and we didn't have anything in there," Steve says,

> . . . and I said, "Listen, we just need to bung some noise down in this middle section; it's probably gonna be some e-bow guitars." He had this African bagpipe, and he said, "Hey listen to what you can do on the synclavier; you can just turn things the other way." I'd never heard of an instrument that could play the sounds on it backwards. With the synclavier you could do that. And so, just for a laugh, after we'd put the

[9] Kunkel was unquestionably the top session drummer of the 1970s and early '80s. His resume includes albums by Bob Dylan, Neil Young, Stevie Nicks, Carole King, Jackson Browne and Linda Ronstadt. He also appeared as one of the doomed drummers in the cult classic "rockumentary" *This Is Spinal Tap*.

bagpipes on there, he said, "Now I'm gonna do it backwards" and flipped the whole thing around. We kind of left it in there, much the same way as when you paint a picture, you just kind of leave a blank space; you might put a bit of scribbling in there to indicate there will be something at a future date.

At first, band mates and producers reacted to the bagpipe solo with shock and bewilderment. After a few listens, however, the consensus was that the novelty of a backwards bagpipe solo further enhanced the song. Like the bizarre baseball-organ solo in Del Shannon's hit song "Runaway," the bagpipe section in "Under the Milky Way" made the song hard to forget.[10]

And yet, even as the album was being sequenced, the producers did not grasp the full potential of the track. Steve recalls:

> I remember sitting down when the album was finished . . . I had "Under the Milky Way" second, where it is now. Waddy Wachtel said, "You don't want that song second, Kilbey." And I said, "Why not?" And he said, "You want 'em to hear some of the good ones before they get to that."

Mike Lembo's reaction, on the other hand, would be quite different.

---

[10] In Australia, there had already been hits featuring bagpipe solos by the time "Under the Milky Way" came out. Less than two years before *Starfish* was recorded, John Farnham had a huge hit in Australia (and in many other countries) with "You're the Voice," which has a bagpipe solo in the bridge and more bagpipes in the song's closing choruses. Steve would almost certainly have heard this, though it's doubtful he would've liked it. And AC/DC's "Long Way to the Top," which has a memorable bagpipe solo, was a top 5 hit in Australia in 1976, and soon acquired anthemic status. The majority of American listeners, however, were quite unprepared for what came blasting out of their speakers halfway through this new Church track.

17

OUR INSTRUMENTS HAVE NO WAY OF MEASURING THIS FEELING

It was the moment of truth. Mike Lembo stood in the doorway, his hulking frame silhouetted by the light behind him.

"Let's hear it," he said, tapping an unlit cigar against his leg.

"Have a seat," Steve said, pointing to the place of honor: a stuffed recliner equidistant from the four monitor speakers. Steve, Marty, Peter, and Richard all sat in swivel chairs near the recording console.

Lembo shuffled in, grunted, and dropped himself into the chair, sighing deeply. He put the cigar in his mouth but still did not light it.

Steve played the first track, "Destination," and looked over a few times to see Lembo's foot tapping quietly against the floor. The band did not need their manager's permission to put any of these tracks on the album, but it was important that he be kept in the loop. If he developed enthusiasm for the new songs, so much the better; after all, he would be more likely to get behind something he actually liked. The harder Lembo worked, the better it was for the band.

When "Under the Milky Way" began playing through the monitors, Lembo's foot stopped tapping. His face scrunched up. Steve couldn't tell if he was concentrating on the music or imagining a lemon he had sucked. When the bagpipe solo began, the right side of his mouth turned upward in a slight grin.

As the song faded away he said, softly, "Stop the tape for a second."

He stared at Steve, and then at the rest of them; he wore an expression on his face as if he had just discovered El Dorado, the mythical kingdom of gold.

"I can get this song on the radio," Lembo said quietly. He paused, then his usual loud squeak of a voice took over.

"When this song is on the radio, when this song is on MTV, you guys are gonna be showered with money."

"Don't you mean *if?*" Steve interjected, his voice catching slightly in his throat.

Lembo looked him straight in the eyes. "Believe me on this one. When this comes out, you will never have to worry about anything ever again."

Steve sighed and ran his hand through his hair. He was already tiring of the hyperbole. "Look, Mike," he said, "they told me that about 'Columbus'."

"FUCK 'COLUMBUS!'" Lembo shouted, squeezing his cigar between his thumb and forefinger and jabbing it at Steve. "Fuck everything you've ever done before!"

He paused for effect, lowered his voice and said, "This song is a hit."

★ ★ ★ ★ ★

Starfish was released in spring 1988 to excellent reviews. The Australian *Rolling Stone* featured the Church on its cover, and the American *Rolling Stone* devoted a feature article to the band. The magazine's well-regarded David Fricke gave the album four stars and penned a review that perfectly encapsulated the themes of the record.

> At its most compelling, the band scrambles the real and the surreal with ease, rattling its stately guitarchitecture with howling north-wind echo and the troubled undertow of Kilbey's enigmatic lyrics. *Starfish* is an album that will disorient and fascinate; shaking its spell will not be easy.

In the UK, Ralph Traitor of *Sounds* likewise gave the album four stars:

> Kilbey's songwriting is not about attack but strategy. You begin to appreciate how ingeniously the Church have amalgamated their '60s inspirations and '80s realities. This is a style that doesn't have to look back

to feel good, but the weight of history leans approvingly on it just the same.

Critics around the world told the band that this was the triumph they had been hoping for. All the Church could do now was sit back and hope the public felt the same way.

After the release of *Starfish*, as the positive reviews started pouring in, the band began to spend more time at Arista's New York offices, doing interviews and helping with promotion. One of the staff at Arista at this time (we'll call him "Greg") worked in radio promotion. When he learned I was writing this book, he sent me an e-mail detailing his experiences with the band:

> Steve Kilbey was either grumpy all the time, or condescending. Lots of people were intimidated by him. [There's] no doubt that he's a really intelligent guy, but he made sure you knew it. He was cruel, I think.
>
> Marty Willson-Piper was manic. He wanted to go through everyone's stockpile of albums and took *everything* he could get his hands on, from Whitney Houston on down. He was also pretty opinionated and adamant about his musical taste.
>
> Peter Koppes seemed to have a chip on his shoulder. Not as popular as Marty, though we figured he was probably a much better and more accomplished musician. Peter also talked a lot about space aliens and religion.
>
> Richard Ploog couldn't have been nicer. Really sweet and friendly. He stuttered.

Greg reckons there was a bit of friction within the band because all the reporters wanted to talk to Steve and Marty, ignoring the other two. "But," he points out, "most bands have that dynamic."

In recent years the band has complained about how Arista seemed to lose interest and drop the Church as soon as their style of music went out of fashion. Still, Greg confirms what others have stated previously: that in the early years, Arista worked hard on the band's behalf, pushing the Church as hard as they possibly could. Greg again:

> The band did have a hit album with us, but we worked our asses off to make it a hit. Probably back then, Arista spent over a million dollars in

Game Theory (Donnette Thayer, center) *(Robert Toren)*

publicity and promotion on *Starfish*. I'm no fan of major labels, but you have to give credit where credit is due."

* * * * *

Steve continued to catch concerts by Game Theory whenever he was in the same town as Donnette's band. He found, to his chagrin, that his growing fame in America made anonymity at these shows increasingly difficult. At one performance in Washington D.C., Steve's very presence elicited more excitement from the crowd than did the band onstage, despite the fact that for most of the show Steve was asleep at the bar, oblivious to the hoopla surrounding him.

Because of her relationship with Steve, Donnette found herself also living in two worlds whenever he was with her. While her bandmates drove from show to show in an older van and slept on friends' couches and floors, Donnette traveled with Steve in rented cars and stayed with him in fancy hotels. This exacerbated the tension that already existed between her and band leader Scott Miller in the wake of their dissolved relationship.

"I'll never forget the one night [my bandmates] dropped us off, still trying to be groovy," Donnette wrote:

> There was this long corridor of perfectly white globe lights for what
> seemed like a mile along the entrance. Someone said, "Do you think
> they'll have showers . . . where we're going to stay?" Someone answered,
> "No, there's a tub that doubles for a kitchen table, that's all." I felt
> tremendously guilty, but not after I found my amp later with all the tubes
> mysteriously smashed.

As if tensions weren't already running high enough between Donnette and her bandmates, Steve unwittingly drove the final nail into Game Theory's coffin when he got Donnette lost on the way to the band's New York City gig. Her angry bandmates went ahead with their show, with a cardboard cutout standing in for their absent guitarist. Game Theory folded for good shortly thereafter. Years later, when asked by Thomas Durkin why the band had ended, Scott Miller said, "Donnette and me breaking up and Enigma Records [going into bankruptcy] were big factors." Recalling the end of the band, bassist Guillaume Guissan describes Donnette as "exponentially self-involved," while allowing that was pretty much par for the course in rock and roll. "In retrospect," he says on his web page, "it's a shame that she didn't part with the band on better terms. The first tour was great and the last was very fun when she wasn't around. She was very enthusiastic at first, but as real success stayed just beyond our grasp she lost interest."

Now that she was a free agent, Donnette began work with Steve on the first of two albums that would be recorded under the name Hex. This turned out to be one of the most inspired and artistically rewarding collaborations of Steve's career. In Donnette he had found a singer whose voice was as beautiful as the music he was writing. The arrangements for many of the songs were spare—often consisting of softly strummed acoustic guitars, ambient keyboard textures, and tasteful electronic percussion—which allowed her voice to float up through the wide open spaces like smoke. As with so many of Steve's projects, the album was written in a spirit of wild improvisation. Describing the process years later on *Shadow Cabinet*, Donnette attributed their inspiration to an unusual source:

The Grateful Dead were doing a week-long concert series at Madison Square Garden which was right next door to the studio where we were working. If you don't already know, Steve likes to do impromptu writing, so the lyrics for many of the songs were written during breaks between guitar takes or what have you. So there's no way some groovy vibrations are not going to sift over from half a billion deadheads and into Steve's waiting ethereal snare. I mainly edited, acting as a blonde thesaurus with a little red pen wrapped up in velvet.

Once the initial recordings had been committed to a Fostex 16-track, the duo then moved on to Gambit Studios (also in New York) to record expanded 24-track versions of the new songs with engineer Bryce Goggin. This multi-draft process may explain why the album has a tighter, more cohesive feel than much of Steve's other non-Church work.

Ever the multi-tasker, Steve divided his time between *Hex* and preparing for the Church's impending world tour in support of *Starfish*. The critical buzz had become a roar, and expectations for this tour were high. The members of the band, however, were already sick of each other after spending so much time isolated and overworked in Los Angeles. Richard Ploog, in particular, was rapidly losing interest in the workings of the whole rock-and-roll machine. Having never cared about success, the drummer had little incentive to deliver. He would just as soon be puttering about in his garden than playing in front of thousands of people.

Marty and Peter seemed mainly interested in what the Church's success could do for their solo careers. If recorded performances from the *Starfish* tour are any indication of the norm, Steve and Marty battled constantly for the audience's attention. Marty would often beat Steve to the mike and talk to the crowd, introducing the next song and so on. As the best-looking member of the band and a songwriter who was growing in leaps and bounds, Marty could scarcely be contained by the Church. His manic stage antics and flashy playing reached their apex on this tour and seriously threatened to upstage the contributions of the other members.

For his part, Steve found his ongoing collaborations with Donnette more interesting than the prospect of furthering the career of his band. He put in a modicum of effort, because he realized the Church was his cash cow, his meal ticket. Creatively, however, he felt himself pulled in other directions.

Richard and Steve, Long Island, 1988 *(Michael Barone/Dana Valois)*

Touring for *Starfish* in 1988 marked the first time that the bulk of the shows were in North America. European dates were limited to two weeks in March and April, and another week at the end of June, while the only Australian shows were in Melbourne and Sydney at the end of April. The North American leg of the tour was extensive, however, covering virtually all of May and June, another month of dates from mid-August to mid-September, and still more shows in October. For the August and September dates, the Church's management set up another package show, as they had with Echo and the Bunnymen two years earlier. This time, the Church were paired with Peter Murphy, former lead singer of the cult new-wave/Goth band Bauhaus, now pursuing a mildly successful solo career. This combination didn't work out as well as the previous one. Murphy apparently expressed displeasure at being relegated to the status of opening act, but realistically there was nothing he could do about it—"Under the Milky Way" was climbing the *Billboard* singles chart, while Murphy would not achieve a similar breakthrough for another two years.

"I met Peter Murphy a couple of times backstage," Steve recalls.

He was like an English public schoolboy. He was sort of effeminate and kind of . . . he was a star in his own head. I'd seen him on TV in Bauhaus and thought, Wow, I bet he's a weird powerful bloke, and then I met him and he was like, "Oh, hello!" One time I heard an argument, and there was this great big tour manager, and Murphy was in a corner going, "Keep that man away from me!" He was really pathetic, and I thought his band was mediocre. His only good thing was when he did "Bela Lugosi's Dead" and the lights would come on and he had that little vampire thing going, but other than that, I don't think he knew what the hell he was actually doing. I think he'd been in a group with some other guys who had been creative, and I think they depended on each other. And he sort of thought, like McCulloch thought, "I am the star, I don't need these guys, people are coming to see *me*," and then he suddenly realized that, left to his own devices, he was a bit adrift."

Not everyone in the audience shared Steve's assessment, though. A friend and former bandmate of mine, who saw one of these shows, told me: "Peter Murphy blew the Church off the stage. He mopped the floor with them. By the time the headliners started their set, it was already over."

Although both artists ostensibly belonged to what American radio rather nebulously defined as the "modern rock" genre, there wasn't much overlap between their audiences. Murphy drew the pale-faced, black-make-up-wearing crowd. Steve had flirted with this style, particularly during his days emulating Marc Bolan, but his focus was now squarely on the music itself. And, although it may be true that Marty and Peter's penchant for tight leather pants made for good camera fodder, the Church did not put a great deal of thought into their look. The band's audience, too, consisted mainly of college and post-college types—many of them bespectacled and maybe wearing nice clothes for the night out, but not putting in much effort beyond that.

Sonically, the Church *did* have crossover appeal to some members of Murphy's audience, but many others exited as soon as their man left the stage. "I'd say about a third of the audience was there for him and probably half of [those] left when we came on," Steve says. "I remember I said into the microphone once, 'It's the biggest retreat of the Goths since the Roman Empire!'"

For a number of other dates on the tour, Arista paired the band with one of Steve's and Marty's heroes: Tom Verlaine of Television, who performed a solo acoustic opening set. This, too, turned out to be a somewhat disillusioning experience, though Steve retained his admiration for Verlaine as an artist. On a personal level, Verlaine was steadfastly frugal, and he bumped heads with Steve—blissfully promiscuous with his finances—a few times on the subject of money. "At one point," Steve says, "I found myself in a Denny's with him and he's like, 'Uh, Kilbey, let me get this straight; I seem to have paid for your French fries!'"

All penny-pinching aside, it was a real thrill for Steve to be on tour with one of his songwriting heroes, and it was quite an ego boost to know that Verlaine was opening for the Church and not the other way around. The band did not waste this opportunity; for their encore every night ("You Took"), they brought Verlaine onstage with them for a three-way guitar duel. During those moments, everyone involved stepped up to the plate and delivered some of the most raucous, incendiary music of their careers. It had quite an effect on the fans too, many of whom consider the Verlaine/Church shows to be some of the best live performances they've ever witnessed.

Sadly, along with these peaks came many troughs. While the band kept the energy level up during its shows, the four musicians often seemed to be pulling in different directions. In particular, friction developed between Steve and Richard, both onstage and off. Ploog would often speed up and slow down his playing arbitrarily, depending on his mood, and because he was the drummer and set the tempo, the band had no choice but to follow him.

To make matters worse, Ploog insisted on bringing his girlfriend along with him for the entire US tour. It wouldn't have been so bad if she had gotten along with everyone, but according to Steve, she seemed hell-bent on making them all miserable. She hated America, she hated traveling, she hated the food, she hated the music. As Steve describes it, she complained the whole time she was on the road with them. Many times after the main set, the band would find her waiting for them in the dressing room. As the band got ready to go back out for their encore, she would say, "You're not going to play any *more*, are you?"

Richard was convinced that she was his soul mate and that they were destined to be a "John and Yoko" couple, spending every waking moment together. But her very presence steadily drove the other band members up the wall. On multiple occasions the other guys asked Richard to send her home.

"He kept tricking us," Steve says. "He'd say, 'Yeah, she's going back next week,' and then next week would come. You'd get to Chicago where she was going to fly back to Sydney from. You'd get back on the bus, and he'd hidden her on the bus. And only halfway towards fucking wherever you were going, she'd appear and he'd go, 'Ah yeah, she didn't go.'"

There have been several theories over the years about Richard Ploog's gradual disengagement from the band, and the term "acid casualty" is of-

ten bandied about. Although no one can be absolutely certain that drugs caused Ploog's subsequent (alleged) mental illness, most agree that LSD exacerbated his condition. His intake had been no stronger than Steve's onetime "acid for breakfast" regimen, but hallucinogens affect every person different-ly. One of Steve's favorite sayings is, "You're only ever one trip away from madness," and it's possible Richard took that one trip.

Richard stayed in the Church for an-other two years, but he sowed the seeds of his departure during the 1988 tour. Perhaps his bandmates hoped he would snap out of it and regain his enthusiasm for the music. They gave him the benefit of the doubt

Richard and Steve, during the US tour, 1988
(Michael Barone/Dana Valois)

time and time again. Ultimately, however, his unpredictability behind the drum set threatened the stability of the entire band.

To this day, all those involved in the situation remain tight-lipped and have not disclosed the exact nature of Richard's malady, assuming it is even known. What *is* known is that Richard very quickly seemed to lose interest in playing in the band and retreated inward. It became increasingly difficult for his friends to communicate with him on a musical level, or even to carry on a simple conversation with him. It was a terrible situation for Richard—but clearly also a growing problem for the Church.

18

THE PURSUIT OF ADULATION IS YOUR BUTTER AND YOUR BREAD

Because of the incessant ringing in his ears, Steve had difficulty concentrating on the two women talking to him. Behind them he could see Ploog hopping about shirtless, a white towel around his neck. In the corner of the dressing room, Peter Koppes sat holding court with three college-age girls and an overly earnest male reporter. Marty was on the phone with his girlfriend in Sweden.

An attractive, waifish brunette approached him, pushing aside—with her eyes—the other two fans.

"Steve," she said, "will you hold something for me?"

He stared at her for a moment, then gave his characteristic smirk. "Okay."

"Hold out your hand."

He held out his hand.

"Close your eyes."

He closed his eyes.

She placed in his hand what felt like a warm, slimy marble.

He opened his eyes, looking first at the girl's face. Her left eye socket was empty—just two flaps of wet red skin. He looked down and saw a sweaty glass eye staring up at him. He blinked, looked again. It was still there. The girl grinned, grabbed the eye, popped it back into her face, scowled at the other two girls, and walked off.

Steve looked around incredulously, hoping his bandmates had seen what he had seen. They had not.

He went to sleep that night visualizing the eye—vacant but also, paradoxically, seeing straight through him.

★ ★ ★ ★ ★

One night, somebody loved us so much they stole all our coats. They loved us so much on a freezing cold night in the middle of Ohio that they took our coats, so we walked outside in our wet stage clothes freezing. How do I deal with that? I don't know. It's like, what do you do? I've had people want to kill me and people want to give me their firstborn. You just kind of get cynical after a while. And then you start using people. You think, if you want to be used I'll use you, and then you get sick of that.

—Steve Kilbey, July 2003

The level of adulation Steve received from his American fans caught him off guard. Sure, there had been zealous fans elsewhere, fans who would sleep with him at the drop of a hat, but only in America was Steve approached by a male fan who asked if Steve would do him the honor of sleeping with his wife (Steve respectfully declined.)

In America the audiences screamed louder, they waited longer outside in the cold for tickets. They clamored more for autographs and visibly trembled when they got in close range of their idols. All this adoration increased exponentially as the *Starfish* album went gold in America. Even though the band was still confined to the "college rock" category in the mainstream consciousness, Steve discovered that college-rock status in the States was the equivalent of royalty everywhere else.

Patrick Boulay, a devoted fan since 1990, sums up this phenomenon:

We are the "converted" I guess. Once you get it—I got it in '90 after hearing "Metropolis" on alt radio, being swept away by the melancholy of "Monday Morning" and "Disappointment," reading the liner notes of *Starfish*, so many transcendent moments really in those golden July/ August days so long ago—you're never quite the same. You realize that, honestly, there isn't a better band that ever put music to tape. Yes, that includes the Beatles. The Beatles are, of course, the greatest band of all time but nobody is "better" than the Church. And that's what makes a Church fan a Church fan. You believe this. You know it. Fuck everyone else. They aren't enlightened. They are heathens.

Steve certainly appreciated this passion for his music—it confirmed, in his mind, the inherent quality of the Church's work. But some fans seemed to want more from him than just the songs, Steve felt:

> In America, you get a lot of these sorts of people who really believe that because you play guitar and you've got some lyrics, that you must know something, that you're on to something.

Thus Steve Kilbey, bassist and lyricist of the Church, became Guru Steve, the unwitting source of wisdom and enlightenment for a strange cult of disaffected American youth (the author of this book among them). In a way it was what Steve had always wanted—the desire to be loved and adored is at the heart of every rock-and-roll dream—but in another way it was tiresome. Steve had already experienced fame twice in Australia. The initial rush that came from being loved by theaters full of people had largely worn off. And these Americans hounded him, peppering him with questions. Hadn't he already given enough? Wasn't a gold record full of beautiful melodies and insightful lyrics enough? It was a difficult thing to deal with.

Because of the pressure from the fans, internal strife within the band, and the pressure of expectation from Arista, Steve smoked more pot on the *Starfish* tour than at any other point in his life. Marijuana had essentially been a daily staple for most of his adulthood, but now he smoked such large quantities of the stuff that he routinely coughed up blood. To quit or even cut down was near impossible. He explained to journalist Michelle Andre: "I knew that one day I'd have to give it up, but now that day has . . . well, that day's come about three years ago, and now I have to stop because it's absolutely ruining me! [But] I don't think I can. I haven't been able to so far." Every single person, from his bandmates on down to the bus driver, was smoking crates of the stuff. Steve ruefully told Andre, "It's the only thing I really like doing."

After one of the *Starfish* shows in New England, a wealthy fan told the band, "I like you; I want you to come out and have Thanksgiving with me." The fan's parents were more than happy to cook for the band, naively thinking (in that characteristically ethnocentric American way) that the Australian musicians would be missing home on that uniquely North American holiday.

The parents turned out to be millionaires. After one look at their mansion, the band's black bus driver refused to go in, saying, "I ain't goin' in there, I ain't fucking goin' in there."

Perhaps out of loyalty to their driver, or perhaps because it is the accepted rock-and-roll way of things, the Church repaid the family's kindness by breaking things and generally making a nuisance of themselves. From the halcyon days of Led Zeppelin throwing refrigerators into the Puget Sound down to Billy Idol setting fire to his hotel room in the 1980s, a bit of destruction has always been part and parcel of the authentic rock touring experience. Whether it was some innate desire to bite the hand that feeds, or a way of acting out the frustrations of being on the road with the same people for an entire year, the Church occasionally slipped into this behavior. They could never entirely escape the corrosive clutches of rock-and-roll cliché.

"Ploogy probably went in the toilet and stuck their toothbrush up his arse or something," Steve says. "I was probably pissed off, out on the back smoking dope. [Looking back], I don't know what to think of it all. I don't know if these people deserve it or not. In my Buddhist moments I go, 'What am I doing treating people like that?'"

* * * * *

By December of 1988, the nearly twelve months of promotion and touring for *Starfish* came to an end. When all was said and done, the Church had performed ninety-four shows across the US, Canada, Europe, the UK, and Australia. At nearly every stop, the band was interviewed by local media, made radio appearances, and did the occasional live and in-studio taping for TV. Management provided the four musicians with heavily booked daily schedules that left little time for rest or sightseeing. Richard Ploog's itinerary for March 11 (during their Madrid stay), for example, included several radio interviews, one TV interview, and ten press interviews over a ten-hour period. Lunch and dinner provided no respite—they were spent with journalists.

As it turned out, 1988 would be the most successful year of the band's history. *Starfish* sold 600,000 copies in the United States alone, while "Under the Milky Way" reached number 24 in the singles chart. Back in Australia, "Milky Way" climbed to number 5, and *Starfish* reached number 7 on the album charts—their best positions ever in their home market. Everyone thought it was just the beginning.

The band members went home for a four-month break before reconvening to begin work on the next album. For Steve, re-entry into civilian life was particularly difficult this time around. After a year of being waited on hand and foot, he had to readjust to Karin's requests to take out the garbage and pick up after himself. America had spoiled him. More specifically, American *success* had spoiled him. Now he was back in Australia a changed man.

To keep himself busy, and to keep one foot continually in the rock-and-roll world, Steve did his first solo live performances. A fateful gig in Perth, on Australia's west coast, set the tone for his solo performing style: a sort of vaudeville comedy-and-song routine that differed radically from his austere, say-nothing-to-the audience Church persona. It wasn't intentional. Steve began the gig with a well-rehearsed, carefully structured set list, but before long, things began to break down. People called out for songs that weren't on the list, and because there were no loud guitars or drums to drown these voices out, Steve felt he needed to address them. He played some of the requests, strumming his way through songs he had never played on acoustic guitar before. He ad-libbed between songs, engaging the audience with rambling, tangential monologues. And, after the fifth or sixth request for "Under the Milky Way," he threw his arms up and said, "How about one of you come up and sing it?" One by one, audience members took the stage to sing verses from the song. One individual did such a good job that Steve let him play a few more songs. While the replacement serenaded the audience with Kilbey compositions, the author of the songs went out to the lobby and ordered a drink, thinking, "What a gig!"

Ever since then, Steve's solo concerts have been an "anything goes" affair—usually with no set list, minimal rehearsal, and maximum audience participation. The shows are either spectacular successes or monumental failures, but they're never boring.

Steve also took the opportunity to finally record a full set of songs with Karin. The resulting album, titled "Charms and Blues," was released under the name Curious Yellow—a pseudonym Karin used for all of her musical projects, with or without Kilbey.

Sonically there were some similarities with *Hex*; once again Steve played most of the instruments and co-wrote most of the tracks, though he ceded the lyrical reins (for the most part) to Karin. But because of Karin's heavy Swedish accent and somewhat limited vocal range, "Charms and Blues" is a more challenging listen than the Donnette collaboration. Still, some people prefer Curious Yellow to Hex. Longtime fan Ernst Kok says, "I think Karin Jansson is to us what Nico was to Velvet Underground fans. I love her Swedish-accented voice; it has this crushed, almost broken quality. It reminds me of Marianne Faithfull. I can listen to that album over and over again."

When the Church met up in Sydney in mid-1989 to begin writing new material, Steve's heart wasn't in it. The band dutifully jammed out some new songs, but musically the material was a retread of everything that had gone before.

Steve remained much more interested in the new solo album he was recording than in the Church project. In fact, he would come home from Church rehearsals every night, switch on his new eight-track reel-to-reel, and really get to work. Whereas the Church material felt locked into the tried-and-true format of two guitars, bass and drums, the solo material was all over the map. Steve felt free to explore different rhythms and more complex melodies. On one track, "No Such Thing," he even ventured into the realm of rap. He often recorded late into the night and then showed up for the Church sessions the next morning physically exhausted and creatively drained.

It was in this atmosphere of malaise and distraction that the next Church album, *Gold Afternoon Fix*, was written. Steve explains:

> After the success, no one really cared. We just sort of drifted along and everything we did was sort of half-assed. Half-hearted. Like, "oh yeah, let's write a song. Sounds alright. Sounds like us." And someone would go, "you should go back and record" and we'd be like, "yeah, alright." "We gotta do this video." "Yeah alright, we'll do it."
>
> And for me, I had made a load of money, I had a load of things going on in my personal life. I was buying new instruments and doing things at home. I was far more interested in writing *Remindlessness* [solo album]

that I was in *Gold Afternoon Fix*. Going in with the Church every day was such a drag. Ploogy mucking about. It was like our brief moment of success de-motivated us.

It's like one of those classic things where a wrestler has just knocked his opponent out and he's lying on the floor, and instead of finishing him off and getting the count, he jumps up on the ropes and sort of taunts the audience. Meanwhile the guy on the ground comes back to life, jumps up and throttles him. That's pretty much what we did.

We were like, "ah, we've made it, we're there to stay, this is our destiny," you know, things will look after themselves from now on; we don't even have to try.

The new Church songs weren't bad per se. All of the requisite hooks were in place. Even on autopilot Steve could produce some interesting material. For lyrical ideas, he returned to his esoteric interests, chiefly the occult, mythology, and ancient history. Whereas the lyrics for *Starfish* had felt personal and intimate, these new songs seemed rather cold and impersonal—trading the relationship themes and social commentary for fanciful science fiction ("Terra Nova Cain") or pithy character portraits ("You're Still Beautiful")—with one major exception. The song "Pharaoh," which became the album's leadoff track, featured a strident opening verse that was anything but veiled:

Hi to all the people who are selling me
Here's one straight from the factory
They sew my eyes up in my sockets
I dip my hand into their pockets.

And later in the song: .

One big man with a big connection
Takes the whole damn ship in the wrong direction
I don't mind him misinterpreting me
I hate it when he gets us lost out to sea

This could be a jab at either Clive Davis or Mike Lembo, though Steve has never explicitly identified the target; the most he will say is that "Pharaoh" is a case of the Church "biting the hand that feeds."

The recording of *Gold Afternoon Fix* was unnecessarily drawn out be-

cause Arista demanded demos of all the tracks before the official recording process could begin. This may have been in order to save time and
money during the actual cutting of the album with paid producers, but
the added requirement of setting down an entire rough draft of the album
suggested a lack of confidence in the band and virtually ensured that the
four musicians—so dependent on that elusive spark of creative spontaneity—would be completely sick of the material by the time the recording
sessions commenced.

In hindsight, the demo recordings are notable because they captured
the last full sessions that Richard Ploog would do with the Church. Even a
cursory listen to these demos reveals that the once solid drummer was on
shaky ground: the beats are tentative; the tempo changes arbitrary. At some
points the old Ploog shines through, but more often he sounds as if he is
about to drop his sticks.

These tracks also offer a rare glimpse into Steve's revision process.
Normally he didn't do much (if any) revising between the composition
and recording phases of an album (continuing to adhere to his "half hour"
rule), but the huge gap in time between the writing and final recording of *Gold Afternoon Fix* allowed him the opportunity to pare down the
songs, trimming away excess verbiage and altering small details. The track
"Laughing," in particular, benefitted from this; it went from four verses,
four choruses, and a staggering four bridges in the rough draft to three
verses, three choruses, and one bridge on the album. The first version is
bloated and repetitive; the final version is lean and builds on a pivotal emotional admission: "I understood before I knew / I realized I'd spend my life
coming back to you."

Once the demos were approved, it was back to Los Angeles for three
months in late 1989 to record the album. Not wanting to change a winning
formula, Arista teamed the band with the production team of Greg Ladanyi
and Waddy Wachtel again, overriding the band's wish to work with ex-Led
Zeppelin bassist John Paul Jones.[11]

---

[11] According to Steve, Jones took a liking to the members of the Church and even had
them over for dinner a few times. Then, inexplicably, he dropped out of the running.
Only years later did Steve discover that the Church's label and management, fearing a
Jones / Church collaboration might turn out too artsy and uncommercial, had vetoed the
venerable musician in favor of the safer (and commercially tested) Wachtel and Ladanyi.

This time, however, what had once been new and interesting had become stale. Years later, writing for the *Shadow Cabinet* web site, Marty summed up the awkward nature of this pairing:

> For them the objective was a succinct, simple, contemporary guitar band that could also get in the charts. (Producers seem to like the idea of themselves as hit makers.) . . . Greg was all Fleetwood Mac and Jackson Browny and Waddy was all AC/DC and Keith Richardsy and we were all psychedelic and moody. Strange Brew! Waddy was always trying to get us to . . . play a groove that *he* felt, whereas we were less restrained, and if an echo was slightly out of time somewhere it wouldn't really matter. It was our glorious synchronised chaos.

This push-and-pull escalated to the point where the relationship between the band and the producers became openly antagonistic. Because Ploog seemed unable to keep a beat, Wachtel recorded him playing small sections of the songs and then looped those recordings. The band would then record to the looped drum tracks rather than Ploog's live playing.

Steve got an apartment with Donnette, which caused further tension between Steve and Richard; according to Donnette, Richard—somewhat illogically—blamed her for the band being in L.A.

Donnette and Steve, 1989 *(Courtesy, Donnette Thayer)*

There was little joy in the official recording sessions for *Gold Afternoon Fix,* and for that reason the original demos—despite all their roughness and rhythmic shakiness—are more enjoyable to listen to than the finished album.

That being said, *Gold Afternoon Fix* should hardly be dismissed outright. In subsequent years, Steve and Marty would disparage the album, and the band's fans duly echoed their view. They have a point; certainly the production lets the material down. The live drumming is sorely missed, and the cold, mechanical feel of much of the record has much to do with that absence.[12]

---

[12] Marty wrote on *Shadow Cabinet* about how the stilted recording process had effectively killed one of his favorite tracks: "['Grind'] was a fantastic recipe that was really badly cooked using a lot of synthetic ingredients when the fresh vegetables were left in the cupboard."

Still, the songs themselves have much to offer. "City," "Disappointment,"
and "Metropolis" all conjure the image of a futuristic gilded age—a new
Babylon slowly imploding amidst the dusty, gold-flecked ruins of an ancient, sprawling city. The album never quite kicks into high gear, preferring instead to drift in eddies of austere, unassuming instrumentation. The
once ubiquitous Rickenbacker 12-string is almost nowhere to be heard.

Gold Afternoon Fix was certainly a puzzling detour after Starfish. Many
fans of the earlier album rejected the follow-up as a failure. One Minneapolis
reviewer declared it an unfortunate descent into the dreaded realm of
"soft rock." But the album managed to cast its own peculiar spell on those
who gave it a chance. Harper Piver, a modern-dance choreographer from
Wilmington, North Carolina, explained to me her enthusiasm for Gold
Afternoon Fix:

> I just loved the fact that the album seemed so completely of another
> world. It was a real mystery—nothing else sounded like it. I'd never heard
> Starfish, so I had nothing to compare it to, but I had Gold Afternoon Fix in
> my Walkman for that entire summer. It was my soundtrack for a while.

And longtime fan Patrick Boulay regards Gold Afternoon Fix as the
Church's best work to that point, and has his own theories as to why Steve
is cold to it:

> You know what I think it is about Gold Afternoon Fix that annoys Steve
> so much? It was supposed to be the huge follow-up to Starfish and it
> didn't sell as well. Plus the Ploog factor. Plus, he probably resents all the
> marketing shit they had to do (the album cover, etc.) where they look
> like alt rock stars. Still, the music is exceptional and I think it's their most
> varied album. Shit, "Grind" is on it, and it's unstoppable.

19
LOST MY TOUCH

Seeing the band live in 1990 may have been an awakening for me and other recent converts, but for the band members themselves it was a time of disillusionment. Because of the earlier success of *Starfish*, public expectations for the follow-up were high. As a result, *Gold Afternoon Fix* sold well on its release in April 1990, and critics gave it respectable—if not ecstatic—reviews. Jim Sullivan's piece in the *Boston Globe* summed up the general feeling: "This is a gentle, agitated, ingratiating record. Its moody charm grows with repetition." *Rolling Stone* once again praised the band, though writer Chris Mundy pointed out the album's chief shortcoming when he said, "[T]he band refuses to break new musical ground, choosing instead to explore further the sound garden it has so meticulously cultivated." David Messer, writing for the Australian *Rolling Stone*, offered a similarly backhanded compliment:

> Despite the pretentious mysticism of their lyrics, despite their outmoded pseudo-Sixties dress sense, despite the fact that their singer has little more than a three-note range, despite the fact that they've been playing the same kind of music for over a decade, I can't help liking almost everything the Church do.

Gold Afternoon Fix may have received respectful treatment, but it was obvious to everyone that the album was a disappointment—the press liked rather than loved it.

When it came time to tour *Gold Afternoon Fix*, Steve, Peter, and Marty were finally forced into a decision about Richard. His recent studio playing had made it clear that he could no longer perform at the high level they required from one another. "It was just time," Steve says.

> He had to go. He didn't really fight very much when he went. We had two bad choices there, and we just took one of them. It was bad how we dealt with it, but after the success, no one cared.

The band replaced Richard with Jay Dee Daugherty, Patti Smith's longtime drummer. Initially, it was hoped that Richard might regain focus after a "sabbatical," and so the change was announced as a temporary one. Jay Dee proved to be everything that Richard had not been in recent years: rock solid in his timing, dependable, enthusiastic, a professional in every sense of the word.

Just as they had done with *Starfish*, the band embarked on a world-wide tour. However, this time the entire itinerary was crammed into a hectic four-month period. The shows were musically very proficient; many of the *Gold Afternoon Fix* songs came alive onstage in a way they hadn't on the album—particularly "Essence," which often culminated in an over-the-top guitar shredding.

Jay Dee Daugherty *(Brian Smith)*

The experience of playing with the versatile Jay Dee temporarily brought back a little of the band's spark. Steve and the new drummer also hit it off quite well on a personal level. "He's a wonderful man," Steve says. "Everything about him was wonderful. It was a real honor to play with him, and it gave the group a little bit of a dying breath to finish the tour. We never could have done that tour with Ploog, the way he was going."

Audience attendance for the shows was good, although it was clear to all that the Church had not made many gains; at best they had managed to retain their *Starfish* audience. Also, because of all the middlemen on the payroll, the band did not earn much for its efforts. In addition to a regular tour manager, Lembo had employed a "production manager," who received a handsome salary in return for doing, in Steve's view, absolutely nothing.

"We had, like, fifteen guys on the crew alone," Steve says.

I couldn't even remember all of them, who they were or what they did. On the European leg of the *Gold Afternoon Fix* tour we lost two hundred thousand pounds, guaranteeing that we would never make any money out of our Arista deal. So we had this huge amount of people with huge losses, and the Church just walking around blindly and not thinking anything of it.

On the *Gold Afternoon Fix* tour *(Trevor Boyd)*

After this financial debacle, the Church decided to get rid of Mike Lembo. Steve explains:

Our manager was just sitting back at home, commissioning us at twenty percent—of course, twenty percent before any of the bills got paid. If we had commissioned him after the bills had been paid he might have been a bit more careful about not having a cast of thousands and all the rest of it. We might have thought about it in a slightly cheaper and more economical way. But of course the imbeciles in the Church are really the ones to blame, and perhaps Peter was the only one who was occasionally saying, "What's going on? How much are we earning? Where's the money coming from? Where's it going to?" I think we were all in some kind of numb zone. I think we all knew that it hadn't worked.

In the move to fire Lembo, the Church were egged on by their tour manager, who had witnessed firsthand the consequences of Lembo's decisions. As is typical of the Church, however, they had no exit strategy, and so Lembo's removal opened up a power vacuum and threw the financial and managerial affairs of the band into further chaos.

These various setbacks did not worry Steve much at the time. He did not comprehend just how quickly the Church's American success would end up slipping through their fingers.

I was egotistical enough to think that now that I was up there, I would be up there forever. I wasn't looking at the signals all around me—mediocre reviews, mediocre responses, and mediocre attendance. Mediocre attitude within the band. I thought, "Aw, there's not a big hit on this album, maybe the next one will have a big hit or something." I thought I was around to stay. I didn't think I would be forgotten so soon.

In October 1990, a few months after the completion of the *Gold Afternoon Fix* tour, Steve undertook a solo US tour. Armed simply with a Guild acoustic 12-string guitar, he took his troubadour persona across America, playing small clubs and reconnecting with the joy of performing music. There was no specific album to promote, though two Kilbey-related releases—his second home-recorded collection *The Slow Crack*[13] and his *Hex* collaboration with Donnette Thayer—had recently been released on American independent labels. In its lack of commercial calculation (and massive road crew), this tour was the antithesis of the *Gold Afternoon Fix* traveling juggernaut. It was also just what he needed at this uncertain point in his career—it was just him, his small audience, and their ongoing musical dialogue.

When it was over, Steve returned to Australia and set about releasing the mammoth double solo album he had been working on all throughout the *Gold Afternoon Fix* sessions. Titled *Remindlessness*, it was definitely a labor of love. The songs were brazenly obtuse—there wasn't a radio-friendly moment anywhere on the eighty-minute collection. The eight-track reel-to-reel represented a step forward in sound quality from his *Unearthed* days, but there were still elements of the project that screamed "homemade," particularly the abrasive, herky-jerky drum programming. It was anything but a smooth groove, but the awkwardness of the drums highlighted, in some ways, the dislocation and disaffection in the lyrics. Easily the least accessible thing Steve had ever put out, *Remindlessness* got a lukewarm reception from fans and critics. Still, Steve earned points in the integrity department, further establishing himself as an artist committed to releasing whatever the

---

[13] The Rough Trade US release comprised the Australian *Slow Crack* EP plus three bonus tracks (previously only available on a Red Eye EP), the most notable being "Transaction"—recorded in a studio in New York and featuring Donnette Thayer on "swan guitar." Interestingly, the song was co-written by Karin Jansson.

hell he felt like, expectations be damned.

If Steve had thought his life was already complicated enough, it was about to become even more so. Having only just begun to settle back into the routine of his life in Australia, he was faced with a new, unexpected development: Karin announced she was pregnant—with twins.

The birth of his daughters Elektra and Miranda brought responsibilities that terrified Steve. He made an effort to embrace his new role as a father and try to integrate it with his life as a working musician, and indeed there were many moments when the realization that he had helped bring these two lovely girls into the world filled him with reverence and awe.

However, when domestic life became too demanding, Steve chose to throw himself more deeply into his work—specifically the release and promotion of a new project titled Jack Frost: a collaboration with Grant McLennan of the Go-Betweens.

The pairing of Kilbey and McLennan was a somewhat odd one. Steve envied Grant because the Go-Betweens were a perennial critics' favorite. True, they had only sold a fraction of the records that the Church had, but they had artistic credibility in spades. Writer David Hutcheon explained the appeal: "[T]hey created a template for literate, mature pop songs . . . . Once you fall for the small-town dramas of 'Streets of Your Town' or 'Was There Anything I Could Do?,' devotion is almost always total." The Church, by contrast, rarely elicited this type of passion outside of their fan base. It seemed the Go-Betweens were one of those anointed bands who, like the Velvet Underground, were not commercially successful, but ended up being written about a great deal. Along with co-frontman Robert Forster, McLennan was often praised as a gifted writer whose songs possessed an intellectual depth unusual in the pop genre.

Steve coveted this kind of acclaim, and he had come to realize that—in McLennan's case, at least—it was justified. In personal demeanor, Grant was intelligent, polite, and unassuming—a soothing presence and a welcome counterpoint to Steve's rougher edges. Like Steve, though, Grant was a walking bundle of contradictions. Ostensibly more a "man of the people" than Steve, who enjoyed nothing more than the chance to while away the afternoon in a seedy bar, Grant also had a certain prissiness about him; he could not stand vulgar jokes and excessive profanity. Taking a cue from

Grant McLennan and Steve Kilbey *(Michael Barone/Dana Valois)*

Steve's family, Grant always referred to his new friend as "Steven."

What solidified the bond between the two men was heartbreak. Grant was still brooding over the breakup of his relationship with fellow Go-Between Amanda Brown, which had coincided with the breakup of the band itself in 1989. And despite the fact that Karin would soon give birth to Steve's children, Steve continued to be deeply torn between her and Donnette; indeed, his indecision was causing him to lose both of them. The songs Kilbey and McLennan began writing directly reflected the melancholy they were both feeling. The end result was a disjointed but oddly compelling collection of forlorn love songs, peppered incongruously with Kilbey surrealism.

Released in Australia by Red Eye, *Jack Frost* was picked up by Arista for American release in an attempt to squeeze a few last drops out of the Church franchise. The album received fair to positive reviews but failed to connect with a large audience. Part of the problem may have been that the two songwriters' styles were too widely divergent to be reconciled comfortably. This was especially frustrating because both men contributed some of their finest melodies and most memorable turns of phrase to the album.

Overall, *Jack Frost* is a fascinating, disjointed mess, scattered as all hell but undeniably alive. Grant enjoyed the experience enough to agree to a second collaboration, yet in interviews he sometimes had difficulty taking ownership of the results. He told the American zine *B-Side,* "It took on a life of its own. It deserted us. It controlled us. We didn't have anything to do with it." It is perhaps telling that in subsequent years, Steve frequently included songs from *Jack Frost* in his solo sets and Church performances, whereas Grant never played them on his own.

Unlike the Church, which aspired to the status of a democracy but largely remained a banana republic (with "Under the Milky Way" as the chief export), Jack Frost was a true collaboration, a fifty-fifty split in every way. Almost every song featured alternating lead vocals from both singers—something which had never been done in the Church and rarely in the Go-Betweens. The album was made purely out of love, and for that reason alone Steve remembers its creation as one of the most enjoyable experiences of his musical career.

20

YOU MAKE ME DRIFT UP AND FLOAT, AND FALL LIKE A STONE

Heroin is a concentrated high. It's like you close your eyes and you can see a whole lifetime. In three seconds you're on the nod. Behind your eyes you've entered this incredible fantasy world. You could have gone to war and met a woman and raised children and become old and died and been buried. And then you open your eyes up and it's a couple of seconds later. It does these time shifts—in the beginning. In the end there was none of that. There was no attempt. I wasn't even looking or thinking or dreaming of getting anything like that. It was purely a cold hard necessity that I had to have, otherwise I'd fall apart. In the beginning, before I was a complete addict, before I'd started shooting it, before my body had developed a tolerance for it, it really put me in a good creative place, with the ideas coming out of the seams. Effortless. I felt like, if I had some heroin, everything I touched would turn to gold.

—Steve Kilbey, July 2004

Steve began using heroin in late 1990, during Karin's pregnancy.[14] It has struck many observers as odd that, having scrupulously avoided heroin and other intravenous drugs throughout his career, he would suddenly begin

---

[14] Many people assume because of the title *Gold Afternoon Fix* that Steve was already using heroin during the making of that album, but that is not so. The title derives from the stock market term referring to the price that is set daily for buying gold.

using in his mid-thirties—at the very moment he was about to become a father. Russell Kilbey offers the succinct observation: "Steve wasn't ready to have kids at that point." Steve himself explains it this way:

> At the age of thirty-five, I had every material thing I wanted. I was comfortable and I'd had this taste of success in America and it disoriented me. Half of me wanted more, and the other half was just like, *You're kidding.* So I was divided right down the middle. My soul was going, *No way,* and my brain and body were going, *More, more, more.*
>
> Up until then I had had a code. It was something I didn't even think about; it was like, *No heroin.* That was just not on. And then eventually, a friend of mine who was very mild-mannered, easygoing—I mean, if it had been some wild . . . if it had been Angry Anderson from Rose Tattoo, or Michael Hutchence, or someone like that, I would have been like, *No*—but the guy I was with was sort of a collegy, mild guy [who] you take home to meet your mum. And one night he said, "I'm gonna get some heroin. Do you want some?" And I was like, *Wow, yeah. Right on. What have I got to lose?*

The sound of *Priest=Aura,* the Church album that followed *Gold Afternoon Fix,* owes a large debt to *Papaver somniferum,* the opium poppy. Steve ingested it in the distilled form of heroin, but the other band members took their share of it in its classic incarnation: opium, the drug of the Romantic poets.

This all came about due to a connection the band had scored during its 1991 "Jokes, Magic & Souvenirs" tour of Australia in support of the video compilation, *Goldfish.* Tasmania, an island off the southeast coast of the Australian mainland, is home to one of the world's largest crops of opium poppies, second only to Afghanistan. Officially it is grown for the pharmaceutical industry—morphine and codeine are both derived from these poppies. But opium can also be relatively easily extracted from them (unlike heroin, which has to be processed), and the Church's source, a Tasmanian fan, had access to the plants. An arrangement was set up whereby the Church would deposit $200 into the connection's bank account, and three days later a shipment of film canisters full of liquid opium would show up on the band's doorstep.

"I remember standing there writing songs," Steve says, "and several members of the band having [a] canister like a feed bag round their nose with their tongues in it, licking the stuff out. Of course, the others who had even a very mild flirtation with these things stopped, and I kept going."

Opium use has some prominent side-effects which doubtlessly made for an interesting studio experience. Often, a few hours after ingestion, the user experiences a wave of extreme nausea which can only be alleviated by lying down or sitting absolutely still (presumably the Churchmen used the tried-and-true anti-nausea remedy of marijuana to take some of the edge off this.) Also, at around the same time as the nausea kicks in, the user begins to itch all over. This can last for several hours. In the opium dens of the late nineteenth century, it was not unusual to find one opium smoker joyfully scratching the back of another, usually a complete stranger. On the far more negative side of things, opium paralyzes the bowels, leading to constipation, and also makes it extremely difficult to urinate. For all the joyous musical experimentation that went on during the *Priest* sessions, there was probably some physical discomfort, too.

The effect of opium on the brain is quite similar to that of heroin, only the euphoria is more subtle: there isn't nearly the same headlong rush as that produced by the more potent, refined H. And while opium was considered for many centuries to be a dangerously addictive drug, the horrors of the modern age have rendered it rather quaint (though opium withdrawal remains a harrowing experience). In other words, for all its seductive and sometimes dangerous properties, opium can't hold a candle to the darker specter of smack. If opium is a warm, softly glowing flame, heroin is an all-consuming, brightly blazing forest fire.

Steve credits the fluid, rhythmic sound of *Priest=Aura* to the band's use of opiates. For the first time, the Church actually sounded sexy—not in the stilted, self-conscious style of the earlier "The Night Is Very Soft," but in a truly languorous, organic rhythm of sensuality. Gone was the impression of a drummer tied unnecessarily to a 4/4 click track. Jay Dee's beats interwove with Steve's bass lines, the two instruments of the rhythm section making love to one another throughout every song. Steve explains,

[It was] the opium. I had really become aware of the concept of bass. *Heyday* was much higher sounding. Up until then, except for *The Blurred Crusade*, we'd never really had an album that was sonically quite right. Jay

Dee also deserves a lot of credit for that. He and I definitely locked in more and started becoming more rhythmic. I was becoming a better bass player.

Another reason for the change in bass sound was the fact that Steve now played exclusively on a Fender six-string bass, allowing him access to a more dynamic range of notes than had been possible on a four-string. Also, because the strings on the Fender VI are so close together, Steve began playing with a plectrum, which gave him a sharp, precise attack on the notes. He could play full chords on the Fender as well as single notes. "There's a lot of bass on that record," he says. "A lot of bass overdubs doing things you may not think of the bass doing."

The afterglow the album seems to have left in the minds of some of the participants belies the fact that the recording process for *Priest* was not entirely harmonious. Ever since *Heyday*, the band had claimed to act as a truly collaborative unit, but this was not quite accurate. Sure, they composed together—but if anything came into the mix that Steve didn't like, it was implicitly understood that he had veto power. This uneasy arrangement almost led to a confrontation during the recording of one of *Priest's* more commercially viable songs. Peter Koppes recalls:

> We were recording a solo for the song "Feel" and everybody was there working together—it was a three-part section. The producer was there, I was there with the guitar, Marty was there, and the drummer, Jay Dee, was there knocking things together. We finally got the whole thing happening in one go. We said, "That's amazing." Then Steve said, "I don't think it's really a good part for the song." And I'd gotten to that point where I just got up, put my guitar away. I wasn't going to stay and fuel the discomfort in the room by defending myself or anything, I just thought, "I'm gonna let that comment stink. I'm gonna let that *smell.*" And for a minute or two no one said a word. And then Jay Dee said, "Well, *I* thought it was just the right part for the song." And then the producer said, "You know, I thought it was the right part." And Marty didn't disagree. So Steve said, "Oh, all right then. Okay."

Even in the midst of creating an exciting, groundbreaking project, the tension that had permeated the band since day one remained, and no amount of opium could nullify it.

Talk to the hand *(Michael Barone/Dana Valois)*

★ ★ ★ ★ ★

What really distinguishes *Priest=Aura* from other Church albums is its origi-
nality. With the band's previous releases, it's relatively easy to spot the influences (two scoops of Pink Floyd here, a dash of Television there, just a pinch

of T. Rex, all cooked slowly in a rich Brian Eno broth), but *Priest* seems to have materialized as if summoned by occult means—fully formed, having no artistic mother or father. The closest any critic could get to describing its sound was "a King Crimson for the '90s." But that comparison, while intriguing, is woefully inadequate. One would expect a King Crimson of the '90s—or of any decade—to embrace oddball time signatures and abrupt tempo changes, but *Priest* is a much smoother beast. When matched with a receptive listener, it almost seems to sync itself with that person's heartbeat, ebbing and pulsing so that it becomes part of the circulatory system itself. Everything chugs along in this manner until the blood pressure surges with "Chaos." And at the very moment that the new feelings of discomfort and anxiety that song induces threaten to overwhelm the listener, "Film" arrives to bring things gently back to manageable levels.

It's easy to see why the Church went for broke with *Priest=Aura*. *Gold Afternoon Fix* had been a concession to the record company, an attempt to give the people what the band thought they wanted, and it had failed. It had sold respectably—over 250,000 in the USA, for example, on the back of the success of *Starfish*—but it hadn't lit a fire in the way that *Starfish* or *The Blurred Crusade* had. If there was to be any future for the band, the musicians themselves had to take the reins.

So it was back to Sydney, back to EMI's Studio 301. No more L.A. and no more of Arista's people calling the shots. The Church brought in a producer of their own choosing—Gavin MacKillop—and got to work.

In addition to showcasing the solid rhythm section of Steve and Jay Dee, the album also finds Marty and Peter playing at a new level of synergy. No longer is there any push or pull between the two guitarists. In fact, the guitar parts weave together so well that it is impossible to tell who is playing what.

Lyrically, Steve approached the album as a culmination of everything he had been working towards since he first began writing. Here he proudly delves into all his favorite subjects: alienation, shifting states of consciousness, love, loss, ancient history, sin, sorcery, and reincarnation—and that's just in the first three tracks. Some songs, like "Kings," contain all of these at once, juxtaposing biblical imagery with jarring modern terminology. Steve is quite proud of this song and likes to single out two lines in particular: "Herod nods beneath the palms / Holds poor baby in his arms." "You can pick up on that and follow those implications," Steve says now:

. . . that Herod finally gets his hands on baby Jesus and he can finally do whatever he likes, but he's had a fix and he's fallen asleep with the kid in his arms. You can analyze it and enjoy it on that deeper level, but if you don't want to do that, you don't have to. It's not knocking you over the head or giving you a load of dates or figures or boring facts. Some critics would probably like it better if I said, "Johnny nods beneath the palms." If you say Herod or Nebuchadnezzar, they'll say, "Oh, I don't want to hear that, it's like school."

The juxtapositions in the lyrics of "Kings," crooned over Marty's digitally-delayed electric-guitar riff, create the sort of disorientation one might experience with time travel. Lines like "shutter speed the bleeding leaves," "stars burn cold beneath the glass," and "Nebuchadnezzar's parking zone" don't make a lick of linear sense but somehow manage to transport the listener elsewhere. And, while the album is not entirely free of Kilbey lyrical clunkers ("Strike while the irony's . . . [dramatic pause] . . . hot!", "Adrenaline is not my mistress," etc.), for the most part Steve manages to juggle his disparate ideas well—blending the anachronisms so smoothly, and singing the lines so earnestly that it begins to seem perfectly reasonable that Herod would be a heroin addict and Nebuchadnezzar would have his own parking space. This is the beauty of *Priest=Aura*. It is a sonic document of that exciting moment when the band ascended to a new level of creative possibility. It stands alone.

So why was the album such a commercial flop? The disparity between fans' reverence for *Priest=Aura* and the general public's reception of the album when it was released in April 1992 is striking. To the faithful, *Priest* ranks alongside *Sgt. Pepper's Lonely Hearts Club Band* and *Exile on Main Street* as a pivotal rock album. To everyone else, it's one of those records that swelled the used bins of record stores everywhere for years after its release, one of the most sold-back albums of the 1990s.

Why this vast gulf? For starters, the Church's casual listeners—the folks who had snapped up *Starfish* in droves—had certain expectations of the band. Ideally, they wanted the Church to deliver more shimmering pop gems like "Under the Milky Way" and "Reptile." They wanted hooks, harmonies, and jangly guitars. When *Priest* delivered longer, atmospheric pieces in a progressive rock vein, the broader public's rejection was swift and absolute. Very few people appreciated what Steve was trying to do with his lyrical telescoping because very few people took the time to listen to what he was saying. And when the promisingly catchy opening chords of "Ripple" segued into the downbeat chorus, this fickle mass of listeners reached—as if in unison—for the stop button.

The critical reaction was more forgiving—but only just. *Rolling Stone*—previously the band's biggest champion in the US—gave the album a mere two stars. Ira Robbins wrote:

> Background noise can't dissipate the album's arid atmosphere or its occasional resemblance to Seventies progressive rock. In tone and temperament, *Priest=Aura* has all the warmth of an undertaker.

Entertainment Weekly's reviewer, Gina Arnold, was more enthusiastic:

> [Kilbey's] evocative use of language, combined with the thick swirl of coguitarists Marty Willson-Piper and Peter Koppes, creates a satisfying sound that could easily suspend any listener's initial disbelief.

And back in Australia, Dino Scatena, writing in *Juke,* seemed one of the few to completely "get it," writing:

> The journey begins with long, wavering strings. They whisper to you, invite you to enter the mystical unknown.
> In a few moments, your world explodes in color and beauty: time becomes muddled, irrelevant. You float through lands of fantasy, meander through kaleidoscopic states of consciousness and emotion.
> The trip ends without warning, throwing your hazy mind back into the lifeless, colorless real world; your soul left craving for me.

For me personally, *Priest=Aura* came along at just the right time. It represented, in a very real way, childhood's end; it was released just as I prepared to leave home for college.

The album disappointed me at first, since it departed even further from the hooks that had drawn me to the band in the first place. But when its spell finally began to take hold, after three or four listens, it did so with a vengeance. I eventually saw it as the band's rebirth, its reinvention. Since I too was about to reinvent myself in a new location, living on my own for the first time, *Priest* became my soundtrack, just as *Starfish* had years earlier.

The music was certainly darker than before. I had no way then of knowing the changes that had taken place in Steve Kilbey's life since the last LP, but it seemed to me the sound of a hard-won maturity, tainted somewhat by a corresponding loss of youthful idealism. Even with my blinkered adoration of the band, I realized that *Priest=Aura* was probably not going to do well commercially. Well, no matter; it was my own private treasure.

Perhaps the thing I loved most about the album was how it felt like one unified composition rather than fourteen individual songs. And of course it passed my litmus test for a great Church CD: I could listen to it while lying on the floor with the lights off and it would transport me to other places and other times. "Chaos" seemed to me the most sonically adventurous piece, and "The Disillusionist" the most lyrically intriguing. I spent a lot of time trying to figure out how much of Steve Kilbey's personality was in the title character, since the song dealt with a rock star who had a singular power over his fans and sometimes exploited that power. If the song was autobiographical, it brought with it large helpings of self-loathing: "His skin looks like he slept in it/or had something rotten kept in it," "They say that he's famous from the waist down/But the top half of his body is a corpse." The song also pointed out how the star himself could be exploited by fans desperate to come in contact with what they perceived to be a more exotic life.

So it was with *Priest=Aura* in my Walkman (and Kerouac's *On the Road* under my arm) that I headed off to college. There would, of course, be much star-chasing and soul-searching in my future.

★ ★ ★ ★ ★

Peter Koppes left the Church after the two-week tour of Australia in support of *Priest=Aura* in October 1992. He had already decided to leave well before the final show, but the fact that the band earned zero dollars for the tour after all expenses were paid confirmed his decision to depart. His primary reason for leaving was that he continued to feel shut out of the creative process—a long-standing complaint that stretched back at least as far as the *Seance* days, if not further.

"With 'As You Will' [from the *Heyday* sessions], I was given one hour to sing that at two o'clock in the morning before we started mixing the album. The song was treated as a B-side from the outset." Peter explains.

> I wasn't really invited to sing another song until "New Season" [on
> *Starfish*] which was treated the same way . . . Once again I had an hour to
> sing it. And they sped it right up. I wasn't very happy with it either. But
> I didn't have the courage to defy anybody particularly. I didn't feel that I
> had any support to do that. I was just pleased that I had a shot at doing [a
> song]. You know, I left the band for good reasons. And that's probably one
> of them: I never felt like I was given the same respect.

Audience recordings exist of nearly every show from the *Priest* tour, and the results are musically uneven. Many Church fans have probably seen the video recording of the Enmore Theatre show (released by the band themselves in 2001); this video—a poor recording of a poor performance—has prompted many to write off the entire tour as a disaster, but it is only a snapshot of one bad night. A few nights earlier, the band had given one of their best performances ever at the National Theater in Melbourne. Fortunately for posterity, an anonymous fan made a high-quality recording of that show, which has been heavily traded ever since.

Listening now to the tape, I am struck by the angry edge to many of the songs. Steve begins the show succinctly, saying "This could possibly be our last time playing here. Anyway, let's get on with it." His singing carries the ragged intensity of some of his earliest performances yet remains, remarkably, on key throughout. (In contrast, on the Enmore video his voice remains flat from beginning to end). Most excitingly, Marty and Peter engage in an all-out guitar war, stabbing back and forth with lean, razor-sharp riffs. Jay Dee undergirds the chaos with precision and power. This is a case of the Church channeling its internal strife into a truly compelling and enthralling performance. And, happily, the band is bolstered by an excellent PA balance, allowing Steve's vocals to come through loud and clear. The lucky few who witnessed this show saw their favorite group go out (or so it seemed at the time) on the highest of high notes.

After a brief period of soul-searching, however, Steve and Marty decided to carry on the Church name. But there would be some radical changes. Jay

Dee's request to be kept on a fixed wage had become cost-prohibitive, so he was let go. Another money-saving measure was the decision to record the next album at Steve's new studio—a facility he had set up with his *Starfish* profits on the first floor of a three-story house he'd bought in Surry Hills. Canadian songwriter Mae Moore (with whom Steve collaborated on her *Bohemia* album) described this somewhat downbeat setting in the liner notes to her *Collected Works 1989–1999:*

> So, we get to the house and two ex-convicts are living there. The place was crawling with enormous cockroaches and my bed was a mattress on the floor. I'm thinking, *I don't think I can stay here.* It was just a little too dark and there were hypodermic needles. I mean, I was prepared to have a new experience but not quite to actually live in that.

As Steve's heroin use crossed over from its honeymoon phase into full-blown addiction, he took up permanent residence in the Surry Hills abode, leaving Karin and his young daughters in Rozelle. He provided for all his children's material needs, but, for a time at least, he took flight from any emotional responsibilities. The only commitment he continued to honor was his deepening relationship with the sweet paradox, heroin.

And yet, out of chaos came beauty. After his stellar creative work on *Priest*, Steve quickly (and seemingly offhandedly) cranked out his finest solo album: *Narcosis.* Released initially as a five-song EP at the beginning of 1992 and later expanded to include four additional tracks, *Narcosis* captured Steve at the tail end of his smack honeymoon: still reeling from the creative possibilities his new drug of choice offered but also well aware of the darkness ahead.

Ideally, the album should be listened to back to back with *Priest=Aura;* the two are companion pieces. *Narcosis* offers a more personal, less expansive exploration of *Priest*'s major themes, coupled with a very real sense of foreboding. In "Fall in Love," he describes his circumstances in the third person:

> Eventually he could derive pleasure from nothing
> The most lurid pornography or the most holy scriptures
> Failed to arouse him from his stupor, his boredom

These clinical observations are counterbalanced with a plaintive chorus: "Fall in love with me, it's not impossible."

"It was strange to watch myself going down a very predictable route," Steve says now.

> I realized that this was the same path a lot of other low-life people—the type of person I was describing—had taken. I was becoming that—and at the same time I could still stand back and see that I was. Yeah, and seeing how it was going to end up. Now that I think about it, there were more verses [to "Fall in Love"], and there was more to the story. And it went on longer, and when we were mixing it, as a whim—although the engineer and the other people were going, "No no no," I just cut it short and grabbed the faders and said, "That's enough." I think it became too personal from there on in. I think it might have involved children or something.

In the creepy, arresting "Sleep With Me," he implores, over and over, "Sleep with me, why don't you sleep with me? / You should try (being used) / Try to understand."

There is something voyeuristic about listening to *Narcosis*; one gets the feeling one is eavesdropping on another human being's disintegration. Which is also what makes it so compelling: it marks the last straining gasp of pre-addict Steve, immortalized on tape.

21
MORE ABOUT THE BLANK YEARS, IN THE WILDERNESS

Steve sat at a wooden desk in his room at the Surry Hills house, arranging a neat line of heroin on the cover of his hardback edition of *Gormenghast*. He pressed an index finger to his right nostril, bent his head down and vacuumed the line into his lungs. Leaning back, he felt the familiar head-rush as the powder entered his bloodstream. He sighed in contentment.

Sitting next to him, on a small sofa, was Susan—a former doctor who had lost her medical license for stealing morphine from a hospital. She and her boyfriend—a drug dealer just released from prison—had taken up semi-permanent residence at Steve's. As a novice smack user, he did not have the established connections these people had, so the least he could do was give them a place to stay, in return for the steady stream of drugs they brought his way.

Susan watched as Steve leaned back in his chair, a dreamy smile playing across his face. She shook her head and said, "What a waste."

Steve's eyes refocused on the room's other occupant. It seemed like an odd statement to have come from the mouth of Dr. Dope herself.

"What do you mean?" he asked.

"When you snort smack, half of it doesn't even get into your blood; it just passes straight through you. That, Steve, is why God invented the syringe."

"Oh." Steve looked at her for a moment, and then asked, "Will you show me how to do it properly?"

"Sure," she said. "Sure."

Susan reached into her purse and took out a small black case. "But wait a little bit. Wait until you come down. Then we'll dip into this." She opened the case to reveal a hypodermic needle, syringe, a spoon, and a small, balled-up ziplock bag containing a block of white powder.

"You're the doctor," Steve said.

A few hours later, Steve came off his nod to discover that Susan had gone. He found her downstairs, reading a book.

"I'm ready," he said.

"Okay," she said. "There's something else I need to get. I'll see you in your room in a couple minutes."

She appeared in his doorway with a length of surgical tubing. "Right," she said, "just watch what I do." She broke off a bit of the chalky block and placed it on the spoon. To this she added an eyedropper-full of water. Then she flipped up her Zippo lighter and held the spoon over the flame, moving it around slightly so that the heat reached all parts of the mixture. When the chalk and the water had combined to form a brown liquid, she dropped a piece of lint into it. Into this lint she inserted the needle and drew liquid up into the syringe. She tossed the surgical tube to Steve and said, "Tie this around your arm, above the elbow. Tie it tight, as if you were making a tourniquet. Then make a fist."

When Steve had done this, she leaned over him and slowly inserted the needle into a bulging vein on his inner forearm. She pushed the plunger down. Then, with the needle still in his arm, she said, "Untie the tube."

As soon as the tube had fallen from his arm, Steve felt a rush of warmth throughout his body. It was like a long, sustained orgasm affecting his whole being—his head, his heart, his hands, his legs, all the way down to his feet. It was everything he had previously felt from heroin, but concentrated and magnified one thousand percent. Wave after wave washed over him.

"Jesus," he said. "Jesus Christ."

He had a heroin pulse.

From that moment forward the priorities in Steve's life shifted. Family, friends, and music all came a distant second to heroin. The man who had been a late sleeper his entire life now found himself rising before dawn, eager to secure his supply of drugs for the day. During the first few months of his addiction he sent others to get the drugs for him. They all ripped him off, and he accepted that. Although the Church's star was fading rapidly in the early 1990s, it was a good time for Steve financially, as he finally began receiving the bulk of his royalties from the *Starfish* years. He had more than enough money to throw around. For a small, blessed circle of junkies, 1993 was the year that Santa Claus came to town; only their Santa had two earrings, dark, slicked-back hair, and a sci-fi villain's pointy beard. Santa made sure that all the residents of the Surry Hills house were taken care of—from the recording engineer down to the random drifter sleeping on the living-room couch.

It was a good life for a time. And then, imperceptibly at first, the money began to dwindle. The royalty checks shrank and no new revenue streams materialized. Steve started making the drug runs alone, cutting out the middlemen. One by one, the welfare junkies were jettisoned. Within twelve months Santa Claus morphed into Ebenezer Scrooge, hoarding his smack stockpile all to himself.

Before long, musical equipment began mysteriously disappearing from the studio. Steve sold his instruments one week and then bought them back the next, his every action timed to the arrival of those magical royalty checks.

He continued recording throughout this period, churning out a staggering number of projects in addition to his work with the Church. Though the music itself remained pure, the motivating factor was money. And the main purpose of the money was to keep the drugs coming.

When he looks back on this period, Steve tends to denigrate his work on those projects, saying that the drugs kept him from being truly engaged in the work. From the typical perspective of a recovering addict, he says:

> I just wanted to get [the music] out of the way. I just wanted to play whatever they wanted me to play, or write what they wanted me to write . . . I just wanted to get some gear in me and sit on the couch and fall asleep.

But Simon Polinski—a talented recording engineer who worked extensively with Steve throughout the 1990s—begs to differ:

I've worked many a time with people who were doing [heroin], who were just out of it. But he wasn't. He was really *on* it. It didn't affect him the same way as it affects most of the other people . . . [It] didn't affect his work or anything. He'd still roll up to the studio with a clean shirt on. He looks after himself. He was never a scumbag or anything in those days. And I've worked with a few . . . you'd think, "Go and put some deodorant on, will ya?" He's not like that. It's quite unique.

Like many others who have worked with Steve, Simon was astounded by Kilbey's improvisational approach to recording:

He'll sit on a synth that's he's never ever seen before—I've seen him do it— he'll just push (random) buttons and then say, "Okay, roll tape," and he'll do a whole pass of just amazing stuff. Not even in key or anything! Weird sounds, there you go, it's on the track and it sounds perfect. He had all these great ideas, and because he's very eloquent, he can really describe to you what he wants and you understand immediately. He can tell you poetically what he wants. On backing vocals he said, "I want this backing vocal to sound like it's silver, so it's gotta be metallic but yet silky." So he'll describe it and then I'll say, "Something like this?" and he'll say, "Ah, yeah."

But if drugs didn't affect the overall quality of the work, they did directly impede the completion of at least two projects. The first was Mae Moore's *Bohemia*, recorded and released in 1992. Moore, a Canadian singer-songwriter in the Joni Mitchell vein, had been paired with Steve by her management at Sony. It was intended to be a mutually beneficial relationship: Steve could have a hand in a potentially lucrative commercial project, while Moore would get the chance to deepen her art through working with the more artistically adventurous Kilbey. For the first few months the collaboration proved tremendously fruitful. Like Polinski, Moore found Kilbey's approach refreshing and challenging; indeed, she credited him with opening up a whole new approach to her songwriting. But eventually the obstacles posed by Kilbey's addiction proved impossible to surmount. In the liner notes to her *Collected Works* Moore writes:

Kilbey, at that time, was in a bad way; really unreliable. This was at the point when we were getting ready to mix the record . . . Steve just didn't show up for a few days. That's when we got Gavin MacKillop to come down and finish the record. Gavin had worked with Steve before, so there was some continuity there. When Kilbey came back to the studio, he was asked to leave because he was being really destructive. [He] never came back. I was disappointed. I was mad at Steven because of what he was doing to himself with heroin, not so much that he let the project down; I was more concerned for him personally. I was really proud of the songs we'd written together. We had a good working relationship.

Steve later explained his disappearance by saying he had lost creative interest in the project and didn't want to work on "songs about fucking Canada anymore." But later, in 1998, his drug problems derailed a project in which he *was* creatively invested: a collaboration with his old friend Frank Kearns (the former guitarist in Cactus World News.) As Steve remembers:

He had this lovely studio [in Ireland], nice house and everything, and I went over there. And of course I ran out of drugs and I became really sick. Especially made worse by the fact that I had brought two weeks' supply with me that was supposed to last me through the whole thing, and I'd used it all up in the first three days. And instead of making a record—which we were supposed to be doing for three weeks—I think for two of the weeks he just found out about heroin withdrawals and sort of nursed me: running around trying to get prescriptions for sleeping pills and cleaning up where I was sick. It was disgusting—a real shock for him. We had sort of a half-finished thing. Hey Frank, if you're reading this book, I'm sorry! I really let him down. It's a shame. I really ruined that one. The whole thing was such a bad, embarrassing, rotten kind of thing.

Often, however, a miserable recording experience could still yield a great record, as was the case with the second Jack Frost album, *Snow Job*, recorded in 1993. The atmosphere in which this album was created was anything but pleasant, but the results were creative gold.

By the time of Jack Frost's second collaboration, Grant McLennan had also developed a taste for smack, although Steve says that Grant's problem was not as severe as Steve's (a statement borne out by the fact that Grant was able to stop using it not long after the album's completion). At any rate, the two quickly discovered that the honeymoon was over; smack had long since turned on them both. Once a source of heavenly inspiration, it now set them at each other's throats.

"I was like a pig, like a little Gollum," Steve recalls, "I've got my precious!"

> I would turn up and use it and he would be sitting there sick, and I mightn't give him any, or I might just give him a tiny little bit, and stuff like that—borrowing money off of each other, one guy running out to get it and coming home obviously out of it and saying, "Ah, there wasn't any." I was probably worse than him. The first Jack Frost seemed so innocent and so much done for the joy of music, and over this one smack had reared its ugly specter.

Despite this dour assessment, the resulting album was a far more successful fusion of the two artists' disparate sounds than its predecessor had been. Stylistically, *Snow Job* was a throwback to the sunny harmonies and jangly guitars of the Byrds and the Mamas and the Papas, with a slight grunge/punk edge. Once again, Steve and Grant split the vocals fifty-fifty, but this time their lyrics blended rather than clashed. On "Angela Carter" and "Running from the Body" in particular, one gets the impression of the two songwriters rowing in the same direction rather than trying to wrest the song away from one another.

After Grant died unexpectedly of a heart attack in 2006, Steve wrote on his blog:

> the record captures the roiling boiling turmoil
> of those days
> i can hardly bear to listen to it myself
> its agony is apparent
> but it bleeds for you
> and it's a great falling apart record
> a la sister/lovers . . .
> (May 7)

> by christ
> these songs fucking rock, baybee
> listen to grants grreat guitar solos

a lotta pentup energy and raw emotion
he was a sensitive guy who could shake it!!
theres some beautiful songs here
I will no longer avoid this record
(May 9)

★ ★ ★ ★ ★

After several months alone in Rozelle with the kids, Karin got the message loud and clear: Steve had gone AWOL from their relationship and from his parental duties. She made arrangements with her family back in Sweden, and in 1994 she and the kids left Australia and moved back to her home country. Donnette Thayer, whom Steve had left hanging in America, also came to the realization that she had no future with him; his heavy drug use coupled with his emotional inertia ensured that their relationship would always remain stuck in neutral. If either of these developments registered with Steve, however, they didn't affect him—at least not immediately. He pursued his addiction with single-minded ferocity. Everything else was irrelevant.

★ ★ ★ ★ ★

Two interesting, if uneven, Church albums appeared in the period after Peter left the band. The first was *Sometime Anywhere*, released in 1994. This sprawling, somewhat schizophrenic collection of songs featured Steve and Marty playing virtually all the instruments, with supplemental percussion provided by drummer Tim Powles. The versatile Powles, who had opened for the Church numerous times in the 1980s as a member of the Venetians, aspired to join the Church full-time. But Steve and Marty were not interested in adding a permanent drummer. The two remaining Churchmen composed all of the tracks on *Sometime Anywhere* without drums, and only needed Tim to replace some of the mechanical beats with more organic flourishes. For the time being, at least, Tim's work with the band was limited to the studio; Marty and Steve intended to tour the material as an acoustic duo, keeping overheads to a minimum.

Marty had much to gain and little to lose from the newly pared-down arrangement. For one thing, the restructuring of the band put him on an even footing creatively with Steve. With only two members composing and recording all of the music, Marty was able to have greater control over how the songs would sound. He also sang more on this album than on previous efforts, singing lead on "Angelica" and "The Time Being," and alternating verses with Steve on the album's first single, "Two Places at Once."

Dare (formerly known as Andy) Mason, the album's producer, shared some details of this track's inception with Church archivist Trevor Boyd:

> The only piece of music that the guys had prepared for the album were the chords to "Two Places at Once." So we started by recording Marty and Steve both playing acoustic guitar. Marty played bass on that one, I seem to remember, and Tim Powles really brought it to life with his drum part. Quite early on Steve suggested that they share the vocals, which had never happened on a Church song. But not only that, he also suggested that they go away and write two verses and a chorus each without reference to what the other was writing. So really it's two songs in one, hence the title. I was convinced the muses were with us on this one when Steve's chorus fit so well with Marty's when they came together [at the end] of the song.

Sometime Anywhere is perhaps the most frustrating listen in the entire Church catalog. On the one hand, it is easily the band's most ambitious and diverse work, representing a welcome reach beyond psychedelic rock to incorporate elements of flamenco, Middle-Eastern music, techno, and even rap into the sonic mix. There is an undeniable energy to these songs that is exciting to hear. The problem is that very little of it actually hangs together, and most of the songs feel as if they were abandoned halfway through. Some of this may be because Steve and Marty used an old friend to produce the album rather than an outside figure. It's a Catch-22, because Dare clearly encouraged and enabled the two songwriters in their creative risk-taking. However, because of his lifelong friendship with Marty, he may have felt too connected to the material to serve as an effective editor once the ideas were on the table.

"Loveblind" is one of the album's stronger tracks—an intriguing glimpse of an avenue the Church might have explored further had they continued as a duo. Marty provides Spanish-accented acoustic guitar flourishes over an insistent trance beat, while Steve's lyrics tell a Philip K. Dick/Raymond Chandler–style story of a private investigator helping a beautiful client track down her missing husband—a man who has literally lost his face. "I pieced together clue by clue just what a faceless man would do," Steve sings. "Who

would he love, where would he go/Places faceless men might know." After
his fruitless search, the narrator has a surprising epiphany:

> In the mirror in my space, there was a man without a face
> I rang my client and I banged on her door
> I told her it was me that we was looking for

This combination of concrete narrative with elements of magic realism, the whole thing shot through with double entendres, is nothing new for Steve. There's nothing particularly poetic or striking about the lyrics. What *is* striking is that he eschews his normally soporific delivery and sings those lyrics in a dynamic melody worthy of a Sinatra/Riddle collaboration, over music that is both mesmerizing *and* up-tempo. It's audio film-noir—that you can dance to.

Of the other tracks, "Day of the Dead" and "Dead Man's Dream" both represent a furthering of the dreamy *Priest=Aura* space-rock style, albeit with a more stripped-down approach. The absence of Peter and Jay Dee is felt most acutely on "My Little Problem," a beautiful ballad that never quite achieves the sonic liftoff it requires.

The instrumental "Eastern" is an exciting, bracing listen, as is "Lullaby"—in which the three wise men address Mary on the event of Christ's birth. It's a fairly straightforward retelling until the ominous final verse:

> A doom is on the child that I can see
> He don't belong in this time with you and me
> His life will not be very long
> Before you know it he will be gone

Then the final line, sung almost cheerfully: "We've been sent to sing a lullaby for you."

A pair of luminous pop gems—"Business Woman" and "Authority"—arrive late on the album. "Business Woman" has been much maligned by both the band and fans in the years since the album's release, due to the fact that Arista made Steve and Marty include the track on the album (rather than as a B-side) despite their protestations.[15] Nevertheless, it is a fine track

---

[15]Marty ranted about Arista's heavy-handedness to Rey Roldon of *Boston Rock*: "I don't think that it's the record company's business, to tell you the truth . . . They have this theory of 'oh, we wanted the record out more in a pop way,' and then we get intellec-

with beautiful harmonies and wry, tongue-in-cheek lyrics that would not be out of place on an XTC album.

On the downside, songs like "Angelica," "Cut in Two" (included on a bonus disc) and "Lost My Touch" are little more than sketches. In the first two, Marty shrieks, barks and bays some less-than-inspired vocal improvisations over and around Steve's slightly more concrete melodies. One example (from "Angelica") should suffice:

> I've got a verbal caress
> I've got it, I've got it here in my mouth
> And it's here for you
> And I'll share it
> This verbal caress is gonna get wet!

As for "Lost My Touch," the less said about Steve's rapping, the better.

Marty's solo contributions are more successful. "Fly Home" is an extended Pink Floyd-style workout, and the hook-heavy "The Myths You Made,"[16] with its thundering, guitar-drenched chorus, is one of his strongest contributions to the Church oeuvre.

The album clocks in at over 70 minutes, not including *Somewhere Else*, the seven-song bonus CD that came bundled with the first 25,000 copies of the album. What is most irritating about this whole project is that the two discs between them contain at least fifty minutes of really solid material. Had it been edited down to that, the album could have been a strong follow-up to *Priest=Aura*. Instead, the bloated disc seems to exist primarily to give the listener's thumb a workout by repeatedly hitting the skip button.

It can reasonably be argued that, on a personal level, Marty became the band's guiding force during this time. Steve receded into the background somewhat, because of his addiction. He was still there creatively, but the day-to-day responsibilities of running the band—including doing interviews and publicity—often fell to Marty. Steve's love and appreciation for his band-

---

tual journalists calling us up and saying, 'What the fuck is "Business Woman" doing on your album?!' So who's fucking making the right decision there? Arista supports us, tries hard, spends money on us and they're working to make our record successful, but that's a gripe."

[16] Included on the bonus disc rather than the album proper.

Steve and Marty performing as a duo *(Brett Leigh Dicks)*

mate deepened as a result of Marty's support and self-sacrifice.

"Marty bore the brunt of my addiction," Steve says.

> He just tried to do his best with whatever the situation was. He never gave me any ultimatums, he just kept trying. Much more than I thought he would. He really hung in there and was a real rock in my life for a while. There were terrible things like me driving along in America stoned and almost crashing the car once, nodding out. And the opposite, when I couldn't find it and how sick and nervous and hyper everything would be to me. He hung in there.

The guitarist who had once quit the band due to his personal issues with the singer now found himself taking care of him. He carried Steve through the worst period without complaint. The subject is not something they discuss with each other now—they are not sentimental men—but a deep bond exists between Steve and Marty that the others don't share.

Arista seems to have put considerable money and effort into their attempt to make *Sometime Anywhere* a success, though—even with the addition of the pop tracks "Business Woman" and "Authority" on the main disc—the album was largely experimental, with seven of the thirteen tracks clocking in over six minutes in length. It was not an easy sell to commercial radio.

The press were decidedly friendlier to *Sometime Anywhere* than they had been to its predecessor. Tom Lanham of *Musician* magazine wrote, "The once-jangling group has summoned up a surreal, bewitching mood piece somewhere between *Wish You Were Here* and *The Wall*, an album that would play well by candlelight in a hilltop haunted mansion." UK magazine *Q* gave the album three stars and said, "The melodies are too soporific to penetrate deeply but you can still get heavenly-lost in several chorus lifts (the best being the sublime AOR leanings of 'Two Places at Once') and textures that would shame a Persian carpetweaver." *Goldmine* called it "a warm, compelling record," and *Pulse* noted that "the Church may be courting career suicide by downplaying its more accessible instincts in favor of mystery and insinuation. But *Sometime Anywhere* is dense and impressive." All told, these were the best reviews the band had received since *Starfish*. But good press didn't translate to the commercial breakthrough that Arista had been hoping for.

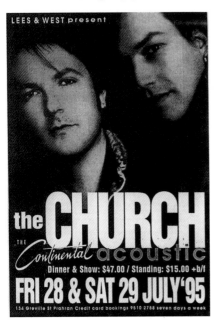

The American tour for *Sometime Anywhere*, in May and June of 1994, was the Church's first time back in the US since the days of *Gold Afternoon Fix*. The experience proved a rude awakening for the pair, demonstrating just how quickly fame can slip away there. Only four years after packing large theaters and halls, they now found themselves performing in much smaller club venues—and it was still not unusual for them to play to a half-empty room. They followed the US leg with similarly scaled-down British and European dates during the latter half of the year, and then swung back through California in January and February of 1995.

As an acoustic duo, the Church was a mixed bag. On the one hand, the stripped-back arrangements permitted greater intimacy; for once, Steve didn't have to shout to be heard above the din of electric instruments and drums. On the other hand, Steve's performances at these shows were wildly erratic, depending on his physical condition. On any given night he was either high or junk-sick. Very occasionally he found a happy medium, and in those instances—such as their performance at the Great American Music Hall in San Francisco in January, 1995—the pair soared, delivering personal, heartfelt versions of songs spanning the band's entire catalogue as well as their solo works. At that particular show, fans got to hear the Jack Frost song "Providence" as performed by Steve and Marty, with the Church guitarist adding new chords and adorning the song with breathtaking lead flourishes that had been wholly absent from the original recording. The duo also performed a hushed, intricate version of "Will I Start to Bleed" from Marty's solo album *Spirit Level*. Both musicians were relaxed and in good spirits throughout the evening, joking with the audience between songs. At one point Steve did a dramatic, off-the-cuff recitation of the lyrics of Free's "All Right Now," investing the words with Laurence Olivier–style gravitas.

In contrast, their set just a few months earlier at the Mean Fiddler in London—featuring many of the same songs—had been essentially dead on arrival; Steve's mind was obviously elsewhere. He was roused only briefly by a fan calling out, "What's with the Captain Kirk haircut?" (Steve was sporting close-cropped, slicked-back hair and pointy sideburns), to which Steve replied, "You look rather like a Klingon yourself."

The higher-ups at Arista, panicking because their once-prized possessions were falling below the cultural radar and the lead singer didn't seem to care, asked Steve to go into rehab. They even offered to foot the bill. Reluctantly, Steve agreed and entered the Betty Ford Clinic during the break between the US and UK legs of the tour. By the time he emerged a few weeks later, Arista had decided to drop the band. Suddenly, for the first time in many years, the Church were without a record contract or any proper management.

Viewed purely from a business standpoint, Arista's decision to let the Church go makes a lot of sense; Steve's increasing reliance on label employees (ostensibly acting on their own) to secure drug connections for him throughout the tour created a legal and ethical headache for the label. And while many in the industry had no trouble turning a blind eye to such things if the musicians in question generated satisfactory profits, the Church's sagging sales had made the band a dubious proposition. Additionally, because of Steve's general lack of interest in the business side of things, he had never gone out of his way to ingratiate himself with the label; he had made no effort to cultivate friendships that might have come in handy at this difficult juncture. With no sense of personal loyalty towards the band, the management at Arista did not agonize too much before giving their former money-makers the heave-ho.

When Morten Skjefte, founder of the *Seance* mailing list, caught up with the duo during their final pass through California, the situation was dire. "The saddest part," he wrote in a subsequent posting, "was to realize the fact that these incredible musicians now are reduced to a small bar-act that have to set up their own gear, hand out flyers and hassle with management about getting paid. There just is no fairness in this business, is there?"

After his stint in rehab, Steve joined Marty for two Church performances at the Borderline in London and then flew to Sweden to reconnect with his daughters. By now, Karin refused to have anything to do with him, but she was very fair about granting access to Elektra and Miranda. For three months Steve stayed clean and played the good father, abstaining from marijuana, alcohol, and even caffeine during this period. This was his first time off heroin and he seemed committed to sobriety as long as none of his drug-using cronies were around. It was a happy period for both Steve and the girls, but all too brief—as soon as he began the European leg of the tour, he missed his daughters acutely. And, detached from his fledgling support system, he quickly fell back into his drug habit.

While the Church were touring in late 1994, an extraordinary album by a group called Fake was released on Mushroom's White Label in Australia. The eponymous release made little impact, and it was not known for some time thereafter that Fake had been a Steve Kilbey project, on which he played all instruments (with the exception of one "Boris Goudenof"—who appeared on many of Steve's side projects in the '90s—on trumpet and electronics), with Sandy Chick (who had previously sung backup on *Sometime Anywhere*) on vocals. Keeping the identities of the musicians secret had been a publicity stunt—it was hoped that the public would be intrigued by this mysterious "supergroup" and buy the album in droves. But this plan backfired disastrously. Not only did the general public take a pass, the majority of Church fans—the album's bedrock audience—also missed out, not realizing *Fake* was a Kilbey endeavor.

Fake took the stylistic fusion of *Sometime Anywhere* a few steps further, adding trumpets and Middle-Eastern accents to the rock/trance/dance hybrid. In terms of lyrics, operating under an assumed identity seemed to free Steve up. It's hard not to read personal overtones into the songs "Back of My Mind" and "I Cannot Feel You." Both can be interpreted as dealing with the complication and disintegration of his relationships with Karin and Donnette, only—interestingly—both songs are from the woman's point of view. Consider this excerpt from "Back of My Mind":

If you fucking think that it's easy for me
To see you in her arms then you're stupid I see
You're talking sweet things, I know what you said
It's the same thing you told me when we were lying in bed

In the back of my mind
I can hear it in the back of my mind
In the back of my mind
I hear your sweet talk in the back of my mind

and from "I Cannot Feel You":

In your presence I feel small
I don't feel I'm there at all
Just a picture on the wall
Tiny boat sinks in the sea
Just the way you sunk in me
Maybe then one day you'll see
That I am not the one you should abandon

On other tracks, such as "Nympho," Steve took the opportunity to lampoon his own famously overwrought, reference-heavy style:

Ivan is so terrible
Attila is a Hun
William wants to conquer me and

Ghengis can have fun
Cause I'm a nympho and I don't care

It's highly debatable whether *Fake* could have been a commercial success, even if it had been promoted properly. It was certainly a lighter and more accessible record than just about anything else in Steve's catalogue. Even so, amidst the catchy dance beats and tuneful melodies there were still many left-of-center elements, such as the instrumental "I'm Sorry Mrs. Hunt There's Been an Accident at the Plant," the quietly menacing "You Gonna Get it Somehow," and the chaotic "Desert Song"—which, with its stomping beat, Middle-Eastern melodies, and wash of background noise could easily have been an outtake from *Sometime Anywhere*. Perhaps it wasn't chart material, but in its successful hybrid of pop music and the avant-garde, *Fake* was a strong effort that deserved a wider audience than it received.

When the Church tour was over, Steve resumed his hectic production schedule. Most of his projects from this period (1995-1996) were recorded at the new Karmic Hit studio in Rozelle, which was much larger than the Surry Hills abode he had recently sold.

Perhaps the most interesting album he produced was Kev Carmody's *Images and Illusions*, an all-star affair whose supporting cast featured Steve, Grant McLennan, Tim Finn (of Split Enz and Crowded House), Andy White, and the Utungun Percussionists. The virtually unclassifiable Carmody—an Aboriginal singer/songwriter who incorporated everything from country to reggae into his politically charged music—found a fertile collaborator in Kilbey. It was a mutually beneficial pairing: Kilbey's talent for providing rich atmospherics suited Carmody's material well, while Carmody's eclectic style pushed Steve—as the album's primary bassist—into musical idioms he not previously explored.

Most significantly, Steve retained the services of the Utungun Percussionists for the next Church album—*Magician Among the Spirits*—which began production following an acoustic "Songwriters' Tour" that sent Steve and Marty around Australia during the latter half of 1995.

The extra space in the new Rozelle studio made it possible for Steve and Marty to set up and play live with Tim Powles rather than jamming separately to pre-recorded drum tracks. Also, Peter Koppes had begun to drift

Steve at Karmic Hit, 1996 *(Andy Voyez)*

back into the picture. His time away from the Church had made him restless, and while he was not yet willing to rejoin his old band, he contributed tasteful "guest guitar" flourishes to several tracks on *Magician Among the Spirits*.

Steve and Marty did not exactly see eye to eye on Peter's reemergence— both were fans of Koppes' style, but Marty felt he could handle all of the guitar duties on his own. And, although it was not stated overtly, Marty was concerned that Peter's return would effectively end his status as equal partner with Steve in the Church. He had worked very hard on behalf of this new version of the Church and believed in it strongly. Around the time of *Sometime Anywhere*'s release he had told *B-Side*'s Sandra Garcia, "The difference between Peter and I, I think, as guitarists [was that] I was able to play as beautifully as him but he wasn't able to play as ugly as I can, you know?" To *Guitar Player,* he said, "The wilder stuff in The Church was always me anyway, because Peter didn't have a wild streak. Peter was soft, which always let me act noisy with the weird noises we have." Steve apparently felt that there *was* room in the mix for Peter's more musical approach, and had extended an invitation to Koppes to participate in the new recordings at whatever level he felt comfortable with.

The prodigal guitarist may have been surprised at what greeted him. Steve's lack of patience—due to his preoccupation with drugs—led him to push his already improvisational recording technique further; the method essentially involved him (and any collaborators) going into the recording studio without previously prepared material and with no preconceived ideas about how the project should sound. They would hole up and not emerge until they had a finished album. The Church had been toying with this technique since *Priest=Aura*, but they now went into overdrive; what once would have taken months would now be thrown together in a matter of days, and the first take was often the one that made it onto the record.

When I interviewed Tim Powles in 1998, the drummer described this unorthodox process favorably:

> I've learned a lot about music through [Steve's] drug use. It's a weird thing to say, but it's true. It's not like I've done a lot myself, it's just I've learned to have to deal with things in a different way. The more drugs someone uses, usually the less patience they have. In the '80s I'd take a week to do the drums for an album. When I first met Steven and started working with him, I learned to do it in a day. That process was an amazingly great thing for me, and it wouldn't have happened if drugs weren't around.

Some of the studio musicians, on the other hand, were taken aback by Kilbey's haphazard procedures. Violinist Linda Neil, who worked on *Sometime Anywhere*, Kev Carmody's *Images and Illusions,* and *Magician Among the Spirits*, recalls, "It was just chaotic . . . Looking back on it I think, My God, how did I do that? They just put me on the spot, threw me in there and said, 'Play!'"

Like the others, however, Neil quickly adapted to the chaos and began to flourish. Indeed, her distinctive playing dominates the albums she appears on. One song on *Magician Among the Spirits*, "Romany Caravan" (for which she received a co-writing credit), was based entirely around her melody line.

> [Steve] wanted me to be involved in the creative process with them . . . That was the impression I got, but I don't think it was thought through. I think they just wanted to throw on a lot of different elements, or that's what ended up happening. I sometimes think he was trying to teach me, you know? Get me my first publishing deal. He was a great supporter of mine; I always appreciated that about Steve.

Magician Among the Spirits, released in Australia in May 1996, is the bastard
cousin of *Priest=Aura*. It possesses the same dizzying atmosphere of experimentation and possibility as *Priest,* but without any of its predecessor's focus
or grandeur. Clearly, heroin was now Steve's albatross rather than his muse.
There is a distinct weariness to his voice throughout the album, a feeling of
junk-sickness captured straight to tape. That being said, *Magician* is not completely downbeat. "Comedown" is the Church's most radio-friendly rocker
since the *Starfish* days—even with Steve singing against the catchy music
of the chorus, "I just can't help wondering / It's such a waste of time"—and
"Ladyboy" is a playful, though perhaps not entirely successful, meditation
on sexual ambiguity.

I have to admit to a real fondness for this album. I love the organic instrumentation and find the band's uninhibited approach to the recording
process exciting and inspiring. It's definitely a musician's record. From a
critical standpoint, though, I acknowledge the album's lack of consistency.
The appropriately named "Grandiose" is, at best, a guilty pleasure—essentially five minutes of guitar wankery, an indulgence the Church would never
have allowed themselves on their early albums. Marty's song "The Further
Adventures of the Time Being," with its lugubrious pace and Yes-reject

Linda Neil and Russell Kilbey at Karmic Hit, 1997 *(Brian Smith)*

lyrics, is execrable. "Why Don't You Love Me"—a song not included on the original album but added to the reissue—qualifies in this writer's mind as the worst Church song ever, thanks to its purple prose, annoying vocal effects, and lack of any discernible melody.

It's easy to see why *Magician Among the Spirits* did not revive the Church's career. In fact, the album very nearly ended it. The band entered into a convoluted agreement to self-release *Magician* on their own label, Deep Karma, to be manufactured by Mushroom and distributed by Mushroom's White Label in Australia and in America by a company called Feedback. This turned out to be perhaps the biggest debacle in the Church's long list of bad business decisions, because Feedback went bankrupt after they had paid Mushroom only one-fifth of the amount they owed for the 25,000 copies of the CD they had received. Accounts vary as to what went wrong, but all sides seem to have been at fault in some way. Clearly the band took some very bad advice from manager Bruce Butler, who convinced them they would see a large amount of money up front from Feedback. Brian Smith from the *Shadow Cabinet* web page recalls Butler stating confidently that the Church had fifty or sixty thousand fans who would buy anything they re-

The master-tape rack at Karmic Hit, 1997 *(Brian Smith)*

corded, and that alternate online sources of information (the *Seance* e-mail list and *Shadow Cabinet*) could be relied on as a conduit to this fan base.

One major problem was that the contract did *not* guarantee the Church a large sum up front. Feedback were to pay the Church for the 25,000 CDs over a 120-day period. But things began to go bad for the company after the first payment was made, and the Church never saw the rest of the money. It's not clear whether the band even received that first payment, which may have been retained by Mushroom to cover *their* costs. In effect, the Church paid to have 25,000 CDs pressed and given away.

There is disagreement amongst the former employees of Feedback regarding that organization's culpability. Brian Dwyer—who worked there during this period—wrote to *Shadow Cabinet:*

> [Feedback] was not interested in putting any money or promotion into *Magician Among the Spirits*. There were no posters, stickers, radio play, etc. I volunteered my free time to put up posters (if they would make some) in record stores and go to radio stations to get some airplay but they were not interested. I have a lot of contacts in the music biz in Chicago that

could have helped a little but that would have been better than nothing. [Feedback] simply didn't give a shit.

Richard Godwin, the company's ex-CEO, countered with the assertion that marketing and promotion had been primarily the responsibility of the band's management:

> The Church's management were to provide ALL of the promotional marketing through two promotion companies, one on the West Coast and one on the East coast. They were also to handle all of the print media marketing to all of the big magazines, etc. We agreed on a street date which we stuck to. The band were supposed to have all of the marketing assets in place by this date. After calling and faxing the band and management for a whole month (at Mushroom) we were finally told that the band was on the road and their management was incommunicado. SIX weeks after the CD was released in the States we were called by Scott Murphy at Mushroom and told that they did not have any marketing companies in place and did we know of anybody good that we could recommend. Total incompetence!!

Christopher Prescott, a lawyer who looked at the contracts, split the difference in a public posting to Godwin:

> It is true that Mushroom and Deep Karma [the Church's own label] didn't "have any marketing companies in place" and that the contract provides that they should have done so, with one based in New York and another in Los Angeles. But the contract also provides that the marketing was to be arranged by Feedback "in consultation with Label and Mushroom." Is it any wonder that an Australian exporting company called Feedback for help in recommending a marketing company? You did say that this was "SIX" weeks late (though the contract doesn't set any time deadlines for promotional activities), but what about your payments?

Regardless of who dropped the ball (and it sounds like everyone did), the fact remains that there was almost no promotion for the record in the US. The little promotion that *did* occur came from Feedback, who clearly did not have the resources (or, according to Dwyer, the enthusiasm) to do more than the bare minimum. A serious flaw in the contract itself was the lack of a timetable for promotional activities. Prescott states that the Church's management was *legally* not at fault because there was no set deadline, but clearly there must have been an expectation that promotional materials would be in place to coincide with the album's US release. No satisfactory answer has been provided as to why this didn't happen, but presumably Bruce Butler was in over his head and there was a cashflow problem on the Church side, which was further exacerbated by Feedback's missed payments. Butler's comments to Brian concerning alternate means of promotion (the Internet), indicate a desire to move away from traditional methods and big companies, but the alternative had not been clearly thought through.

As usual, the band did not scrutinize the fine print of the deal until it was too late. Other than the T-shirts and band newsletters Steve had hawked in the mid-'80s, they had never had much involvement in their own marketing. Having been signed to EMI in their infancy, the Church were about as far removed from a DIY band as you could get. Now their management told them they could self-release their music and it would sell itself. Hadn't *Starfish* gone gold? It all sounded perfectly reasonable to two guys who'd always been content to let the "straights" take care of the business end.

Due to the promotional fiasco, *Magician Among the Spirits* was essentially ignored by the American press. It received little notice in Australia, either, and the attention it did receive was generally negative. Marty, back home in England when the house of cards collapsed, gave a rather bleak assessment of the Church's current state on *Shadow Cabinet*:

> At this stage the Church, although perceived by some as a good, as well as successful, band, does not have a record deal and nobody is exactly banging down the door. So we retire to contemplate our options. Steve and I are lucky because we both have our own studios and can put something together that only needs to sell moderately well (subjective) for us to benefit financially. But since (the distro company) went down and we made nothing from the last two years of our work, we are somewhat on the back foot. We don't have ready-made back up records just in case the last one falters. We still have to make the next record. It isn't cheap as we live in different countries. The will is there, the money is not.

One creative bright spot of 1996 was the release (on Australian indie label Phantom Records) of *Pharmakoi/Distance Crunching Honchos With Echo Units*, credited to the Refo:mation. This side project was essentially the Church without Marty. During interviews for *Sometime Anywhere*, Steve had openly speculated on what that record might have sounded like with Peter instead of Marty. *Pharmakoi* served the purpose of satisfying his curiosity in that regard. Peter used the album to cement his comeback, proving once and for all his status as the Church's great sonic architect, and disproving Marty's previous statement that Peter was the less adventurous of the two guitarists. Partly due to the positive experience of working on this album, Peter made the decision to rejoin the Church full-time. "I just thought, next time I should get kicked out rather than leave," he says now about his decision.

> That was the attitude I had. I needed to assert myself more in the band . . . I had been working as a session guitarist. [Steve and I] had worked together doing solo stuff, and we'd made the Refo:mation. That was basically a reaction against *Magician,* I guess. You could look at it from a different perspective: maybe Marty joined the Refo:mation rather than me rejoining the Church!"

The re-infusion of the Koppes magic into the mix certainly served as a creative catalyst for the other musicians. On every track on *Pharmakoi*, layers upon layers of guitars wash over Steve's fragmented lyrics, carried aloft by Tim Powles' intuitive rhythms. A true collaboration, *Pharmakoi* celebrates the unadulterated joy of inspired improvisation. In keeping with the democratic spirit, the album even features a lead vocal from Tim Powles, on "Take Your Place." Tim described the song's inception:

> Steve thought "Take Your Place" should be an instrumental and I disagreed. And he said, "Well you sing something then." And it sounded like a challenge and I said, "Okay." So I took him on at his own game . . . in the sense that when Steve writes a song he normally listens to it for about three or four times and then walks downstairs and sings it, and that's it. So I sat there and rolled it a couple of times and wrote down some words and then went downstairs and sang it. That's it. I basically looked at it as a challenge and it worked out.

Lyrically, *Pharmakoi* is Steve at his most Dadaist. The man notorious for not revising his words took things even further here, making up many of the lyrics in front of the microphone with the tape rolling. This explains such head-scratching lines as "You got a mind like magazine / You got a taste like Florentine / And a lot that's in-between" (in "She Comes in Singing").

There is one significant exception to this loose approach: the ballad "The Moon and the Sea," which is a tightly crafted imagistic poem. The soul-searching lyrics ("Sometimes I can't tell what I'm doing here / Am I supposed to be a clown or a buccaneer / From the vaguest clue to the faintest idea") hark all the way back to the themes of "The Unguarded Moment." Both songs deal with insecurity and uncertainty; "The Moon and the Sea," however, contains the added component of lost love, exemplified by the poignant line: "Alone in this room with the moon and the sea / Listen to the space where she used to be / Another life away." This song, with its gentle bass and eddies of echoing guitar, serves as

Steve Kilbey and Tim Powles, "solo" gig, 1997 *(Matt Packham)*

the emotional axis around which the rest of the album slowly turns.

Taken as a whole—even allowing for the hokey rapping on "Traitor" and the occasional foot-in-mouth lyric—*Pharmakoi* is one of the best Church albums of the 90s. Don't let the Refo:mation name fool you—this is more of a bona-fide Church record than either of the two preceding official albums.

Perhaps one of the factors that contributed to the lack of inhibition in the Refo:mation sessions was the understanding that no one was going to make much money from it. True enough, when the album came out, on a small label and with little fanfare, it didn't reach much of an audience beyond diehard Church fans (and even many fans remain unaware of this album's existence). Also, because it did not feature the Church name, *Pharmakoi* received virtually no reviews, even from the Australian street press.

The Refo:mation chose not to tour, for fear that rehearsing the songs and playing them again and again each night would rob them of their spontaneity. That's a shame, as some of the songs—with the support of a tour and the right marketing push—could have received significant radio play, even if the album as a whole may have been too left-of-center for a mass audience.

★ ★ ★ ★ ★

With his finances and music career in a shambles, and no meaningful companionship save that of fellow junkies, Steve had just one lifeline left—his children. Whatever impulses had caused him to hole up in Surry Hills when he should have been spending more time with them had long dissipated, as had the creative euphoria he'd experienced during those early days of heavy drug use. As soon as the kids had left for Sweden he had begun to miss them, often dreaming about them and even crying himself awake. Elektra and Miranda approached life with innocence and wonder, qualities that had been lacking in Steve's world for quite some time. During his brief clean stint in 1994, he had realized that fatherhood was something he actually enjoyed; spending time with his kids made him feel young again.

Steve came to the realization that, by living half a world away, he was missing the most crucial years of his daughters' lives. He did not want to let this happen; he saw his daughters as a part of his life he wanted to hang on to—as much for his own sake as for theirs. So Steve made the decision to sell everything he owned and move to Sweden. It took him just a few months to dispose of all of his earthly possessions. Had he been thinking straight, he could have made a lot of money auctioning off his belongings to fans. Instead, he simply threw open the doors of his house and sold everything at rock-bottom prices. What he couldn't sell he threw away.[17] When he boarded the plane to Sweden in late 1997, his personal belongings consisted of a small carry-on bag and the clothes he was wearing.

---

[17] Marty commented at the time to *Shadow Cabinet* webmaster Brian Smith: "If you saw what he was getting rid of, you would weep."

22

HAPPY HUNTING GROUND

Brian Smith seems an unlikely savior for a psychedelic band. Tall, soft-spoken, with a shy grin that lights up his face, the Maltese-born, Australian-raised Church fan has no interest in Steve's two key obsessions, drugs and spirituality. He favors hard science over the metaphysical, which makes his Church obsession hard to explain. "When I try and reconcile being a Church fan with this reality-based obsession of mine," he says, "the only conclusion I can come to is that I'm not letting the Church's music do what Steve has said he wants it to do: take you to another place. I *see* the other place, I appreciate how beautiful it is, but I know I'm only visiting and that it's not a patch on reality. I think I'm paying more attention to the projector than the film."

Brian's main interests outside of the Church are computers and science fiction, particularly the meticulously detailed sci-fi world of *Babylon 5*. The Church's music, in its inherent spaciness, *does* serve as a nice soundtrack for these otherworldly pursuits. The extremely detail-oriented Smith (he once carried on a protracted argument with a *Babylon 5* producer over the show's "control panel design" on one of its space ships) is naturally drawn to the Church's stellar musicianship. A classically trained musician himself, he particularly admires the inventive guitar interplay between Peter Koppes and Marty Willson-Piper.

Brian's web site, *Shadow Cabinet*, which continues to be the single most comprehensive site devoted to the Church, began in the 1980s as a scrapbook. Starved for information on his favorite band, Brian began cutting out and saving any Church-related items he could find in the local press. The first such clipping came from a gossipy Valentine's Day column in a Melbourne newspaper. The author had asked a few Australian celebrities what they would like for Valentines Day. Steve Kilbey's response was, "to wake up in bed covered by ten beautiful women." Brian duly clipped this and pasted it in his scrapbook as entry number 1.

Eventually, the scrapbook began to bulge at the seams from the articles and photographs Brian had accumulated. Some of the pictures were his own (he took his camera to several concerts and captured the band in full flight); the rest came from newspapers, magazines, and the short-lived Church fan club newsletter of the late '80s.

Here's where Brian's passion for computers came in. Naturally, he staked out his own corner of cyberspace early on, and by 1995 he had begun to upload scans and transcriptions of the items in his Church collection. Before long, other fans started sending him their archives, too. Eventually his site came to include audio samples, videos, a Church-themed chat room, and a collection of Steve Kilbey's short stories and poems. "I wanted to be the best," he says matter-of-factly.

> I wanted *Shadow Cabinet* to be the place where people went for information on the Church. Other fans started sites to fill certain niches, and that was great, but no one had the sheer scope of what I had. I always remember being a Church fan with nothing to read about the Church—no interviews, no reviews, nothing. I wanted the next fan who felt *Starfish* wriggle into their brain and seize hold of it to say: "I've got to know more . . . Hey, there's a nice web site with all sorts of good stuff to read." I'm a gateway drug, baby!

The band quickly took note of Brian's efforts. The first official contact came from Steve, who happened upon *Shadow Cabinet* while doing an internet search for the Church. His e-mails were characteristically brief, but he offered his support and gently chided Brian for getting some of his lyrics wrong. Within that first year, their cyber-acquaintance carried over into real life. During one of their first face-to-face meetings (at a Kilbey solo show) Steve invited Brian backstage, fired up a joint, and offered the smoldering spliff to his fan.

"I've never even seen a joint before," Brian said.

"What planet did *you* grow up on?" Steve asked.

"Nerdsville," Brian replied.

Steve exhaled and chuckled to himself. "So you've never done any drugs?"

"No, I have no interest."

Steve took another toke and then said, "Actually, that's good."

Steve quickly warmed to Brian. The fact that he harbored no pretensions and was unapologetically "square" impressed Steve. Here was a passionate fan who, despite his fervor, would not compromise his values to curry favor with his hero. Steve trusted Brian and gradually began using Brian's site as a platform for major band-related an-nouncements. The other band members followed suit. During the period in the 1990s immediately following *Magician Among the Spirits*—when the Church had no record label, no management, and no PR—*Shadow Cabinet* became the band's lifeline. For a brief time, Marty had his own section on the site titled "Questions with Answers," in which he gave detailed written responses to fan questions. Peter

Steve Kilbey and Brian Smith, 1996

gave the site an exclusive interview, titled "Peter Koppes Peers into the Shadow Cabinet." Apart from his contributions to this book, it may be the lengthiest interview the circumspect guitarist has ever done.

In its heyday, *Shadow Cabinet* served as a conduit for some rather un-orthodox messages. The strangest of these was undoubtedly when, after a concert, Steve handed Brian a napkin on which he had scribbled a personal ad. Brian dutifully put it online, so for a brief period (presumably until Steve sobered up) *Shadow Cabinet* served as a dating service for Mr. Kilbey.[18] Also, when both Steve and Marty found themselves in financial difficulties, they turned to *Shadow Cabinet* as a place to auction off their guitars and memo-rabilia.

2009 marks the site's fourteenth anniversary—an impressive feat in the ephemeral world of cyberspace. The web site has certainly waxed and

---

[18] The number of people who responded to this solicitation (assuming anyone did) re-mains unknown.

waned over the years; at one point it almost ground to a halt, not due to burn-out on Brian's part—his fervor continued unabated—but simply because real life intruded: he got married and moved from Australia to the US. Still, he regrets having given the perception that he was neglecting his duties.

> I remember getting an e-mail from a fan, and it read, "Where did you go? We *need* you—people are depending on you!" That actually made me feel pretty guilty—like I was letting the band and the fans down.

Brian has never received any financial compensation for his work on behalf of the Church, though the total number of hours he has logged while archiving the band's history must be staggering. Although the band now has its own official site, *Shadow Cabinet* continues to be the one-stop destination for information on the band's history and catalog.

It would be remiss of me not to mention five additional fans who had an equally large impact keeping the Church enterprise going during those difficult years. First and foremost, the late Morten Skjefte helped establish the Church's online presence in a big way with the *Seance* e-mail list in the early 1990s. During those exciting early days of the Internet, when cyberspace was a playground for the adventurous, the disaffected, and the clinically insane, *Seance* served as a powerful grassroots organizational tool, the significance of which the band did not fully grasp at the time. Most people came across *Seance* by accident—that's certainly how it happened for me. In 1994 I was a junior at the University of Georgia and had just discovered how fiendishly addictive web surfing could be. One afternoon, after trolling through the various Usenet music groups, I posted a message to rec.arts. music-alternative, writing, "Does anyone still listen to the Church? They're one of my favorite bands but they seem to have dropped off the radar. Do they still tour?" Within a matter of hours I received a response, probably from Morten himself, with instructions on how to sign up for *Seance*.

Getting on the *Seance* mailing list was like receiving an infusion of much-needed nutrients. Up to that point, I hadn't fully realized how starved for the Church I was. But once I got plugged in, I passed many blissful hours— hours I should have spent studying—engaged in heated dialogue with oth-

ers who shared my particular addiction. Friendships were formed, many
of which survive to this day. More crucially, *Seance* helped get the word out
to all of us about what the Church were doing and where they were touring. All it took was for one fan to catch a show listing in the local paper and
within minutes that information would be disseminated.

Concurrent with the Church's emergence on the Internet, two
Englishmen, Trevor Boyd and Michael Farrant, each launched a Church
fanzine—*North, South, East & West* and *The Maven*, respectively. Despite being thrown together on the slimmest of budgets, both zines were treasure
troves. *North, South, East & West* frequently featured lengthy, exclusive interviews with all four band members, while
The Maven became a Church's collector's
paradise, with indie record stores and fellow
traders offering their wares on its pages.
Thumbing through these zines now, I am
impressed by the ingenuity, craftsmanship,
and love that must have gone into their as-
sembly. In the age of advanced desktop publishing, it is relatively easy to put together an
attractive zine on a small budget, but in the
early '90s, Trevor and Michael's "software"

Steve Kilbey and Trevor Boyd, 1994 *(Courtesy, Trevor Boyd)*

consisted simply of scissors, tape, a word processor, and a lot of heart.

Trevor, like Brian, was directly involved in keeping the band afloat. He
singlehandedly organized Steve Kilbey's successful 1998 solo performance
in London, and he personally printed and marketed Steve's book of prose
and poetry, *Nineveh / The Ephemeron*. More than likely, Trevor Boyd lost money hand over fist in his dedicated service to his favorite band.

On the subject of fans pouring money into their favorite band, Kevin
Lane Keller spikes the curve. A successful businessman, Dartmouth profes-
sor, and longtime Church fan, Keller approached the band during their *Box
of Birds* tour and essentially offered to be their patron. As a fan, he had a
strong interest in the Church's continued existence, and as a wealthy entre-
preneur, he had the ability to help fund that existence. From 1999 through
2005, he poured thousands of dollars into the band and helped coordinate
their US tours. In return, he received an "executive producer" credit on most
of their albums during this period. It's very possible that the albums *After*

Everything, Now This and *Forget Yourself* would never have been made without this cash infusion.

Finally, David Barnard is responsible for a very successful bulletin board called *Hotel Womb*. "The Womb," as its denizens affectionately call it, came into being in 1999 during the Church's *Box of Birds* tour. It first existed as a place for fans to post their reviews of individual shows as the tour unfolded. But these things tend to take on a life of their own, and before long the Womb became a focal point for all things Church-related. If fans wanted to meet up before shows, they posted to the Womb. If someone had a question about a specific lyric, they posted to the Womb. If inquiring minds urgently needed to know Steve Kilbey's shoe size, they posted to the Womb. Eventually, the intellectual scope of the Womb expanded beyond the Church. Egos still chafe in the aftermath of the mind-to-mind combat that took place on the site during the US invasion of Iraq.

Most importantly, *Hotel Womb* is Steve Kilbey's favorite Church-related site; it's his direct window into how any given album is being received by his audience. He reads the fan reviews regularly and those reviews do have an influence on how he perceives his own work. He's even been known to make the occasional posting himself, under an assumed name.

23
WISH I KNEW WHAT YOU WERE LOOKING FOR

A man in Belfast kissed his wife goodbye. Even as he held her close, he was fingering the ticket in his pocket. Halfway across the world in northeast Georgia, USA, a poor college student dipped into his savings account, withdrew $550, and called British Airlines. He was behind on his rent and his electricity was about to be shut off, but the voice beckoned.

From all over they came. Parallel lines began to converge. Newlyweds on a European honeymoon made a slight detour. An Italian businessman took two days off from work. On a flight out of Sydney, a young woman stared out the window at clouds that looked like white billowy cotton candy. She wondered if he was going to play that song.

I first met my idol, Steve Kilbey, in 1998, not long after he had moved to Sweden. If one were to make a chart of our respective musical careers, this meeting would occur at the lowest point of Steve's, which was also the highest point in mine—the time surrounding the release of my CD, *you speak in too many voices,* and the modest but generally positive critical attention it received.

A few months into the New Year, Trevor Boyd made the announcement on the *Seance* mailing list that Steve would be playing a solo acoustic concert in London in April 1998, at a club called the Borderline. I immediately wrote to Trevor and, with little preamble, offered my services as an opening act.

That night I lay awake wishing I could take the e-mail back. I imagined

Trevor and his cronies sitting around his computer, laughing at the nerve of this American kid who had e-mailed him. I was still unaware that Steve had hit a new low in his career and his life, and that the idea of a small-time singer/songwriter with an independent release opening for him might not be completely unreasonable. No, I believed I had done something outrageous and stupid by asking to play on the same bill with the Church frontman.

To my pleasant surprise, Trevor got back to me promptly, asking me to send my CD and press clippings. He really liked it, and within a month I had secured the gig. Friends of mine who knew about my ten-year obsession with Steve Kilbey simply refused to believe it. They saw Steve through my eyes, and to me, of course, Steve was a god. Like Othello, my friends demanded "the ocular proof." I was only too happy to show them the e-mail from Trevor that read, "You have got the gig, man!" I carried the message around with me! In that same small town, quite probably at the same time, the members of R.E.M. were basking in the glow of their new eighty-million-dollar record contract—but in my eyes *I* was the one who had struck gold.

Trevor gave me the lowdown on payment: I was to receive a hundred dollars for a half-hour performance (the Borderline's standard payment for an opening act), but I'd have to take care of my own travel and accommodation costs. The flight from Georgia to London cost over five hundred dollars. Lodging for a four-to-five-night stay was over two hundred dollars (actually, an incredible bargain). Even offset by my gig earnings, I would still be looking at a loss of at least six hundred dollars to open for Steve. I was a pizza cook and telemarketer at the time, so money was short. Nevertheless, my response was: "Hell yeah, I'll do it!"

I arrived in London four days prior to the show and spent my time exploring the city. My reaction to the town was very different from Steve's (he famously detested the place). I immediately fell in love with my surroundings and maxed out my credit card on books and CDs that I couldn't find stateside. I had never been there before, but most of my childhood had been spent watching imported British programming on PBS: *Monty Python*, *Fawlty Towers*, *Black Adder*, countless drama series, and, of course, *Doctor Who*. So this trip felt like a sort of homecoming.

On the afternoon of the show, I met the handful of devoted Church fans who were waiting outside the club to catch the sound check, and prepared myself for meeting the man himself. Trevor, a tall, thin man with salt-and-pepper hair and John Lennon spectacles, asked if I was nervous about my upcoming performance. "I'm not nervous about the show," I said, "but I *am* nervous about meeting Kilbey." Trevor responded that Steve could sometimes be difficult.

"He can't be all *that* bad," I said. "I mean, I've met Michael Stipe, and he was a total asshole. Steve can't be any worse than that."

Trevor looked at me for a moment, as if he were weighing whether to tell me what was on his mind. Finally, he said matter-of-factly, "There's something you should know: Steve is a heroin addict."

I was crushed, though in retrospect, I'm not sure why. Steve had always been up-front about his enthusiasm for drug experimentation. But it was one thing to imagine my hero smoking a joint or dropping a tab of acid, quite another to imagine him tying off and sticking a spike in his arm. Whenever I thought of the word "heroin," it usually followed hot on the heels of the name Kurt Cobain. Most junkies' lives didn't have happy endings.

"Has he ever tried to quit?" I asked.

"Yes, but it didn't take. Honestly, I don't think he will ever give it up for good. He enjoys it too much." He paused, thinking to himself, then said, "Steve's a genius. I guess a certain license comes with that."

First meeting: Steve Kilbey and Robert Lurie, 1998

My first impression of Steve Kilbey himself came when he took the stage for sound check. I was startled by his size. He wasn't overweight, but he was a large, imposing figure, or at least he appeared that way on the elevated stage. Then there was the voice: that rich, sonorous baritone that just seemed to rise out of him as he tested out two new songs: "Buffalo" and "Louisiana."

We were introduced after the warm-up. Trevor said something along the lines of, "Steve, this is Robert. He flew over from the States to do this gig."

"Hello Robert," Steve said matter-of-factly, giving me a firm handshake.

It suddenly dawned on me that though I had traveled thousands of miles to meet and play for my hero, I had absolutely nothing to say to him. I suppose I also realized in that instant that any kind of normal human interaction with this man would be difficult. For one thing, it would require some curiosity on his part about where I was from, what I did for a living, what my music was like. But he really had no interest in these details. A deep panic set in, simultaneously gnawing at my gut and sending my thoughts racing.

And yet . . . and yet . . . when I did my sound check, he listened. When Trevor and the fans were getting ready to depart for dinner, Kilbey insisted they wait until I finished my songs. But when we all sat down in the restaurant, this man who had previously been so gracious and considerate drummed his knife and fork on the side of the table, quite clearly bored. He gave one-word answers to questions before returning to his private, internal rhythm.

"Steve, why don't you tell us some of the jokes you were telling in the car last night?" Trevor prompted.

Kilbey thought for a moment, then replied, "The giraffe walked into the bar and said, 'The highballs are on me.'"

One side of his mouth curved up into a smirk. He lapsed back into silence as everyone laughed.

Before long, I was summoned back to the club to set up. My chief concern at that point was my own performance, and I forgot, briefly, about Steve Kilbey. As it turned out, I was blessed with an enthusiastic reception from the Borderline audience that night—they had come prepared to listen to acoustic music, so they were very attentive. It was a decent showing on my end as well, and I left the stage happy.

Then it was Steve's turn. I slipped back into the comfortable role of fan and observed the proceedings.

He emerged from the dressing room wreathed in pungent marijuana smoke, a large stocky man with an oddly feminine face. He already had his guitar strapped on and one hand—puffy, riddled with red pinpricks—rested on the fretboard. His glassy eyes gazed out, unfocused, indifferent. He walked slowly to the stage entrance. Paused. Took a deep breath. Walked out, duly noting the applause and cheers, the surging crowd. He reached down and plugged in the guitar. Began strumming. In one miraculous moment, he was transformed. His frustration, arrogance, weakness vanished. The Magician took over. The argument he'd had the day before with the

mother of his children was forgotten. The cravings were, for the moment, nullified. "That was a different man/ You know he's never been here." The hangers-on, the sycophants who had so annoyed him only minutes before were now old friends. No longer forty-four, he was ageless. "Looking for the blue and the green/Constant in opal, aquamarine/But you could not find yourself that way." He finished the first song and sighed.

Steve at the Borderline, London, 1998 *(Trevor Boyd)*

"I really don't have anything planned for tonight. What do you want to hear?"

"Antenna!"

"Reptile!"

"Milky Way!"

"Ahh." An idea occurred to him. He strummed two chords repeatedly, the open strings droning. The notes floated out into the crowd.

"Remember when I told you/you were pretty lost." His voice had grit in it now, a light touch of sandpaper. He kept his eyes closed. The first verse flowed by, the strumming becoming more insistent. The second verse came in a jangling flood. The third followed close behind. "All I have, all I need, all you got is providence." The last verse spilled out like tears.

On the flight home, I had a hard time reconciling my conflicting emotions. On the one hand, I was ecstatic to have shared the stage with Steve and made an impression on his audience. On the other hand, I was utterly disillusioned with Steve himself. During the weeks leading up to the gig, I had constructed an elaborate fantasy about how well we were going to hit it off, about how we might even end up collaborating on music.

Not only had my unrealistic expectations been deflated, but Steve and I had barely even carried on a conversation. His iciness had caught me completely off guard.

Given this disheartening experience, I asked myself a tough question: What exactly did I *want* from Steve?

I had no answer.

24

ANESTHESIA'S COMING TO YOU

Steve hurried down the Stockholm street, clutching his coat tightly about him. The air bit into his skin. Icy snowflakes blew to and fro. For once in his life he was late to buy drugs. Lou Reed had sung of "waiting for the man," and indeed that's how it was for Kilbey—endless waiting on street corners, jonesing, feeling the sickness come on with the predictability of a hangover. But today he had encountered some difficulty getting the money together, and so he was late. Now he walked quickly, hoping Erik was still waiting. He scanned the sidewalk ahead, looking for the tall figure he knew so well. Other people walked by, paying him no notice, making their way quickly to their own destinations. Then he saw his man. The tall, blond Swede stood across the street looking nonchalant, his hands thrust deep in his pockets, collar turned up around his neck. The two briefly made eye contact and Erik nodded. Steve's adrenalin surged. My connection! Relief! He ran out into the road, forgetting momentarily that he was in Sweden, not Australia, and that the cars here drove on the other side of the road. Before Steve had time to jump back, a huge black Mercedes plowed straight into him, hurling his body into the air. He crashed back down onto the hood of the car, landing on his right arm. The driver had by this point slammed on the brakes and careened onto the sidewalk. Steve lay crumpled in the gutter.

When he came to, his first thought was of Erik. He tried to raise his head to look for the dealer, but it was difficult. A policeman and the driver of the Mercedes stood over him. Slowly, gingerly, Steve sat up.

"Sir, an ambulance is on the way," the officer said. "Don't move too much."

"I think I'm okay," Steve muttered.

The officer spoke quietly to the driver of the car. "I need to ask this man a few questions privately. But I need you to stay nearby. I will need to speak to you as well."

"Of course," the man said. He looked once more at Steve, wiped his brow, then walked off.

The officer leaned down so his face was close to Steve's. "So what happened?"

Steve told him, leaving out the reason he had been in such a hurry.

"Did he slow down?"

"I don't think he really got a chance to. I pretty much jumped right out in front of him."

"I see," the officer said. He walked away.

Steve stood up, his body swaying dizzily. He walked away from the curb over to a building and leaned against it. Again he scanned the street for Erik, but Erik was nowhere to be found. There was a numbness in his right arm and his legs ached where the car had hit him, but Steve's thoughts were, as always, on the smack.

After a few minutes, the policeman walked back over to Steve. "How are you feeling?" he asked.

"I don't know. I think I'll be okay."

"Do you intend to file charges against the man who hit you?"

"I can't charge him; I just ran across the road and it wasn't his fault."

"He was going too fast."

"It still wasn't his fault."

The officer leaned closer, to the point where Steve could smell his breath. "Listen," the policeman said, "there would probably be a lot of money in it for you if you filed charges against him."

This gave Steve pause. A lot of money meant a lot of heroin; it meant not having to scam and hustle so much to make ends meet for every fix.

"No," Steve said eventually. "That wouldn't feel right." He craned his neck, looking again for some sign of Erik. This whole mess was taking up a lot of valuable time.

An ambulance pulled up, lights flashing and siren whining. The back door opened and a paramedic got out.

"Where's the man who was hit?" she asked.

"He's right here," the officer said.

"It's okay," Steve said. "I'm fine."

"Sir," the woman said, "you need to go to the hospital. You were hit by a car. Something may be broken. You could have internal bleeding."

"Really, I'm okay."

The woman felt his arm carefully. Steve continued to look around for Erik.

"This doesn't feel good," she said. "We're going to take you to the hospital."

"I am absolutely *not* going to the hospital."

The paramedic gave the policeman an exasperated look.

"I'll tell you what," the officer said to Steve, "if you can lift your arm above your head, you're free to leave."

There are many tales of mothers who have been able to lift up a car to free their child trapped underneath it. Steve summoned up a similar kind of strength to lift his broken arm. "AAAAAAGHHHHH!" he exclaimed as he slowly raised his right arm above his head. The paramedic's eyes opened wide. The cop shrugged. "I guess we have nothing more to do here," he said.

Steve walked away. As he trudged up the street, looking still for his connection, the Mercedes owner walked quickly alongside him. "I want you to have this," he said, thrusting some banknotes under Steve's nose. "I really appreciate you not filing charges. Go and buy yourself a beer or something."

Steve gratefully took the money with his left hand, muttered "Thanks," and walked on, quickly now, looking around furtively. No sign of Erik. He was about to cross the street when he heard a whispered "Steven."

Erik stepped out of a doorway.

"About a week later the arm started to swell and go black," Steve recalls.

A few people said, "You'd better go and have that looked at." And of course it was broken in three places. The real pain was not the breaking of it; it was when I had to have it reset. Later on everyone was saying, "You could have gotten like $200,000 for that if you had charged the guy. It wouldn't have been him that was paying, it would have been the insurance company." You know, I could have made a fortune out of it. I could have said, "I'm a musician, I can't play anymore," or any old bollocks. And I would have made a load of money. But I didn't. All I was concerned with was getting the smack.

Fortunately—in fact, rather astonishingly—the arm healed with virtually no impact on Steve's bass playing.

> My arm's got a little bit of a kink in it. And sometimes on a cold or damp day it's a little bit achy. But other than that, it didn't affect things at all. I was so lucky there. I can't believe that.

★ ★ ★ ★ ★

As could have been expected, the move to Sweden didn't cure Steve's heroin addiction; he merely brought his problem with him. And it took very little time for him to establish drug connections in Stockholm.

Life as a junkie dad certainly had its surreal moments. Steve would drive his daughters to a support group to meet with other children of drug-addicted parents. Waiting outside, Steve often recognized his drug buddies in the parking lot, bringing *their* kids to the meetings.

Drug addiction is a spectrum. At one end you have the hopeless cases who degrade and debase themselves in order to keep the supply line intact. At the other end are people who manage to hold on to their jobs and maintain some semblance of a functioning life. Steve may have had a ferocious appetite for heroin, but he always did his best to provide for his daughters and shield them from his problem. On that point everyone agrees. "I don't want people reading this to think that the kids were going through a real deprivation or anything like that," he says.

> This was Sweden in the 1990s. Where they lived with their mother and her husband was a beautiful apartment; they had everything they wanted. Sometimes when they came to my place, I didn't have a fridge full of food and stuff. Maybe it was baked beans on toast every night. It just wasn't the way it should have been. I'm lucky that all the people concerned went with me as far as they could go in trying to make it work.

It's a very dodgy thing when the children's father—someone who loves them and wants the best for them—is also a drug addict. It's like, where's the line? Do you go, "No, you can't see them at all till you clean up"? —which means the father and the children may never see each other again—or do you let him have them for smallish chunks of time? It's a very fine line, and I think all the people concerned did their best. Luckily, nothing really bad ever happened. It wasn't as bad as it could have been, but it was bad.

Perhaps the biggest impact on the children came from the subtle psychological effects of being left alone. When the girls were old enough to fend for themselves in the apartment, Steve would sometimes go out to get his fix. Of course in the drug world things don't always run to schedule, and on those occasions he would sometimes be gone an hour—or an afternoon—when he had promised to be back in two minutes. "I would imagine it was terrible for them," he says.

> Now of course they are old enough to know what was going on. They've forgiven me, but I think it will go on having an effect on them forever, a bit like a slow release. They may think right now, "It's okay, Dad," but they still don't understand the full import of what it did to them. I loved [my daughters] and took care of them and fed them, but when you're an addict drugs always come first, and it definitely affected them.

That inner conflict comes through loud and clear on *Hologram of Baal*, the album the Church recorded at Karmic Hit and released in 1998. It opens with "Anesthesia," Steve's unabashed paean to narcotic bliss, and it closes with "Glow Worm"—a love song about his daughters. The latter is as nakedly honest a song as Steve is ever likely to write. Over a deceptively simple guitar progression, he sings, "As a broken soul below / I always wanna be living in your glow . . . I wanna tell you everything but I can't find the words." Reading these lyrics in the context of the songwriter's turbulent life lends them an added poignancy. Here we see Steve Kilbey's heart unencumbered by elaborate metaphors or arcane references.

Much of the strength of *Hologram of Baal* derives from the firm guiding hand of Tim Powles. The scrappy drummer had become a fully fledged band member right at the moment when everything around him was going to shit. Peter had finally rejoined, and Marty was divided between the Church and his other projects—"hedging his bets," as Steve puts it. Steve himself—the once and future king—was essentially a zombie. Sensing this gaping power vacuum and being a go-to kind of guy, Powles took the reins and, through sheer force of will, bent these disparate, short-fused personalities to the task of creating a uniformly strong album.

Tim Powles *(Kevin Keller)*

Tim is the type of person who radiates confidence. With his no-nonsense, workmanlike demeanor, he comes off more like a mechanic than a musician. His close-cropped hair and muscular build reinforce this image. I had the opportunity to meet Tim during the US *Hologram of Baal* tour in 1998, and found his grounded personality a refreshing (and essential) contrast to the flightiness of his band mates. We talked at length about his role within the band.

"If I wasn't there, there would *be* no band," he said. "It's as simple as that."

> Even the other guys acknowledge that that's an absolute fact. It's only because of my nature and my temperament and the fact that I know everybody that the band's together. Because they're a very *very* volatile, complicated three-way thing. I'm just a very patient person.

He went on to explain his process of producing *Hologram of Baal*:

> The album would not be here without me. It's not because I'm great, it's just 'cause I did it. That's what the Church needed: someone to come along and do it. We had no record company; we had nothing. We had to put something together ourselves and the thing that I think I'm particularly satisfied with is that the picture in my head of *Hologram of Baal* is exactly the picture on that CD that you hear . . .
>
> I definitely erred on the noisy side on *Hologram* but I thought, no one is going to sit up and listen to the Church again if we sound like *Heyday* . . . The songs to me are fairly timeless, classic Church songs, but with the production I've tried to bring in new elements.

The album had originally been titled *Hologram of Allah*, but after Powles suffered a series of nightmares involving an impending Fatwa, the band changed the deity in the title to Baal, an ancient Phoenician god (a choice perfectly in keeping with Kilbey's famously obscure allusions). The title itself was a red herring—it had nothing whatsoever to do with the content of the songs. A number of listeners attempted to read into it a connection with Bertolt Brecht's post–World War I play, *Baal*, but Steve insisted there was no link.

Steve's involvement in the recording of *Hologram of Baal* was minimal— he played bass on only half the songs and contributed occasional acoustic and electric guitar. Tim and Marty shouldered the remaining bass duties. And while Steve may have sung lead on every track, nearly all the backing vocals—from the elaborate harmonies on "Buffalo" down to the random whisperings on "Lizard" (a B-side from the sessions)—came from Tim.

Steve during the recording of *Hologram of Baal* (Trevor Boyd)

Peter came to the table with a fresh new guitar sound. "It's a style kind of like a keyboard, a Hammond organ approach to playing guitar," he says.

> I'd been trying to create a more cinematic, panoramic atmosphere. Some of it originally came about through trying to recreate "Under the Milky Way" live. After we did *Priest* I discovered this fabulous device that allowed me to recreate those string sounds—even on an acoustic guitar, and I used that on *Hologram*.

Lyrically, *Hologram of Baal* has no central, cohesive theme. Steve careens madly from mythology and surrealism in "Ricochet" to concrete narrative in "Louisiana." Both "Buffalo" and "Tranquillity" hark back to the delicate beauty of the Church's early ballads, though everything is rendered here more garishly. The effect is akin to taking one's sunglasses off and staring across a sunny landscape; there is much beauty, but the excessive light can be blinding.

"The Great Machine" holds court in the center of the album like a freakish, uninvited third cousin. With lyrics such as "The shadows run for phantom trains/Slowly blowing out their brains/Society dames down the drain," the song is indefensibly pretentious. It is also—maddeningly—hypnotic.

But no description of this collection of songs can be complete without a mention of the elephant in the room: "This is It." The lyrics are a stark examination of the hanging death (officially ruled a suicide, though some speculated it was the result of auto-erotic asphyxiation) of INXS frontman Michael Hutchence. In the final verse, Steve's love of puns takes on its darkest manifestation ever:

> Sometimes you come upon a fork in the road
> What was waiting there he never could have known
> Split-second difference, one tiny percent
> Yeah, he came and he went

Elsewhere in the song, Steve appraises Hutchence's disillusionment and death through the lens of his own experience:

> Watching things you put up start to crash
> Even though you've got a fistful of cash
> Watching the future, it bursts on through
> I was one of those who used to envy you.

Over an ominous chord progression, Steve repeatedly intones "This is it, oh baby this is it." One cannot hear the song and come away unaffected. And one also cannot avoid wondering how much of the song is about Hutchence and how much is about the songwriter himself.

Hologram of Baal reestablished the Church as a musical presence. The album was released at home by Australian powerhouse Festival Records and abroad by respected indie labels Cooking Vinyl (in the UK) and Thirsty Ear

(in the US) and received positive reviews across the board; Both *Select* and
Uncut gave it the coveted five stars, and several US weeklies, including *Seattle*
Weekly and Atlanta's *Stomp and Stammer*,
included it in their annual top-ten lists. In
the Australian *Rolling Stone*, David Nichols
wrote, "[T]he Church circa '98 have a grace-
ful push, a groove heralding new life . . .
.these oldies are back with a vengeance."
Dave Simpson wrote in the *Uncut* review,
"*Hologram Of Baal* sees the Church reunite
for what must be their finest album. While
their contemporaries spawned numerous
imitators, nobody has ever really sounded
like the Church. Nobody could."

The world tour in support of *Hologram* was
very successful (perhaps partly because the
Church hadn't toured outside Australia as
a full four-piece band in eight years). They
played remarkably well, trotting out some
old hits along with the edgier new material, and winning over some new converts
in the process. A particularly touching mo-

Peter and Steve on the *Hologram of Baal* tour, 1998
(Carrigan Compton)

ment occurred during the Atlanta show I
attended. The band played the song "Two Places at Once," which features
the line "I've been waiting, seems like eternity / I've been waiting, waiting
for you." When the song reached that point, many in the audience—while
singing along—pointed at Steve. The wry half-smirk dropped from his face;
he found himself unable to greet such unabashed love with his customary
irony.

25
DON'T GO LOOKING FOR ME

> Steve spent a lot of time thinking about spiritual things and reading books on religion and mysticism and Buddhism. I inherited a lot of his books when he moved back to Australia—everything from Norse mythology to Indian/ Eastern stuff. He would probably call himself a Buddhist if anything. In Sweden we call people like him searchers—looking for the answer to the big question and becoming frustrated at not finding it. It's probably on the tip of his tongue sometimes.
>
> —Martin Krall

Martin Krall and I have something in common: we both first met Steve as fans of his music. Martin's initial experience with his hero, however, was far more pleasant than mine—probably due to Martin's appealing personality. Honest and unassuming, he immediately engenders a feeling of trust from people who meet him. This is what Steve responded to, and what led them to eventually share an apartment in Sweden.

"When I was about twenty-three," Martin says,

> I read in *Raygun* that there was a second Jack Frost album out, but none of the record stores in Sweden knew about it. I called distributors and they didn't know about it either. So I looked up Steve's number in Australia and called him. He told me he was coming to Sweden the next week to visit his kids and he brought the Jack Frost CD along with him.

Guitars, *Box of Birds* recording sessions in Sweden, 1999 (Kevin Keller)

The matter-of-fact way Martin relates this story highlights a cultural and personality difference between us. It made perfect sense to him to simply pick up the phone and call the creator of the music he was looking for. He didn't give it a second thought. Had I been in his position, I probably would have rehearsed the conversation a hundred times before making the call and then blown it anyway.

My many conversations with European fans over the last few years have convinced me that this sort of paralyzing hero-worship is almost exclusively an American phenomenon. I had always laughed at the footage of teenage American girls fainting at the sight of the Beatles, but surely some small manifestation of that was evident for many years in my approach to the Church. And I'm sure that's what put Steve off when he met me and others like me.

Not that Martin was shielded completely from Steve's dark side. "He's a lovely person," he says, "but because of the position he's in, a lot of people want things from him. So he can be quite arrogant, and maybe that's one of the things you and your readers *don't* want to know about him. But he *is* a great person and a great friend."

Steve and Martin roomed together for much of the time Steve lived in Sweden. Martin remembers him as a quiet, considerate roommate, spending most of his time reading and taking care of his daughters. He kept only one guitar in the apartment and did very little music writing, instead carrying around notebooks and jotting down his reflections and random thoughts. Martin believes that most of these were thrown away during the constant traveling and moving around.

Of Steve's twin daughters, Martin says, "They're quite lovely kids—cute, outgoing, dancing and singing. They have very different personalities."

Steve offered his own description of Elektra and Miranda years later on his blog:

> elli is the most like me of all my kids
> she looks like me
> she can act like me too
> restless, flippant, iconoclastic
> easily bored n argumentative
>
> minnas always been slightly smaller than elli
> and tends to be victim to ellis bully
>
> when they fight n argue its always in swedish
> a loada yibber yabber sometimes followed with a slap
> elli wont stop taking minnas stuff
> n minna wont stop being outraged by it . . .
> do they love each other?
> yes
> do they like each other?
> not that much

26
I'VE BEEN LISTENING TO MYSELF TOO LONG

Steve stared out through the bars of his holding cell door, reflecting on the strange sequence of events that had led to his present situation. He wasn't sure what exactly had put him in this contemplative frame of mind; perhaps it was the large black guy who, only moments earlier, had sexually propositioned him. Or maybe it was the shivering, emaciated crack fiend in the corner who had offered him some rock. At any rate, Steve was thinking it had been a long, twisting road from Baby Grande to this police station on Manhattan's Lower East Side.

Mind you, he wasn't feeling guilty about trying to buy heroin. This was New York City, after all. Visiting New York without partaking of the street H would be like traveling to ancient Rome and skipping the baths. No, what he felt absolutely gut-wrenchingly awful about was missing the gig. In his several years as a junkie he had never once missed a performance, no matter how sick or otherwise indisposed he might have been. It was a point of pride. He *always* showed up for work on time. But now the NYPD had intervened, going typically overboard (Did he *really* need handcuffs? Was he that much of a menace to society?).

The evening had started easily enough; he had hit the streets, putting to work that sixth sense all junkies possess. (Another point of pride: no matter what city he was in, he could always suss out where the dope was.) But then it had all gone to shit. How was he to have known that, between now and the last time he'd gone looking for drugs here, Rudolph fucking

Giuliani had scrubbed the Big Apple squeaky clean? How could he know that the mayor of New York had turned this cesspit of vice and violence into a bright, shiny McCity? And how the fuck was he to know that the greasy, hygiene-impaired hoodlum he had solicited was in fact a police officer? Was it his responsibility to keep up with such things?

His already dark mood turned decidedly fouler when he thought about how this arrest could set back his plans to establish residency in the United States. After all, Natalie was expecting twins. He wanted to be here in the states for that. Most of all, he didn't want to see his relationship with Natalie torn apart by his deportation.

* * * * *

Given his consistently tight-lipped stance on personal matters, it's not surprising that the subject of Steve's wife was off-limits in our interviews. Once again the veil of Kilbey secrecy has been lowered in order to protect the privacy of those closest to him. I *did* catch one glimpse of Natalie Kilbey during my visit to Sydney, across a crowded room. She seemed to glide into focus—a radiant blonde in a long, flowing white skirt, grace personified. She has been described by a couple of Church fans as an "earth mother" type, but that label doesn't quite fit her. The woman I saw in Australia might perhaps be the mother of the sky, or the crystal-clear waters of Bondi Beach, but she seemed to have little to do with the coarse soil of the earth.

Well, she must be special, at least, because it was out of love for her that Steve abandoned the magical forests and snow-capped hills of Sweden for . . . Delaware. I suppose one could argue that he was once again trying to put his difficult past behind him, but really, Delaware? There could only be one reason for such a drastic move and that would be pure, unabashed love.

The story of their meeting in 1998 sounds like something out of a Cameron Crowe screenplay. Natalie was a passionate Church fan, in her mid-twenties at the time. Originally from West Virginia, she was an active member of the *Seance* mailing list and had spent the previous few years in fervent correspondence with other fans. She already loved Steve Kilbey, albeit as an abstraction. She may have even had pictures of him on her wall. But when the two finally met, during the *Hologram of Baal* tour, it was Steve who was smitten.

Steve and Marty, recording *Box of Birds* in Sweden, 1999 *(Kevin Keller)*

It was a whirlwind romance, involving many trips between Sweden and Natalie's home in Delaware. And in 1999 Natalie gave birth to twin girls—Steve's second set, though these two, Eve and Aurora, were fraternal twins rather than identical ones.

The New York arrest effectively outed Steve as a heroin addict. He and those close to him had done an excellent job over the years of keeping his "little problem" a secret from the public; in fact, the band's management at first tried to make the arrest sound like a pot bust, but as soon as the first reporter showed up at the court hearing, it was all over. Immediately, the Church bulletin boards went into overdrive, some anguished fans asking "How could he???" and others countering "It's none of our business." Steve's picture even made the front page of Australian newspapers for the first time in many years. The Sydney *Daily Telegraph* stated, "Steve Kilbey is still regarded by many veteran music critics as one of the finest songwriters this country has ever produced."

It was the type of publicity you couldn't buy.

An interesting footnote to the story is that the Church played the first and only Steveless gig in their history while the errant frontman sat in his cell that night. There was a sort of karmic justice to the fact that Marty—having been the one who had abandoned Steve on the eve of the Hamburg

Peter, recording *Box of Birds* in Sweden, 1999 *(Kevin Keller)*

gig in 1986, now found himself in the opposite position—holding the band together in Steve's absence. He did a remarkable job of it, leading Tim, Peter, and road manager Ward McDonald (on bass) through barnstorming versions of "Day of the Dead," Neil Young's "Cortez the Killer," and "Two Places at Once." Not knowing most of the lyrics, Marty channeled Steve and made them up on the spot. Elsewhere during the set, Peter sang lead on his excellent solo composition "Make a Move on Me" and the traditional Irish folk ballad "She Moved Through the Fair." To further stretch out the show, Marty performed five solo acoustic numbers. The audience was very supportive and enthusiastic throughout.

The album the Church were touring to support was a collection of covers called *Box of Birds*, an album Steve now says he regrets.

> Cooking Vinyl were very keen on a live album. The day that Tim and Marty were in London and actually taking it to them, I sat down and listened to this record they were giving them and it was just horrible. It was leaden you-had-to-be-there kind of stuff; it didn't translate at all. The singing was all out of tune. It sounded like me barking along with a bunch of guys on a headlong descent down a hill. So they went in there and said, "Steve doesn't want to give you the live album. But guess what? We're going to give you an album of covers instead!"

What emerged was a quickly-thrown-together collection featuring some very interesting choices (The Monkees' "Porpoise Song," Hawkwind's "Silver Machine," and the aforementioned "Cortez the Killer," among others), boasting generally good playing but marred by poor production and a lack of imagination. Most of the covers were simply note-for-note recreations of the originals and, in Steve's words, "never really added anything on to the original versions that they didn't already have. I wish it had never come out. But for the amount of people who bought it, it might as well not have."

The short-term consequences of Steve's arrest were minor. He was not deported. He was sentenced instead to community service, cleaning up the New York subway. While he was doing this, he met an older black man who later proceeded to take him to some of Harlem's seediest drug dens. Thus a brand new connection was forged, courtesy of the American justice system.

The long-term impact of the arrest, however, was more significant. Ten years later, Steve still has difficulty entering the United States due to the flag on his record and the American government's increased scrutiny of foreign visitors. Every world tour the Church books has an air of uncertainty until the last moment as Steve waits for his papers to clear—and consequently the band's visits to the United States (still their largest market) have been significantly curtailed since 1999.

27

TILL THE DAY COMES WHEN YOU REALIZE

Many years ago I told myself that I could never be happy without heroin, and indeed, getting off of it is the hardest thing; people have no idea. It's like, honestly, I've been hit and had my arm broken by a car; I'd go through that a hundred times rather than go through one more heroin withdrawal. I'd put out my hand and say, "Bust my hand up," rather than get addicted to heroin and get off it, because it's hell. That's why everybody is still out there doing it, because it's hell to get off. But then one day, for some reason, it just burned itself out. It wasn't like I used my free will. The desire just left me, like an evil, unclean spirit. One day it just left me.

—Steve Kilbey, July 2003

Steve stood on the beach on an early spring morning in 2000, holding his daughter Eve, now one year old. His wife stood next to him with Eve's twin, Aurora. Natalie's long hair blew behind her, exposing a young face still glowing with the joy of new motherhood. Steve turned his eyes to the water, watching the waves crash and foam and recede from the rocky Delaware coast.

He realized, for the first time in years, that he was happy. It didn't have to do with the fact that he'd been clean for three months. No, he had been through that whole routine before; during the first month it was always impossible to sleep, and then you spent the next two months feeling beaten down and exposed to the elements. Only after three months did the body begin to adjust, producing serotonin to take the place of the opiates. But it was not that. Steve felt that whatever dark spirit had descended upon him when he first became an addict was now gone. He knew with certainty that he would not hit the streets in a few weeks to score drugs. Neither would he do it in a few months or a few years.

He was happy. But there was a bittersweet edge to the happiness—he had decided not to tell Natalie or anyone else in his family about his new re-solve. They had heard him promise, time and time again, that he was going to quit. After a decade of broken promises, nothing he said about drugs had much effect. Maybe the promises themselves had worked against him. It was best to just let his family realize, over time, that he had finally done it.

Another thought occurred to him as he looked out over the waves, one that surprised him: he missed Australia. When he had left, he had told every-one he was doing it because he hated the country—its politics, the mentality of its people. In reality, he had been trying, halfheartedly, to pull himself out of his nosedive, to get away from the dealers and enablers who had helped make heroin a daily part of his life. But of course his problem had followed him to Sweden, and all of those elements had re-established themselves as quickly as a virus in a fresh host.

Now a lot of those dealers and enablers in Australia were gone—dead or missing. Maybe now he could go back—live in Bondi, on the beach, in the clean air. Look out on a shore covered in white sand instead of these ugly black and gray rocks; a place where he could swim on a March morning in-stead of standing by the water in a coat and scarf, shivering. And he thought of his two young daughters, and how Australia would be a vast playground to them. He could get them, and his wife, away from this land of strip malls and chain restaurants. After living in the rain, snow, and sleet for years, he just wanted to feel the sun again.

He looked at his wife, who was smiling at him.

"Let's go for a walk," he said.

★ ★ ★ ★ ★

For ten years, heroin had held Steve in its grip. It had come to dominate nearly every aspect of his waking life. Now, in order to survive without the drug, he needed to fill the void with new obsessions, new passions. He need-

Kilbey in the zone. Berlin, 2002 *(Stefan Horlitz)*

ed a distraction. To fulfill this role, he turned to . . . Internet chat rooms.

In hindsight it makes a certain amount of sense; ten years of addiction had complicated Steve's relationships with his friends and family. They loved him and stood by him, but that love was guarded. Steve was damaged and unreliable.

The fans, however, continued to adore him. They embraced him and forgave all his flaws—which seemed mere trifles in comparison with the beautiful music he kept giving them. So Steve began frequenting the Church chat rooms in search of affirmation. And it must be said that he gave as good as he got. For hours on end he regaled the habitués of the *Antenna* site with his spontaneous poetry and dry wit. He very quickly developed a friendly shorthand with three of the regulars: Brian Hutton, Amanda Magnano, and Tony Pucci. And, while he may have arrived there to get his ego stroked, he eventually formed genuine friendships with these three.

Music was the one aspect of Steve's life that had been relatively untainted by his addiction. On the one hand, heroin use had caused radical changes in his composition process, and certainly the Church's internal instability in the early '90s had left him somewhat adrift, but overall his abilities as a singer, lyricist, bassist, guitarist and composer had actually grown. The frequenters of *Antenna* loved and appreciated this music, which was, after all, Steve's life's work. He could chat with them and feel good about himself. And so he did.

I stumbled upon the chat room in 2001, when I was living in south Georgia, teaching English. Not having much of a social life beyond my work, I gravitated to the community of fans I found on Antenna. With the sun going down and the cicadas making a racket outside, I often sat hunched over my laptop, pecking out what I believed were pithy one-liners and waiting patiently for responses from the faceless individuals on the other end. It was there that I encountered a different side of Steve that I hadn't seen in London, one that Simon Polinski sums up effusively when he says,

> There's not an evil bone in his body. He's the sweetest man I've ever met. He's very kind . . . He's a gent. Absolute gent. And if he does crack the shits, it's for a nanosecond. And then he's red-faced and embarrassed about it.

Peter Koppes, Berlin, 2002 *(Stefan Horlitz)*

Steve and I blundered in at the same time and became reacquainted—
and it was the gregarious Steve that I now encountered. Although he was
grandiose, sarcastic, inscrutable, and sometimes just plain obnoxious, I
found myself warming to him in a way that I hadn't in London. He gave no
acknowledgment of our former encounter—I wasn't even sure if he remembered me—but we developed a way of speaking to each other through David
Bowie lyrics. That was *our* shorthand. And, believe it or not, eight years later
Steve can still recite some of our online exchanges almost verbatim. Why
he would retain this information at the expense of other, more important
details is anyone's guess. I may never completely agree with Polinski's over-
the-top assessment of the man, those chat sessions in 2001 at least caused
me to stop thinking of Steve as a callous prick.

Steve made many of his online visits during down-time from the Church's
2002 European tour: a semi-acoustic affair in support of *After Everything
Now This*. That album, released after a lengthy delay, heralded a return to
the hooks and atmosphere that had so drawn me to the band in the first
place. As for the stripped-down, quieter approach the Church experimented
with on the road, Steve himself had mixed feelings about it. To my ears, at
least, it was a success. Acoustic interpretations of "Radiance" and "Song for
the Asking" really brought out the subtleties of those songs. Steve's voice
projected beautifully across the small theaters, clubs, and auditoriums. And
multi-talented Australian singer/songwriter David Lane became a virtual
fifth member of the band, playing piano throughout the set. Visually, it
was certainly not a rock-and-roll spectacle—the usually hyperactive Marty
Willson-Piper spent most of the set on a stool—but the core audience (the
loyal fans) had not come for the theatrics.

Looking back a few years later, there is a general consensus amongst the
members of the band that in 2002 they had not properly thought this new
approach through. Certain songs like "Comedown" and "Electric Lash"
had new arrangements befitting the acoustic format, but many of the other
songs were played as they had always been, not taking into account the difference between acoustic and electric guitars. This may have been due to
the fact that, prior to the *After Everything* tour, Steve had repeatedly stated
that the live versions of the songs should always more or less approximate
the arrangements that had appeared on record. It was almost a mantra for

him. But working with different instruments forced the band to rethink this approach. Future tours would bear witness to this conceptual change, as the band would become increasingly more comfortable with the idea of re-imagining their classic material on a fresh canvas. Ultimately, this approach would revitalize the Church as a live band.

The fact that *After Everything Now This* turned out as well as it did defies all logic. The band itself was now more geographically fragmented than ever. During the drawn-out recording of the album, Steve was hopscotching between Sweden, Delaware, and Australia. Marty was splitting his time between London and New York, Peter had relocated to the Blue Mountains, west of Sydney,[19] and Tim lived in Sydney itself. Perhaps because of the long-distance separation, as well as Steve's problems, relationships within the band had become even more strained than normal—there was no strong sense of shared commitment because the Church's future seemed perpetually uncertain. As a result, the writing and recording of the album proved a long, drawn-out process that occurred in fits and starts in several different studios in at least three countries—typically not the sign of a project going well. And Steve's heroin use (still ongoing when the project began in 1999), which had once so reliably greased his creative wheels, had ceased to provide him any feeling of euphoria and had turned his life into daily drudgery. Add to this the fact that he was not always able to procure a steady supply of marijuana—something as necessary as breathing for Steve—and one might conclude that the obstacles in the band's path were insurmountable.

And yet the album exists, in spite of all the forces working against its creation, as one of the Church's finest achievements. *After Everything Now This* is rich in texture and unified in tone; it touches on all of the band's previously established strengths while moving forward into new and exciting territory. As with *Priest=Aura*—the album it most resembles in terms of mood and pacing—the musicians effectively subsume themselves into the larger collective entity, fusing their musical personalities to the point where it is difficult to discern who is doing what. Peter and Marty, in particular, blend seamlessly. Gone are the telltale jagged riffs that would normally distinguish Marty's playing from the smoother atmospherics of his bandmate.

---

[19] He would move again—to Queensland—not long thereafter.

Steve, *Box of Birds/After Everything* sessions. *(Courtesy, Trevor Boyd)*

Instead, the guitar lines weave around each other, creating complex melodies and rarely breaking out into individual solos.

Steve contributes some of the best bass playing and singing of his career. After a few years playing his instrument with a plectrum, he returns here to using his fingers, plucking lazily, allowing the notes to drop softly in alongside Tim's light pitter-patter. And his voice—the band's signature for many years—has never been as soft and vulnerable as on these tracks. There is a fragility as he reaches for certain notes—an insecurity, almost—as if it could all collapse at any moment. But he comes through every time, penetrating to the emotional core of this beautiful music.

And the lyrics—well, they encompass his spiritual side in all its omnivorous questing, but without the pretension of past efforts. While his words here may lack the grandiosity and scope of his work on *Priest=Aura*, they compensate for that with a beguiling intimacy—a heartfelt communication between Steve and his listeners recalling *Starfish*'s "Lost" fourteen years earlier. On this album, particularly on the nakedly emotional "Seen it Coming" and the softly grooving "Song for the Asking," Steve is in confessional mode. Yet his openness on these two tracks does not preclude him from exploring ambiguous and esoteric subjects elsewhere. Take, for instance, "Night Friends," which appears to evoke Madame Blavatsky's notorious night visits from the "secret masters" (elevated beings from the astral plane who allegedly made nocturnal contact with the Russian mystic and other "spirit sensitives.") This interpretation is supported by the lines "Waiting, we've been waiting/For other worlds to sync up to our own . . . Trying, we've been trying/To make contact with night friends so alone."

As with many Kilbey songs, though, the perceived meaning seems to take an abrupt left turn towards the end. The final verse, at first listen, seems a muddled mess:

> Loving, we've been loving
> But sometimes hate is better
> You can't keep out the killers with love, man
> Hating, we've been hating
> But only love can heal up the hate (all right)

It certainly doesn't have the sort of poetic flow one would normally associate with Kilbey's work; nevertheless, on close examination it reveals itself to be just the sort of paradox he revels in: Neither love nor hate can solve the conundrum the world finds itself in (love doesn't stop bullets, but, in the end, neither does hate), and so the human race is one great dog chasing its own tail. It's a hell of a way to end a song, flipping the Lennon aphorism and giving us no solutions, only problems (and what this revelation has to do with the "night friends" is anyone's guess). But that's one of the things that makes the Church so interesting: the band draws much from the music of the '60s, but it refuses to embrace that era's reliance on simplistic answers to complex problems. And, because Steve has never allowed himself to fall into the category of being a "message writer," he is able to obliquely explore these issues without feeling pressure to offer up empty solutions. "Night Friends" is not a masterpiece by any means—it's a little too disjointed to be a serious contender for that appellation—but it is a striking and original piece of music. Guest musician David Lane wraps the whole package up in some beautiful piano work—his spare, almost jazzy phrases falling through the air alongside Peter's equally restrained guitar textures, landing in front of and behind the staggered beat. The quietness of the song belies the fact that it is one of the most daring and experimental compositions in the Church oeuvre, the centerpiece of one of the best albums the band has ever made.

28

IN SHALLOW DREAMS, LIFE WAS BEGINNING TO TAKE A SHAPE

My loneliness broke like a fever at the end of my month-long stay in Australia in July 2003. Ahead of the Church's impending two-night stand at the Sydney Opera House, fans from all over the world began trickling into the city. My routine up to this point had been marked by lengthy, intense conversations with one or more of the Kilbeys, followed by days of walking around Sydney by myself. Now the house phone, which for weeks had been largely silent, began ringing off the hook. People I had never met in person but knew from Church bulletin boards—Brian Hutton, Nikki Ruggieri, Sue Campbell, Amanda Magnano, Ernst Kok, Danny Burton—were all converging on Sydney. Some, like me, had traveled a long distance. Brian made a weekend trip from Dundee in Scotland to see the shows. Ernst flew in from Europe. Sue—my pen-pal for almost ten years—drove up from Melbourne, as did Amanda. Danny came from Queensland, and Nikki from Steve Kilbey's hometown of Canberra.

I met Danny and Nikki on the night of the band's secret warm-up gig at the New Civic Hotel. I noticed them as I walked up the steps from the train station. Danny was tall and broad-shouldered, the archetypal rugged Australian male, with blondish hair, ruddy complexion, and an easy grin. Nikki was an attractive brunette in her thirties, with a warm smile and faint laugh lines around her eyes.

Danny reached his hand out. "Robert Lurie!" he said. I shook it. Nikki gave me a warm hug. I was a bit taken aback by the fact that they had immediately spotted me, even though we had never met.

"How did you know it was me?" I asked.

"The picture," Danny replied.

"Picture?"

"Yeah, the one of you and Kilbey. It's all over the net."

I was speechless. Then I remembered I'd e-mailed that picture to another fan, Tony Pucci, two weeks earlier. This was how the world of Church fandom worked: any new information, especially pictures, spread like a virus.

"You're famous," Nikki said, laughing.

"Only by association," I replied.

We walked briskly towards the club, making small talk. I felt instantly comfortable with these two; it was easy to forget that our relationships had been forged in the nebulous realm of cyberspace. We did, after all, share a common reference point in the band we followed. Despite the fact that we

Nikki Ruggieri with Steve Kilbey, Sydney, 2003 *(Robert Lurie)*

lived in different parts of the world, had different politics, watched different sports, and worshipped at the altars of different cultural icons, we all knew the lyrics to "You Took." We had all listened to *Magician Among the Spirits* in its entirety . . . many times. Danny and Nikki felt like family. With them it was perfectly okay to admit that I had spent the bulk of my school years transcribing Steve Kilbey's lyrics into notebooks when I was supposed to be taking notes on lectures.

We talked about the Church over dinner, too. There was the standard discussion of favorite albums, favorite songs, etc. Because Danny had been following the band since the early '80s, he probably had best understanding of their overall career, and their place within Australian music history. Nikki and I had caught up on the earlier albums after the fact, but Danny had been there when they were originally released, eagerly listening to each new one as it came out. And whereas my only experience of their 1980s tours was via bootleg tapes and CDs, Danny had seen every Church tour since the beginning. He still remained intensely loyal, though he did claim the band had hit their live peak on the *Heyday* tour of 1986. From that point on, he believed, the energy had abated somewhat, even as the musicianship remained stellar.

Nikki, as it turned out, had never seen the band in full electric mode, having only witnessed the *After Everything Now This* acoustic tour. Of course, Danny and I went on ad nauseam about the Koppes/Willson-Piper twin-guitar assault.

Different fans have varying levels of intensity. Danny, being an überfan, seemed to own every pressing of every album. He had all the fanzines, a sizable collection of videos, and the obligatory stash of bootlegs. I too had a formidable collection of Church paraphernalia. Nikki, on the other hand, maintained a sense of perspective. She loved the Church, of course, but she was primarily interested in the music. Whether a particular copy of an album was on Carrere or Mushroom didn't matter much to her. I was thrilled to engage in detailed discussions of Church minutiae with Danny, but I appreciated Nikki's grounding in the real world.

The show that night taught me a lot about the Church's underground popularity. Even though the warm-up gig had only been announced that very day on the band's web site, word had traveled fast. The Civic was packed. A line ran up the stairs from the basement venue and clear around the block. The people in this line seemed to be of all ages and stripes. Some were in Goth outfits that perhaps suggested a primary loyalty to bands like the Cure and Bauhaus; others were more like us—apparently wearing whatever they had happened to throw on that morning. They all talked excitedly about the impending performance; rumor had it that the band would be debuting material from the upcoming album.

Having purchased our tickets early, we managed to bypass the line and get to the concert room ahead of everyone. Everyone, that is, except for the other diehards, who had gotten there even earlier. One of these I knew straight away: the lovely Sue Campbell, my long-term pen pal. I felt as if this woman were an old friend, someone with whom I had shared many memories, and yet this was our first face-to-face meeting. She had the kind of smile that draws all eyes towards it. Sue was a good ten years older than me, but when her face lit up with that smile, I could swear she had cracked the secret of eternal youth. The first thing she did was give me a big hug and say, "It's great to finally meet you!" We fell effortlessly into conversation, like the old friends that we were.

One by one the fans began to congregate in front of the stage. It was a fairly low stage, so we sat cross-legged directly in front of it; this was going to be like watching the Church in our living rooms.

When the club had filled completely, the band emerged from backstage. There was no fog or light show; in place of such theatrics, a selection from Vangelis' *Blade Runner* score played in the background as the band members took up their instruments. They started with a new number, the aggressive "Sealine." It was a good way to begin the show—a heads-up to the audience that the Church would not be spending the evening dwelling on the past. The first four songs of the set were all from the new album, and they sounded promising indeed. "Telepath" was classic Church: a steadily building wave of claustrophobic momentum over three insistently strummed chords. The intriguingly named "The Theatre and its Double"[20] featured some neo-flamenco flourishes from Marty, and "Nothing Seeker" was the Church at their hardest-rocking. The older songs they *did* play were solid guitar-and-bass numbers that fitted in well with the new material.

It was interesting to watch the four of them crammed onto the tiny stage—I had never seen them in such a confined space. It was not the most visually exciting show I had ever seen—there was little room for dramatic movement, after all—but musically it was the Church at their most polished. Assisting in this impression was an excellent sound mix, with instruments and vocals evenly balanced.

They closed the show with "Magician Among the Spirits." As the band drifted into the hypnotic wash of guitars that marked the beginning of the song, Steve kept looking off into the corner, frowning deeply. Finally, he brought the song to a halt, exclaiming, "You there! Yes, you—and your friend!"

Two young women broke from their conversation and stared at Steve.

"There was a reviewer who wrote about one of our shows recently,"

---

[20] The title is borrowed from Antonin Artaud's manifesto in which he proposed a "theater of cruelty."

Peter and Steve at the Civic, secret gig, Sydney, 2003 *(Robert Lurie)*

Steve continued. "He said that when we did this song, it was the closest thing to a real seance that he had ever experienced." He paused, scowling at the women, and then practically spat out his next words: "But it's awful fucking hard to create that mood with you fucking carrying on over there!" In that instant, "Old Steve"—ornery, cantankerous, difficult—rose up and shattered, momentarily at least, the carefully constructed image of "New Steve"—the friendly bloke down the block, doting father, happy middle-aged artiste. It seemed to me that Old Steve reared his head these days primarily where the music was concerned. He took "Magician Among the Spirits" seriously, even if the audience didn't. It didn't matter that this was an impromptu gig in a small nightclub; he wasn't going to let anyone fuck with his song. He expected them to listen. The Church wasn't in the business of providing background music for casual socializing. If he had to be difficult in order to get this point across, so be it.

Once we had all settled back into the mood, the song did become quite magical. It had the sleepy vocals and the slowly slithering bass line of the album version, but in the middle the song seemed to wake up, as if the spirits in question had made their appearance. And while Marty may have been on auto-pilot, perfunctorily plunking away on the bass, Steve and Tim seemed to be genuinely possessed, crying out, in turns, "Make it all right!" "Make it all right!" The song ended in a controlled meltdown, guitar feedback collapsing upon itself, ominous E notes echoing into oblivion, all awash with the white noise of cymbals rapidly pounded with mallets. And with this, the Church of 2003 left the stage. It was damned impressive—the entire show having been performed on the band's terms, with no concessions to the audience's wishes other than the obligatory "Under the Milky Way."

And what did the audience think? Hard to say. The diehard fans—always a forward-looking bunch—were ecstatic. The band had given a lengthy preview of a new album that would not be released for another three months. Anyone else, well . . . at least they left knowing that the Church were a band very much committed to living in the present.

After the show, many of the fans lingered, sipping drinks and talking about what they had just seen. Steve came out to talk with them, soliciting advice on the new material. "Old Steve" went back into hiding.

★ ★ ★ ★ ★

Newly clean, and having finally gotten Natalie, Eve, and Aurora to Australia, Steve threw himself back into his songwriting with a new sense of focus, entering into the most prolific period of his career. The positive effects of his sobriety are obvious to everyone: Kilbey's lyrics and singing have never been better. That being said, the Church has yet to release an album that matches the focus and power of *After Everything Now This*. They came close with the follow-up—*Forget Yourself*—but in the effort to create something spontaneous and raw, a stylistic reaction against the polished beauty of its predecessor, the band managed to sabotage one of the strongest batches of songs they had assembled in years. Two songs in particular—"Sealine" and "Song in Space"—are woefully ill-served by their recorded versions. The Church had already been performing the new material for months by the time the album was released in fall 2003, and many fans (including those of us who'd attended the show described in the previous section) had grown accustomed to the lean, propulsive live renditions of those two tracks. In contrast, the same songs come across as flat and sluggish on record. Part of the problem lay in the band's insistence on using first takes. During recording, Steve had been reading Jimmy McDonough's Neil Young biography, *Shakey*, a book that breathlessly extolled Young's slapdash, intuitive recording style. But what worked for the grungy, power-chord rock of Neil Young and Crazy Horse didn't necessarily work for the more layered music of the Church. Certainly, the band's goal of creating an album vastly different in style and attitude from *After Everything Now This* was an admirable one, but in this instance the sonic change of pace did not yield quality results. A minor comfort to fans was the fact that all the songs on *Forget Yourself*—from "Nothing Seeker" and "Telepath" on down to "Maya"—sounded fantastic live. On the road, the band increased the tempo and amped up the energy. But hearing the live versions often proved bittersweet; while reveling in the sonic wallop, one could not help wondering at the album that might have been.

Curiously, most of *Forget Yourself* sounds as if it was recorded with the EQ turned completely off. Individual instruments are often hard to discern, and sometimes the bass vanishes from the mix completely. Steve's disconcertingly loud voice floats dizzily above this bed of sonic mud. As Greg Hatmaker, a regular contributor to *Hotel Womb*, quipped, "Maybe if I try listening to the songs through a string and a soup can, I will forget how much it already sounds like they were recorded that way."

There were dissenters to this view. In fact, a small but vocal contingent of fans took to the message boards to proclaim *Forget Yourself* a virtual second coming (significantly, many of these listeners had not yet heard the live renditions of the songs.) The most articulate and fervent of these evangelists was American fan Tony Pucci, who wrote:

> I can truly say that it is one of the best CDs I've ever heard in my life . . . It is epic. It is raw. It is very powerful. It left me stunned. I am challenged as a musician by the very high standard FY sets . . . I actually, when "Sealine" went into "Song in Space," turned it up as loud as it could go and shouted to the world, "Oh my god! This is a f*cking awesome CD!" And then the beauty of "The Theatre and its Double," with a chorus in that song to make you weep . . . Marty's gravelly voice on "See Your Lights" . . . so immediate and human. All of the songs are so special. The beauty of "Maya" and "June." I could make a CDR of "June" 15 times in a row, and listen to it all day! And in all songs, the brilliant melodies of SK . . .

perhaps his best ever. You can hear the joy he has as an artist in his voice. He loves what he is doing . . . making the best music of his life.

While eventually conceding some of the production shortcomings, Tony continues to champion the album as one of the band's best.

The Church later released the completed outtakes and B-sides from the *Forget Yourself* sessions on a separate CD entitled *Beside Yourself.* In a number of ways, I find this limited-edition release to be a richer, more satisfying listen than its parent album. For one thing, more attention seems to have been paid to the mixing and the mastering process, resulting in a crisp recording with a deep, sensuous bass groove. This material was generated in the same mood of free-form experimentation as the much-maligned *Magician Among the Spirits*, but here the approach works. *Beside Yourself* has a number of standouts, including the exquisite intro track "Jazz" and the climactic "Cantilever," a sprawling epic that harkens back to "You Took" but outdoes it in both intensity and dynamics.

Record stores in Australia quickly sold out all the copies of *Beside Yourself,* and one Aussie journalist went so far as to proclaim it one of the band's fin-

The Church at the Sydney Metro, *Forget Yourself* tour *(Captain Mission)*

est albums. The irony of a supposedly throwaway album besting the official release was repeated a year later in 2004 with the acoustic album *El Momento Descuidado*. This intimate, quickly recorded project was initiated by a small label called Liberty Blue that had distinguished itself with a series of "unplugged" albums from notable Australian artists (including former Kilbey collaborator Stephen Cummings). When the label solicited the Church for an acoustic album, the band readily agreed, and took a two-day break from the recording of the next "official" album to hastily rearrange some old classics and record them live to tape. In addition to reworked versions of "Metropolis," "The Unguarded Moment," and "Under the Milky Way," the band tracked four new songs exclusive to the release, including a surprisingly successful country pastiche titled "Till the Cows Come Home."

Many of the rearrangements of the old material were quite radical. Rather than simply play acoustic versions of tried-and-true chestnuts (as they had essentially done on the *After Everything Now This* tour), the band chose to deconstruct and rebuild from the songs from the ground up, often making fundamental changes to structure and tempo. For example, "Tristesse"—which had become something of a sacred cow in the Church catalogue—is sung on *El Momento Descuidado* by Marty Willson-Piper. In place of Steve's relaxed delivery, Marty affects a strained, Dylan-inflected drawl. Strangely, it works, nestled as it is in a comforting bed of chiming acoustic guitars and mandolins. But the most moving of the retooled tracks is Peter Koppes's "A New Season." In recent years Peter's voice has settled into a pleasing rasp somewhat akin to Mark Knopfler's. On this new interpretation of the *Starfish* classic, Peter accompanies himself on piano with minimal augmentation. The appearance of Marty's starkly beautiful solo on nylon-string guitar halfway through the track ranks as one of the Church's most sublime musical moments.

More than anything, *El Momento Descuidado* showcases the quality and depth of the Church's songwriting. Stripped of electric guitars and elaborate soundscapes, lyrics and melodies shine through like simple, unadorned jewels.

Like *Beside Yourself*, *El Momento Descuidado* flew off the Australian shelves and quickly sold out of its initial run. Cooking Vinyl snatched up the disc and mass-released it in the UK and US. And, irony of ironies, the CD received better US distribution than any Church album since *Sometime Anywhere*; copies were quite easy to find in large chain stores as well as the always-reliable independent retailers. In several ways *El Momento* overshadowed *Uninvited, Like the Clouds,* the Church's new electric album that was released shortly thereafter. *Uninvited* is certainly a fine effort—it contains, among other things, the strongest and most focused lyrics of Steve's career—but the music adds nothing new to the Church's sonic toolbox. If anything, this album serves as a nice summary of all the styles the Church have mastered by this point, from the jingle-jangle pop of "Easy" to the moody claustrophobia of "Real Toggle Action." It even boasts a worthy *Priest=Aura* throwback in the extended opening track "Block." But no new ground is being staked out on *Uninvited,* whereas *El Momento* seems fresh and exciting in contrast, even though it sports only four new songs.

One of the largest problems plaguing the post–*Priest=Aura* Church is the issue of quality control. *Uninvited, Like the Clouds* suffers, as have many of the other releases, from a lack of editorial discipline. Historically, this has been the downfall of many artists who have won their coveted creative freedom. But history also points to a possible solution: In the 1920s, American authors F. Scott Fitzgerald and Thomas Wolfe—both wildly talented but (especially in Wolfe's case) excessively wordy writers—flourished under the firm and discerning editorial eye of Maxwell Perkins; Perkins elevated editing to the level of art, working with the extraordinary raw material these writers gave him and helping to shape that material into powerful literature—and thereby forcing Fitzgerald and Wolfe to live up to their own potential. Perhaps the Church need their own Maxwell Perkins—a talented and trusted outside producer who is sympathetic to the band's aims and yet not afraid to raise the bar higher when the occasion demands it; an expert surgeon who knows when, where, and how much to cut. From *Magician Among the Spirits* onward, the band has enjoyed complete artistic freedom; it has not had to respond to the demands of a strong-willed producer. I would argue that this has been absolutely essential in the Church's development—it has allowed them to experiment, to stretch out creatively—but I also feel it is time for the pendulum to swing in the other direction. It is time for these fine musicians to take everything they have learned and create the great work they've had in them for so long. The *only* reason we have yet to see a Church equivalent to *Revolver* or *Abbey Road* is that the Church have not found their George

Martin; the raw materials for such an achievement are certainly there, but the benevolent guiding hand is missing.

Steve once told me, quite vehemently, "No one has *ever* told me what to write." And that's a very good thing. But perhaps it is time that someone told him what *not* to write. It's time that someone said, "Steve, this line about 'Your husband ain't no Ben Affleck' is really jarring; I'm sure you can do better." Or: "Do you *really* need to use the phrase 'fat baby's dick'?" (Both these ill-advised turns of phrase marred *Isidore*, Steve's otherwise excellent 2004 collaborative project with Jeffrey Cain of Remy Zero.)

The only person who could consistently make those kinds of hard-line calls is someone far outside the Church's circle: someone who is a philosophical ally but not a fan.

★ ★ ★ ★ ★

When I last saw Steve, in 2006, his life seemed to be in a pretty good place, and every indication points to continued stability in the years since then. On his return to Australia, Steve settled comfortably into the role of being a full-time dad (in 2006 Steve and Natalie welcomed a new addition to the family: Scarlett Virginia Kilbey). His modest but consistent income—comprised primarily of royalties from "Under the Milky Way" and "Unguarded Moment," plus the proceeds from online sales of his artwork—has made it possible for him to be a daily presence in his younger daughters' lives. The only major downside to the relocation is that he is only able to see Elektra and Miranda—who remain in Sweden with their mother and stepfather—a few times a year.

Steve has apparently not used heroin since 2000, and claims to use marijuana sparingly when at home (relative, at least, to his heavy use on the road).

In the late 1990s, Steve had said in an interview that he would never be able to get back to the health and spiritual well-being he had enjoyed during the *Heyday* period. But he has certainly come closer to that earlier idyll than anyone would have thought possible. Sloth and indulgence have been replaced by exercise and meditation, and the results have been striking.

Steve's attitude towards Australia has also undergone a radical change. He now thinks of it as the most beautiful place on earth, a country he is more than happy to call home. The problem is, Steve has spent so much of his life coming from a place of opposition—opposition to musical rivals, to "straight" society, to prevailing attitudes of morality, to his own geographical location—that his current struggle to be a "regular bloke" in the mold of his father is ultimately a losing proposition. He can act the role in fine fashion for limited periods of time, but a part of him will always be an outsider. It's no accident that he feels a strong affinity for Kurt Vonnegut's book *A Man Without a Country,* for Steve, by his own design, is a soul in isolation. This cannot and should not change, because it is the core of his art.

It must also be acknowledged that one of the principal factors that cemented that sense of isolation in later years was the Church's failure to achieve lasting mainstream success. Indeed, I am forced to the rather startling conclusion that failure *saved* Steve Kilbey, both creatively and personally, because failure prevented Steve from getting fully sucked into the self-aggrandizing and materialistic lifestyle that fame affords—a spiritual malaise that often translates to creative death. One need look no further than the careers of Eric Clapton, Sting, Elton John, and Rod Stewart to see that this is the norm rather than the exception in the rock world. Also, by his own admission, Steve became complacent after experiencing just a *touch* of fame. Had he been swept into the whirlwind of American stardom, *Hologram of Baal, After Everything Now This*, and *El Momento Descuidado* might not have happened. I'm not saying he would have "sold out" in the traditional sense, but the band certainly wouldn't have worked as hard as they did on those projects. *Hologram* and *After Everything*, in particular, represented a very real struggle for the continued existence of the Church. That urgency fueled the creative process. Had they been cocooned by fame and wealth, Steve and the others likely wouldn't have felt that pressure or made that effort.

On a personal level his lack of success may have saved his life from completely spiraling out of control. He remarked once that the only difference between his situation and Keith Richards' was that Keith had enough money to indulge a lifelong heroin addiction, whereas Steve had become stretched thin after only a few years. Steve had no palace on the French Riviera to ransom for his pound of smack. Eventually his resources dried up and he was forced to make a choice.

Steve plays Cupid, San Francisco, 2006 *(Tracy Nunnery)*

29

ALL I EVER WANTED TO SEE

Ten years ago, on the plane back from England, I had asked myself what it was that I wanted from Steve Kilbey. Now it seems quite obvious. Steve is the father of my art. My fledgling career as a songwriter and musician is the direct result of the seeds his music planted in me, and like any dutiful son I craved acknowledgement and approval from that creative father. It was the same insatiable desire that had driven the young Bob Dylan all the way from Hibbing, Minnesota to the ailing Woody Guthrie's bedside in New York. Only, my first meeting with my progenitor had not gone off as well as I had hoped.

Most rational people would have given up at that point. But I am anything but rational. My craving for a connection with Steve sublimated itself into a desire to learn what had made Steve Kilbey the artist that he is today. I wanted to know his story, the full story. I felt there was much in his experience that I and many others could benefit from. Primarily, I was curious to know how one writer could go from "Jet Fin Rock" to "Tristesse" in a single lifetime. What was his secret?

At the end of the day, the answers to these questions proved surprisingly pedestrian: Steve Kilbey became "Steve Kilbey" by feeding his active imagination at every opportunity—reading voraciously in literature, history, and metaphysics; experimenting with altered states of consciousness; challenging himself to branch into new mediums if ever his creativity waned. Coupled with this internal work, Steve pursued his professional goals with single-minded focus, to the exclusion of all other considerations. Consequently, by the time of his first big break, he was already a seasoned performer and accomplished songwriter. From the Beatles through Beck, this has been the time-honored formula for artistic success and longevity: Always keep your eyes open to the vastness and complexity of the world. Document it. Celebrate it and eviscerate it in equal measure. Work, work, work. And if ever you find yourself losing your innate sense of wonder, alter your perceptions. That's what I learned from Steve. It is ultimately a better and longer-lasting gift than mere affirmation.

Throughout the writing of this book, one question has continued to pop into my mind: If Steve and I had met as fellow musicians, without the baggage of the fan/idol relationship, would we have become friends? After much careful consideration, I would have to say, sadly, no. Steve Kilbey has a dual personality; "Old" and "New" Steve continue to vie for control of the host. As one fan wrote to me a number of years ago, "One moment Steve can be the loveliest guy you ever met, the next a right bastard." It is definitely true that when he turns his charisma high-beams on you, Steve Kilbey can be hard to resist: he is funny, charming, gregarious, full of fascinating anecdotes and insights—the kind of person you would want to be sitting next to if you had to endure a long train ride. But, despite Simon Polinski's effusive praise, Steve can also be dismissive and cruel; he has a deeply rooted narcissistic streak that his diligent practice of Buddhism and numerous acts of generosity may often suppress but can never completely kill. If he's in a foul mood, which can be often, other people would be well-advised to keep their distance—they are likely to be insulted or ignored. The maddening thing is that there is no way of telling which Steve you're going to encounter at any given moment, and who is going to be the object of his disdain. Since getting to know him, I've had the opportunity to introduce friends and loved ones to him. Sometimes it goes quite well; for instance, when he learned that my friend J.R. was a classics scholar, he became more enthused than I have ever seen him, peppering J.R. with questions about his studies and trying to get him to speak in Latin. But more often than not I find myself apologizing to friends for Steve's behavior. One told me recently, after meeting him, "As an artist he's brilliant, but as a person Steve Kilbey is a total diva. I don't envy your position at all."

A solitary moment. *Uninvited Like the Clouds* tour, Australia, 2006 *(Captain Mission)*

A lot of fans rationalize all this by saying, "He's a genius; we've got to make certain allowances for him." I find that unacceptable. In the words of my friend, "Being extremely competent at something does not give one free license in one's behavior." Twenty years ago Steve's less-pleasant side might have been explained away with the "pressures of stardom" excuse. But Steve is no longer famous. He is not being mobbed by fans everywhere he goes. The Steve Kilbey of 2008 is a multi-talented, everyman artist—the frontman of a hard-working, underappreciated band that needs all the goodwill it can get.

To be fair, Steve is well aware of his shortcomings and would be the last person to make excuses for them. And it must be said that he has come a long way from the surly young man who once insulted a 30-year-old guy in a guitar shop for being "over the hill." Indeed, Steve is now quick to apologize if he realizes he's said something nasty, and in his blog he has repeatedly extended an olive branch to the multitude of former friends and colleagues he has alienated over the years. He is clearly trying, and, in the final analysis, that is probably all anyone can reasonably ask of another human being.

One side benefit to the experience of writing the book is that Steve seemed
to warm to me during the time we spent working together. The one interview we had scheduled turned to two, and then three, and so on. The
project ended up taking seven years—far longer than either of us could have
anticipated. But he never stopped being available; he remained on call to the
very end.

In turn, I grew less intimidated around him. Some of my happiest moments in Australia were listening to Steve tell stories at Gertrude & Alice's
coffee shop. He had a way of drawing me into his world—to the point where
I could visualize every character and incident he described. The tales of his
childhood and adolescence were like a bizarre, exaggerated version of my
own upbringing, with the Australian landscape standing in for the snowy
streets of Minneapolis.

But Steve was always quick to rouse me if he sensed I was falling too
deeply under his spell. On one occasion he said something along the lines
of, "There are very few people in the music world who work harder on their
songs than I do." I agreed enthusiastically, which provoked an unexpected
flaring of his temper.

"Listen, Lurie," he snapped. "The only reason I'm even talking to you is
because I know you aren't a fucking yes man. So don't start being one now,
just because I'm cooperating!"

It stung. But when I thought about it later on, I respected him for saying
that. After all, how many other rock stars would dress down their biographer for liking them too much?

30
YOU'RE STILL BEAUTIFUL

July 22, 2006: As I watched the Church maneuver their way through an acoustic set at the Marquee Theatre in Tempe, Arizona, I thought about how things had changed—both for the band and me—since that pivotal concert at the Northrop in Minneapolis sixteen years earlier. First and most obviously, age had worked its bittersweet magic on all of us. Of the band's three founding members on stage, only Peter Koppes seemed to have dodged time's bullet; with his thick, curly hair, boyish smile, and trim physique, he looked almost exactly as he had in the "Unguarded Moment" video in 1980. Marty, on the other hand, had undergone a startling transformation; his once wiry frame was now saddled with beer poundage, and his long, flowing hair was crinkly and streaked with gray. Despite this physical decline, his manic energy and facial elasticity enabled him to appear, paradoxically, a good fifteen years younger than his actual age. He retained his handsomeness through sheer force of will; consequently, the audience's eyes were still drawn to him.

And then there was Steve himself: the self-inflicted psychic wounds had lent him gravity and sadness, and certainly he had not come out on the other side of fifty physically unscathed: his hair had thinned considerably and his beard was almost entirely white. Yet his face remained astonishingly youthful—hardly a wrinkle other than the signature crow's feet, and no slack to his skin whatsoever. He retained his strong chin and angular features and had shed much of the "junkie weight" he'd gained during the nineties. All told, he was a man who had narrowly avoided the rock-and-roll curse: despite a pro-

Rob Dickinson of Catherine Wheel, with Steve and Marty, San Francisco, 2006 *(Tracy Nunnery)*

longed, dangerous liaison with one of the nastiest of drugs, he looked closer now to the effervescent Paul McCartney than the shrunken Keith Richards. But it had been a very close call, and Steve knew it.

In addition to physical changes, the band's music had changed as well. Steve's singing represented the biggest leap forward: he had become a master of his vocal instrument, knowing just when to emote and when to pull back, delicately cradling certain phrases in the way Sinatra had on his quieter songs. In fact, his voice had improved so dramatically over the Church's twenty-six-year career that any objective listener, if presented with both *Uninvited, Like the Clouds* and *Of Skins and Heart,* would likely conclude that the two albums featured different singers.

In terms of structure and playing, the Church of 2006 was a far more daring and sophisticated animal than the Church I had seen in 1990. In the earlier years, the Church's MO had simply consisted of playing the songs harder and faster than the recorded versions—amping them up in such a way that the sheer energy of the performance compensated for the shaky harmonies and sloppiness of the musicianship. But now the band chose to radically rearrange the structure of these songs—just as they had on *El Momento Descuidado*—and no longer shied away from quietness and subtlety. Also, the musicians regularly switched instruments onstage—Steve alternating between bass and guitar, Peter playing guitar, keyboards, and mandolin, Tim jumping back and forth between drums, keyboard, and percussion, and Marty pulling off the impressive feat of switching effortlessly from guitar to bass to drums. Unlike previous onstage attempts in this direction, the different musical perspectives now enhanced the quality of the music; this was due in no small part to Steve's much-improved skill on rhythm guitar (His uneven playing had previously been the weak link in such experiments). The Church had figured out how to shake things up, jolting themselves—and their fans—out of the complacency that had long threatened to engulf the whole enterprise.

In terms of stage demeanor, Steve had abandoned his aloofness in favor of direct interaction with the audience. Both the intimacy of the acoustic presentation and the smallness of the venue facilitated this change of approach. The new rapport between band and concertgoers served the musicians well, especially when Marty ran into technical difficulties midway through the show. Steve simply told jokes, noodled on his bass, and carried on conversations with the crowd while Marty fixed the offending effects box.

Because of all these factors, the Marquee performance was the best Church show I had ever seen. While I'm sure the band would have gladly traded the warmth of this small show for the opportunity to play a packed Northrop Auditorium again, they made the best of their diminished stature. We, the fans, were the beneficiaries—receiving a sonic reward for our dedication and tenacity.

Certainly my own life had gone through some drastic changes during the span of time between the Northrop and the Marquee. With regards to the Church—a band I had once worshiped as a substitute for a God that was, to quote Steve, "invisible to me"—I now knew three of the musicians on a personal basis. It was a level of familiarity I could never have dreamed of in years past. But in getting that access I too had traded something away: the all-consuming passion, the fanaticism that had so animated my teenage and early adult interest in this band. I felt a certain sadness at having lost that fervor, but also a sense of relief. The understanding that my favorite band was comprised of complicated and fallible *men*, rather than *gods*, came as both comfort and inspiration—comfort because flesh-and-blood humans are easier to contact, talk to, and relate to than deities, and inspiration because the achievements of these conflicted, sometimes frustratingly difficult individuals opened the possibility that other mixed-up people (such as myself) might also be capable of creating substantive and lasting work.

Despite the ebbing of my youthful fanaticism, however, Steve's lyrics and melodies continued to exert a hold on me. There had been the fear that, when subjected to intense scrutiny, these lyrics might collapse under the weight of serious analysis, as Michael Stipe's (and, to some degree, Robert Smith's) had as I'd gotten older. But such fears had proved unwarranted. Yes, many of Steve's songs were flawed—probably due to his reluctance to edit his work—but those flaws only served to throw the strengths of his writing into sharper relief. On balance, his body of work was one of which he could be justly proud, and one that I was proud of having devoted such a significant amount of time to studying.

Backstage more changes were apparent. For one thing, there were no groupies. Steve made a point of phoning his wife before and after the show, and Peter and Tim were equally diligent in keeping in touch with their spouses. Tim had even brought his daughter on the road with him; she was one-third of the all-female road crew for this tour. The band's manager, Tiare

The otherworldly Peter Koppes, 2007 (Stefan Horlitz)

Helberg, was Marty's long-time partner. As might be expected, the once hedonistic band had settled into a relatively calm lifestyle befitting four middle-
aged men. Of the four, only Steve appeared to smoke marijuana habitually.
Peter enjoyed a post-concert glass of wine, and Marty seemed to be the sole
patron of the heavily stocked beer chest that followed the band from show to
show. In that ice chest, nestled amongst the many neglected beer bottles, sat
the carton of chocolate soy milk that served as Steve's drink of choice.

But this apparent tranquility can never completely belie the palpable
tension that continues to exist between the members of the Church. Marty
and Steve have come through the fire together, and the bond between the
two comprises perhaps the strongest and longest-lasting friendship within
the band. But creatively there continues to be a tug of war between Steve's
inclination towards atmospheric psychedelia and Marty's more straightforward rock sensibility. Peter, by his own choice, has kept himself outside of
this push-and-pull, but his outsider status is problematic. By not engaging
head-on in creative conflicts, he may have protected himself from unneeded
stress, but he has also come to feel that he has less room in which to maneuver. It was this very real musical wall that caused him to create the layered,
ethereal sound—a wash of guitar atmosphere—that has been his signature
since his return. As one fan put it, Peter provides "the sky in which Marty
soars." But it has been a long time since Peter himself has soared, and I get
the sense that he misses that.

From my observations in Tempe, I found it hard to imagine the future
of this turbulent band. Serious personality conflicts continue to go unad-
dressed—conflicts that cause the members to spend as little outside time with
each other as possible. On the other hand, when they took the stage together
at the Marquee, those conflicts melted away and the chemistry that had existed since the band's first rehearsal in 1980 took over once again. My sense,
from talking to Steve, Tim, and Peter, is that they value that chemistry—and
its possibilities—above all other considerations, and will continue to explore
it as long as they can. Their issues and lack of patience with each other may
have resulted in their being one of the world's least-rehearsed bands, but come
soundcheck, night after night, the four of them will all be there, drawn back
in spite of themselves. With the Church, what remains, however improbable,
is real, tangible magic—ultimately unidentifiable and unexplainable.

After the show I found Steve backstage, alone, sprawled out on the leather sofa, cooling himself with a small Japanese paper fan. Without raising his eyes to me he said, "Lurie, do you know how to roll a joint?"

I shrugged. "I'm not very good at it," I said.

He looked up and smirked. "Well what fucking good are you, then? Guess I'll have to do it myself." He sat up, leaned over, and retrieved some rolling papers and a ziplock bag of marijuana from a backpack resting near his feet. I took a seat next to him. As he concentrated intently on his new task, I said, "I think tonight was some of the best singing I've ever heard you do."

He chuckled softly, raised the joint to his lips, licked the edge of the paper and sealed it tight. "I can see it now," he said, "*On that sweltering night in Tempe, Steve's singing was the best it had ever been. The culmination of a magnificent career.* Is that how you'll write it?"

"Something like that."

And then we sat together quietly, in that dark room, allowing the pungent smoke to fill the empty spaces. I think we both understood that this would be our final meeting.

When he had smoked the joint down to a nub, I stood up and said, "Well Steve, I'm heading out."

He stood up as well and said, "I'll walk with you to your car; I need to get out of this room."

Stepping out the back door of the theatre, we were immediately hit by the 105 degree temperature of the Arizona summer night. Even at one o'clock in the morning, under a completely dark sky, it was the type of heat that could pummel a person senseless.

The concertgoers and autograph-seekers had by now gone home, so we were left to traverse a large, barren parking lot. As we made that asphalt trek, I thought about the fact that the imposing man who sauntered beside me was the living, breathing author of the music that had set the course for my own career. Even during my numerous moments of extreme frustration with him, I had never lost the sense of awe I felt in his presence.

As we reached my car, Steve broke the ponderous silence to ask, "What did you think of the show overall?"

"I loved it," I said. "And I appreciate the fact that, this far along, you're still making the music that you want to make. You're not trying for that big hit."

He leaned in a little closer and said, almost conspiratorially, "I don't

Steve Kilbey, Orlando 2006 *(Brian Smith)*

really even know how to write a hit."

He grinned and stuck out his hand.

"Goodbye," he said, "mate."

I shook his hand. "Bye," I said. "Steve, thank you."

That "thank you" contained my whole life.

I watched as he walked away, his head bobbing to the sound of his own internal song. Eventually, he crossed the threshold between the glow of the lamplight and the darkness that lay beyond.

I didn't follow him.

THE FINAL WORD

From Steve Kilbey's blog *The Time Being* (February 18, 2007)

bios fear

yessaday i read my biography again
i guess i was sposed to be checking for any inaccuracies
i dont really care about inaccuracies that much
i mean what does it matter what year singsongs was recorded..?
actually
and im sure rob lurie is reading this . . .
hes done quite a nice job . . . ..
weird to suddenly see my story from his perspective . . .
i mean come on lurie..
you were some seriously uptight little fanboy . . . or what
and it was yer rite of passage to divest your psyche
of my unintentional superimposition
you see it happened to me too
with my fave popstars
but i was never lucky or unlucky enough to get to meet 'em
so i never gotta chance to do what lurie has done
and its strange to think
that i was casually writing n playing
and looking how i did . . . with my smirk n all
and somewhere out there
this teenage american kid in some suburban wilderness

is grokking it all
taking it all in
and
taking it all too seriously
just like me with marky boland n david boogie
except . . . .
anyway rob got a masters degree for this book
and now i envy him
i mean cant someone confer a fucking honarary ornery masters degree on
me?
cmon ya know i got more poetry in my little thingo
than all them professors at fucking harvard n yale put together
cmon give me some quals!
anyway i wasnt looking forward too much to the drug part
but lurie handles it with aplomb
and his "imagined" bits arent too far off the mark..
most of em anyway
and lurie attempts to come to some kinda understanding of my paradox
that is i can be so nice
or i can be so not nice
and hardly anything in the middle
and its funny that lurie puts the boot in a bit at the end
and he reckons that the fambley manne thing is an act
and my everyman pose is faux
and really im the same old prick
and rob youve hit the nail on the head actually
and its great to see that i can still perplex you after all these years
and its great that occasionally your sense of frustration
because you wanted to shake my unbeknownst influence ages ago
and youve taken your obsession
and robby baybee
i like your book
i enjoyed it
theres a few bits gonna get me into trouble maybe . . . .
but in the end
he does say that my stuff stood the test of time

but he eventually comes to a conclusion that
it was kinda worth it
your heroes are never gonna be exactly how ya hoped
lurie should thank his lucky stars
that he did meet me as the stocky thinning haired everyman
and not the glamourous little prick he worshipped
or he woulda gone home with his delusions shattered
ive tried to change since those days
and i have changed as a natural process as well
like everyone
of course that old sk is still in the sub-strata somewhere
that nasty disinterested one
and to tell ya the truth
how could you be interested in every stranger
that ya met by the bucketloads in those days
jesus i was a arrogant turkey . . . .sometimes
im not good at meeting people
it aint one of my skills
smalltalk n schmoozing
actually i dont care . . .
and man between 1986-1990
i met rob luries in every city of this world
guys who loved ya so much . . .
they wanted some intangible fucking thing . . .
i didnt know what it was
they didnt know what it was
except maybe i get em a deal with arista n produce their album
or something
anyway when it became apparent
that you werent interested at all
they often become argumentative n nasty
not understanding that
youre in the middle of a long tour
and its late
n yer stoned and or drunk

n very tired
n you cant even remember the lyrics
some fresh scrubbed "college" kid in boise is querying you about
as i said before
if youd let me loose on my heroes
im sure i woulda come home with cuffed ears
but it sure was tedious meeting some of those guys
lurie . . . i didnt even remember meeting him
till i read a little thing hed written about meeting me in london
during my "tired n emotional" phase
and his piece was brutally honest but he could still see
something in my shambles that kept him going
i completely perplexed him with my unintentional carryon
and he wrote it well
ya see rob thinks he hasnt gotta naxe to grind
but i wonder if he can perceive that he does
?
and that is
when you go n worship someone that much
well
you sorta feel like . . . ..
well its hard to explain . . .
you feel a bit annoyed or something
that youve spent so much effort on them
instead of getting yer own thing together
its great to have influences
its impossible not to
but when the time comes
ya gotta make the break
which is the difference between me n him
i made the break
and he didnt
now rob i hope ya dont mind me analyzing ya here on my blogge
i get a bit of analysis in ye olde bio n ya gotta suffer the slings n arrows
i think its a real good read and its written pretty well
a style emerges and i enjoyed it

i wont cringe at all if i see it in a bookstore
does this mean you can say authorised?
wow i read this book about david bowie some guy wrote
that was not authorised
jesus naughty david
with his thing for black womens bottoms
n the shadow that infested his swimming pool
and the cocaine
and the cocaine
and the . . .
did i mention cocaine?
i guess him n that biographer dont speak much these days . . .
ha ha
so i say
read robs book by all means
theres some hilarious stuff in there
like pryce surplus and his bitter rant
about how i lack any credibility and how i can never have it
gee pryce uh didja see the five star review last week in the age?
and simon polinski saying what a diamond geezer i am
cmon polinski, get fucking real, olde bean
im a bastard and ya know it
ha ha
rob it was interesting to revisit my self thru your eyes
i felt good when id finished reading it
and i also felt happy for ya too
cos it IS a good book
and you finally got something concrete outta all that kilbey carryon
you turned it round my son
youve done well!
ah . . . .
dont it bring a little tear to yer eye?
no?

SOURCES

Note: All anecdotes and quotes, unless otherwise identified in the text, are drawn from personal interviews conducted by the author.

The following people were interviewed and/or contributed information to this project:

Michael Barone, Patrick Boulay, Trevor Boyd, Anthony Collins, Joyce Cooper, Stuart Coupe, Brett Leigh Dicks, John Kilbey, Russell Kilbey, Steve Kilbey, Peter Koppes, Martin Krall, William Lawrence, Dare Mason, Linda Neil, David Nichols, Simon Polinski, Tim Powles, Andy "Rekkids," David Studdert, Pryce Surplice, Donnette Thayer, Clinton Walker, Nic Ward.

I have also drawn on the following additional sources:

Andre, Michelle. "Steve Kilbey Interview," *Ears and Mouth,* January 1988.

Arnold, Gina. "The Church: Priest=Aura," *Entertainment Weekly,* March 20, 1995.

Beck, Chris. "Steve Kilbey," *The Age* (Melbourne), July 1997.

Boyd, Trevor. "A Young Person's Guide......to the Church," *North, South, East and West*, issue 3, 1995.

Brunetti, Frank. "The Church: Persia," *RAM,* October 12, 1984.

"Canberra," *Wikipedia,* en.wikipedia.org/wiki/Canberra, September 13, 2008.

Gassuan, Guillaume. "Game Theory," *Guillaume Gassuan Home Page,* www.gassuan.com/Music/Game%20Theory/Game%20Theory.htm.

"Church Man One of the Best," author unknown, *Daily Telegraph* (Sydney), October 8, 1999.

"The Church: Sometime Anywhere," *Pulse* (author unknown), July 1994.

"The Church: Sometime Anywhere," *Q* (author unknown), May 1994.

"The Church: The Blurred Crusade," *Sounds*, 1982.

"The Church Working Plan (Richard Ploog Itinerary, March 10, 1988)," Reproduced in *The Maven*, December 1996.

Cohen, Marci. "Jack Frost: The Perfect Marriage," *B-Side*, August-September 1991.

Cook, Richard. "Holy Rollers," *Sounds*, 1986.

Coupe, Stuart. "The Big Kiss Off: Another Stuart 'Little Sleuth' Coupe Novel," *RAM*, August 5, 1983.

Coupe, Stuart. "Unguarded Kilbey," *RAM*, March 5, 1982.

"Cultural Cringe," *Wikipedia* (en.wikipedia.org/wiki/Cultural_cringe).

Doe, John. "The Church: Oh Ye of Little Faith," *Roadrunner*, 1981.

Durkin, Thomas. "Interview with Scott Miller of the Loud Family," *Angrylambie*, www.angrylambie.com/scott%20miller%20interview.htm, November 12, 2003.

Dwyer, Brian et al. "MATS and Feedback – What Happened?" *Shadow Cabinet*, www.shadowcabinet.net/archive/albums/mats.htm#feedback, July-December 1997.

Eliezer, Christie. "Play Melancholy for Me," *Juke*, April 21, 1990.

Fricke, David. "The Church: Heyday," *Rolling Stone* (US), February 27, 1986.

Fricke, David. "The Church: Starfish," *Rolling Stone* (US), April 21, 1988.

Garcia, Sandra A. "The Church: The Angelic Assassin and the Gypsy Sorcerer Are Working Their Special Magic Again…," *B-Side*, August-September 1994 .

Goddard, Kent. "The Church: Of Skins and Heart," *RAM*, June 12, 1981.

Grubblesnutch, J. Wallace (pseudonym). "Earth to Kilbey … Earth to Kilbey," Unidentified Australian street press, 1986 .

Holdsworth, Bill. "The Church/Real Life: Her Majesty's Theatre, Brisbane." Juke, September 17, 1983.

Irvin, Thomas. "Peter Koppes Speaks to Thomas Irwin," *Shadow Cabinet*, www.shadowcabinet.net/archive/interview/sckoppes.htm, 1998.

Kilbey, John. "The Brother Ode (part 1)," Karmic Hit MySpace Blog, www.myspace.com/karmichit, October 27, 2006.

Kilbey, Steve. "Church Fan Club Letter," 1983, reprinted in *North, South, East and West,* issue 1, October, 1994.

Kilbey, Steve. *Earthed, Nineveh + The Ephemeron*, Impressed Publishing, 2004.

Kilbey, Steve. *The Time Being*, www.stevekilbey.blogspot.com, 2005–.

"Steve Kilbey Interview," WNUR (Chicago), November 1984.

Lanham, Tom. "The Church: Sometime Anywhere," *Musician*, no. 190, August 1994.

Lee, Joe. "Baby Grande," *Canberra Musicians*, www.geocities.com/canberramusicians/babygrande.html.

Lewis, David. "The Wonder of Wombats," *Sounds*, 1981.

McFarlane, Ian. *Encyclopedia of Australian Rock & Pop*, Allen & Unwin, 1999.

McPhie, Scott. "Chris Gilbey: Memories of the Church," *Shadow Cabinet*, www.shadowcabinet.net, 1999 .

Messer, David. "The Church: Gold Afternoon Fix," *Rolling Stone* (Australia), June 1990.

Miller, Debbie. "The Church: Remote Luxury," *Rolling Stone* (US), October 25, 1984.

Moore, Mae. *Collected Works 1989-1999* (liner notes), Epic (Canada), 1999.

Mundy, Chris. "The Church: Gold Afternoon Fix," *Rolling Stone* (US), May 17, 1990.

Newquist, H.P. "The Church," *Guitar Player*, December 1994.

Nichols, David. "The Church: Hologram of Baal," *Rolling Stone* (Australia), Issue 553, October 1998.

Nichols, David. *The Go-Betweens*, Verse Chorus Press, 2003.

O'Donnell, John. "The Church: Starfish," *Rolling Stone* (Australia), April 1988.

Plume, N.D. (pseudonym) "The Church: Seance," Unidentified Australian street press, July 1983.

Press Release, *Delicatessen 3: Cooking Vinyl Sampler*, 2001.

Robbins, Ira. "The Church: Priest=Aura," *Rolling Stone* (US), 1992.

Robert, Terri. "Stargazing—The Church Reach Skyward," *Juke*, April 2, 1988.

Robertson, Donald. "Is This the Taste of Victory: The Thoughts of Chairman Kilbey," *Roadrunner*, May 1982.

Roldan, Rey. "Two for One Sail," *Boston Rock*, Issue 142, July 1994.

Rundle, David. "The Church at Salinas: Review," *NSEW*, issue 8, 1997.

Scatena, Dino. "The High Priests," *Juke*, April 25, 1992.

Schmidt, Michael. *Lives of the Poets*. Vintage, 2000.

Simpson, Dave. "The Church: Hologram of Baal," *Uncut*, 1998.

Skjefte, Morten. Miscellaneous postings, *Seance* mailing list, 1995.

Smith, Michael. "Rattling on Heaven's Door," *Juke*, July 18, 1981.

St. John, Ed. "The Church: Seance," *Rolling Stone* (Australia), July, 1983.

Sullivan, Jim. "The Church: Gold Afternoon Fix," *Boston Globe*, February 22, 1990.

Taylor, "Dr" G. "The Church: Sing Songs," *RAM*, 1982.

Thayer, Donnette. "Shelter," *Shadow Cabinet*, www.shadowcabinet.net/
   archive/dthayer, 1998.

Thomas, Dave. "The Church: Remote Luxury," source unknown, 1984.

Thompson, Stephen. "The Church: Sometime Anywhere," *Goldmine*,
   July 1994.

Traitor, Ralph. "The Church: Starfish," *Sounds*, 1988.

"Waddy Wachtel," *Wikipedia*, en.wikipedia.org/wiki/Waddy_Wachtel,
   September 11, 2008.

Walker, Clinton. "The Church Undergoes a Revival," *Rolling Stone* (Australia),
   February, 1986.

Walker, Clinton. *Stranded: The Secret History of Australian Independent Music
   1977-1991*, Sydney: Pan Macmillan Australia, 1996.

Wallop, J. C. (pseudonym). *The Tale of the Old Iron Pot*, NSW, Karmic Hit
   Productions, 2007.

Washington, Peter. *Madame Blavatsky's Baboon*, Schocken, 1996.

Weissman, Abby. "Here's One Church That *Won't* Corrupt You!" *The Aquarian*,
   August 6, 1986.

Willson-Piper, Marty. "Questions with Answers," *Shadow Cabinet*,
   www.shadowcabinet.net/archive/seance/martyfaq.htm,
   www.shadowcabinet.net/archive/seance/martans2.htm.

"Marty Willson-Piper Interview," KTCZ Cities 97 (Minneapolis/St Paul),
   February 15, 1990.

"Marty Willson-Piper Interview," KCRW *Snap* (radio show – Santa Monica),
   August 25, 1988.

The World Book Encyclopedia: Volume I, Chicago, World Book, Inc., 1983.

ALSO AVAILABLE FROM VERSE CHORUS PRESS

INNER CITY SOUND
EDITED BY CLINTON WALKER

"The bible of Australian punk"—The Age

The bands that spearheaded the late 1970s punk scene in Australia—the Saints, Birthday Party, Radio Birdman, and the Go-Betweens—are among the most important of their time. INNER CITY SOUND is the classic account of the explosive development of that scene. Original articles from fanzines and newspapers, together with almost 300 photographs, vividly portray the creative ferment of the period and the dozens of bands that sprang up in the wake of the pioneers. First published in late 1981, INNER CITY SOUND soon fell out of print. It became a lost classic, so sought after that it has been bootlegged like the rare singles listed in its discography. This new edition contains 32 extra pages of articles, photos, and discographic data, which take the story through to 1985, when Nick Cave, the Go-Betweens, the Triffids, and others began to break through internationally.

192 pages, 285 photos, paperback.

THE GO-BETWEENS
DAVID NICHOLS

The Go-Betweens recorded six albums that are among the finest work of the 1980s, earning them a reputation as "the ultimate cult band" and the lasting esteem of their peers, from R.E.M. to Sleater-Kinney. In 2000 they returned to making records—and received the best reviews of their career. David Nichols relates their story with wit and verve, and since—unlike most groups—the Go-Betweens had personalities as well as talent, their biography is compelling reading, not just for committed fans but for anyone interested in the current music scene.

288 pages, 85 photos, paperback.

HIGHWAY TO HELL: THE LIFE AND DEATH OF BON SCOTT
CLINTON WALKER

SECOND, REVISED AND UPDATED US EDITION

The definitive account of AC/DC's rise to fame, when the raunchy lyrics and charismatic stage presence of singer Bon Scott, along with the guitar work of Angus and Malcolm Young, defined a new, highly influential brand of rock and roll. Drawing on many interviews and featuring a gallery of rare photos, Clinton Walker traces the band's career through the life of their original front man, from small-time gigs to international success, up to Scott's shocking death in 1980. AC/DC's undiminished superstar status ensures that Bon Scott's presence continues to be felt strongly. HIGHWAY TO HELL offers the full story of this seminal rock figure.

HIGHWAY TO HELL has been updated for this edition. New details that have come to light in recent years about the last hours of Scott's life have been added, enabling the author to dispel persistent rumors and myths and once more set the record straight.

312 pages, 40 photos, paperback. (Not available in Australia)